ONE DAY IT'LL ALL MAKE SENSE

ALSO BY COMMON

I Like You but I Love Me

The Mirror and Me

M.E. (Mixed Emotions)

ONE DAY IT'LL ALL MAKE SENSE

A MEMOIR

COMMON

WITH ADAM BRADLEY

ATRIA BOOKS

NEW YORK LONDON TORONTO SYDNEY NEW DELHI

ATRIA BOOKS

A Division of Simon & Schuster, Inc.
1230 Avenue of the Americas
New York, NY 10020

First Atria Books hardcover edition September 2011

ATRIA BOOKS and colophon are trademarks of Simon & Schuster, Inc.

For information about special discounts for bulk purchases, please contact Simon & Schuster Special Sales at 1-866-506-1949 or business@simonandschuster.com.

The Simon & Schuster Speakers Bureau can bring authors to your live event. For more information or to book an event, contact the Simon & Schuster Speakers Bureau at 1-866-248-3049 or visit our website at www.simonspeakers.com.

Designed by Suet Yee Chong

Manufactured in the United States of America

10   9   8   7   6   5   4   3   2   1

Library of Congress Cataloging-in-Publication Data

Common (Musician)
    One day it'll all make sense : a memoir / by Common with Adam Bradley.—1st Atria Books hardcover ed.
        p. cm.
1. Common (Musician) 2. Rap musician—United States—Biography.
I. Bradley, Adam. II. Title.
    ML420.C656A3 2011
    782.421649092—dc23
    [B]
                                                2011021691

ISBN 978-1-4516-2587-5
ISBN 978-1-4516-2590-5 (ebook)

I dedicate this to the Most High God
from whom all blessings flow.

I also dedicate this to my mother,
to Omoye, and to my grandmother.

CONTENTS

FOREWORD
DR. MAHALIA ANN HINES

"You have a wonderful son." "He is such a good person." "His spirit is so great." These are comments I often hear from perfect strangers. Most of them know my son only as Common, not by his given name, Rashid. But each of them speaks as if they have a personal connection to him. My favorite comment of all, though, is "I want to be your daughter-in-law!"

Every time I hear comments like these, it makes me smile. It makes me very proud to be his mother. Friends and family say, "Rashid hasn't changed. He's still the same as he was before the fame." That makes me feel even more proud. I'm surprised they think he *would* change. I know he's an entertainer and some say he's a star, but in my mind those words only describe what he does, not who he is.

I'm often told that Rashid is who he is because of me. "You are such a strong mother. You've taught him so much." Sure, I would like to take all of the credit for who he has become, but I can't. He's always been his own person—even as a child—and he's certainly become his own man.

Sometimes I listen to him and I have to ask myself, "Who is this? Why is he so wise? Did he really come from me?" There's so much about him that's still a mystery, even to me. What I do know, though, is that I like him. I really like him. Of course, I love him, too. As mothers, we always love our children—but we may not always *like* them. I often tell him, "I would like you even if you weren't my son."

What do I like so much about him? I like praying with him, talking with him, and learning from him. He has a way of putting things into perspective for me when I'm stressed out or worried about something. I remember talking to him about my niece, Bianca, who had come to live with me after my sister, Stella, had died. Bianca was only twelve and she was so angry at everyone, angry at the world. She was angry at her mother for leaving, angry at God for taking her away, and she was even mad at me for still being here. I did everything I knew to do for her, but nothing really helped. She barley graduated from high school and I helped her move on to college away from home. It wasn't long before she was running into problems there.

That's when I called Rashid. I was so worried. I even thought that if my sister were here, Bianca wouldn't be struggling quite so bad. I said to him that I thought if she came back to Chicago where her family was she might do better. He said "Mama, I know you want the best for Bianca. I love her, too. You have to do what you think will help her, but you need to understand that wherever Bianca goes she will take herself with her." It was simple wisdom, but it was a difficult truth. So I let Bianca tough it out away from home and before long, she found her own path with our love and support.

Have I always liked Rashid? Maybe not always. I really didn't like him when he decided to leave school to become a rapper. I didn't even know what rapping was nor did I think that one could have a career in it. I am embarrassed today when I say I didn't know he was even rapping as a teenager. Sure, I knew he could write. He always got As in English. I knew he used to spin on his head to music all the time, but I certainly didn't know that spinning on your head could lead to a career.

Remember, I came up in the '60s where doors finally started opening for African Americans to get an education, which would lead to getting a good job. You'd have that job for life. So why didn't my son want to finish college and get a good job for *his* life? I didn't understand it and I didn't like it, but I loved him and I tried to be supportive as he struggled to follow his dream.

I even went to one of his first shows one night at the House of Blues. I have to admit, I was excited. I was proud that my son was an entertainer. He was excited that I was going to be there, I think. But my excitement started waning early into the show. All I saw were people jumping around onstage and hollering—angry, loud, and more often than not cursing. I wasn't sure who should have been onstage and who shouldn't. I even saw audience members jumping onstage trying to take the mic.

At some point in the show, Rashid seemed to feel like he had to defend his own microphone. I think he even hit someone. My excitement quickly turned to fear. My pride turned to worry, but somehow the show went on. My best friend, Barbara, and I just sat there in amazement. I knew she didn't say what she really thought because she didn't want to hurt my feelings. We sat there in silence looking at one another. Actually, I think by now we were standing because everyone else was standing and throwing up their hands.

With all that chaos going on, I tried to listen closely to the words in Rashid's rhymes. He wasn't quite talking and wasn't quite singing, but something in between. It had rhythm and spirit and a little bit of soul, too. But it sounded to my ears like a foreign language. At one point in his performance, Rashid jumped off the stage and into the audience. Barbara and I looked at one another and we sat down. We had been there since 9:00 p.m. He was supposed to come on at 10:00, but he ended up coming on just after 1:00 in the morning. By 3:00, the show was over and Barbara and I were exhausted.

Well, I thought, *at least I'll get to see his dressing room.* We were escorted backstage—if you can even call it that. Rashid's dressing room was not as big as my bathroom. It was full of Rashid's loud, smelly, and I think drunk (or on the way to being drunk) homeboys. When Barbara and I entered the room, they tried to straighten up out of respect for us, but there was only so much they could do. I gave him a hug—all the while looking at who was in there—told him he did great, and left.

As I drove home I thought to myself, *how could I have not known he was into rapping?* His friend Derek's mother and father knew about it. They were even driving him around to gigs with

Derek and giving them money for equipment. I wondered if some of my money had gone toward his early rapping career. I'm sure it did.

But on the way back from that first show, I knew exactly why Rashid hadn't told me about his rapping earlier. You see, he knew me and he knew that if I had known I would have tried to stop him. Knowing why he kept it a secret didn't help the hurt. I was disappointed in him for not confiding in me. I was angry with myself because as a mother I should have known. I had really missed the boat on that one. It had sailed, but I was determined it wouldn't dock. This was not what I wanted for my son, or for me. I was embarrassed to tell anyone my son was a rapper. But this was his life not mine, so I had to step back. I decided I would give him three years of emotional and financial support to establish his career. If he couldn't do it by then, he would have to go back to school. In my mind, I knew he would be back in school in three years, maybe fewer. Little did I know. . .

Over time, rap changed and so did Rashid. He became a conscious rapper. His lyrics expanded to represent more of what he was about and not what others—be they friends or record labels—thought he should be about. He became his own artist and his own man.

Today I am proud to say my son is a rapper. My friends call me the "hip-hop grandma" because I not only talk about his songs, but about Nas's, Tupac's, Jay-Z's, and Kanye's, too. Even though I often find myself defending rap in front of people who don't have a clue about my son or what he does, I'm happy to do it. I have been in social situations where someone will mention that my son is Common and that he's an entertainer. They'll ask me what he does. I'll say he's a rapper. I can see by their blank looks that they don't know what to say and they don't know what to make of him—or of me. So, I make it easy on them. I'll ask, "Do you have children?" If they say yes, I'll say, "Ask them who Common is." Most of the time, their kids will say, "He's one of the dopest rappers with meaningful lyrics." And, you know what? They're right!

But Rashid is more than just a rapper. He's an actor, an author, a speaker, and according to no less an authority than Dr. Maya Angelou, a poet (smile). As wonderful as all of that is, those are only things he does, not who he is. When I'm asked to describe him I say he is the best son a mother could have, a good father, a great and loyal friend, a fine husband-to-be, a spiritual believer, and a practicing Christian—not necessarily in that order. In this book, you too will have the opportunity to get to know not only Common, but also Rashid. You'll get to know the artist and also the complex soul I'm proud to call my son.

Throughout this book, Rashid opens his heart. He tells his story. He shares very personal experiences that are sometimes too personal even for me. But, if his openness and honesty can touch hearts, change minds, and help others to reflect on their lives in a way that will allow them to see the God within them, then I'll even forgive him for telling my personal business, too!

PROLOGUE

Dear Reader:

When I was eighteen months old, my mother and I were kidnapped at gunpoint. My father held the gun.

At least that's one side of the story. I first heard about it all from my aunt long after it happened, when I was already a grown man. I asked my mother, and she told it to me one way. I asked my father, and he told it to me another. The story I'll tell you begins where my mother's and my father's tales come together and continues past them into the separate corners of my parents' truths. Somehow in telling it, the story becomes my own. Somehow in telling it, it all starts to make sense.

My father, Lonnie Lynn, was a Chicago playground legend. They called him the Genie because he'd make the basketball disappear right before your eyes then make it reappear at the bottom of the net. At six foot eight, he had NBA size and the skills to match. He was nice around the rim and had a sweet stroke from inside eighteen feet. But he talked back to coaches. He missed practice. He developed a habit. He was out of the league before his career really began. For all his gifts, he played just one year of professional basketball, for the Denver Rockets and the Pittsburgh Pipers of the ABA.

Around the same time, his relationship with my mother was falling apart. He was getting high, keeping drugs right out in the open on the nightstand. He'd react to the slightest provocation. One time my mother locked him out of our apartment, and he shot out all the windows. When he was sober, he was a loving man, but when he was high, he was somebody else.

"I was out of basketball," my father later told me. "I was struggling. My lowest point came in December of 1972, when you were nine months old. I weighed one hundred ninety-five pounds, less than I had coming out of high school. That's what the drugs had done—or, rather, what I had done with the drugs. By the time I got back to Chicago, I was back near my playing weight at two hundred thirty-five pounds. I was ready for my last chance."

His last chance came with a tryout for the Seattle SuperSonics. They knew about my dad's past troubles, and they were concerned. They wanted to know he was a family man. Problem was, my folks were separated, heading toward divorce. So, early one morning, my father packed everything he owned into the backseat of a rented Dodge Charger and drove to Eighty-eighth and Dorchester in Chicago's South Side, where my mother and I lived.

Here is where my parents' stories diverge. "He took us out of the house at gunpoint, handcuffed me to the front seat, put you in the back, and started driving across the country to Seattle," my mother says.

"You and your mother got in the front seat with me," my father recalls, "and we started out on Interstate 90 heading west."

I can imagine my mother seething inside—not panicked, not defeated—waiting for her moment. My father must have known this too. Part of him might even have feared her, a strange thing since he was the one at the wheel. She had this indomitable spirit; it only grew stronger when she felt her child was in danger.

What could she do? When we stopped for gas, she says he handcuffed her to the steering wheel. When she needed to use the restroom, she says he stood outside the door. The situation must have looked hopeless to her.

My mother escaped with me early one Sunday morning. She recalls my father pulling off the highway to get gas; there were no plans to stop for food, no plans to sleep. She complained of a head-ache and asked my father to bring her something for the pain.

He came back to the car with a bottle of pills. My mother took two like the container directed then somehow managed to put the rest in his can of Coke as he gassed up the car. When he got back in, he took a big swig of soda then threw the can out the window. It wasn't long before he started feeling the effects.

"Did she drug me? I don't know," my father told me later. "All I know is that I made the decision that it was better to sleep during the day and drive at night while you were sleeping."

We stopped at a roadside motel on the outskirts of Madison, Wisconsin. I wonder what people saw when they looked at us. A beautiful family on a cross-country trip? A doting mother holding her child? A loving husband clutching his wife close by his side? Did they see the family we were or the family we might have been?

My mother told me that my father had just enough time to handcuff her to the bed, sit me on the couch, strip off some of his clothes, and fall onto the mattress, his feet dangling off the edge. Soon he was snoring away. Once he was fast asleep, my mother says she started working her small hand against the cuff, folding her fingers in on themselves and pulling until metal scraped skin.

"Rashid," she said in a stage whisper. "Rashid, baby, go outside and play. Mommy will be there soon."

Something in her eyes must have told me, young as I was, that this was no time for games. I followed her instructions and slipped out the door. Her hand finally free, my mother followed after me. She made it to the lobby and told the man working there to call the police.

"Next thing I know," my father now says, "I wake up and there are two policemen standing over my bed. One of them's got a shotgun on me. The other's pointing a pistol. I raised my hands up above my head and turned my eyes to the sky. I can remember seeing a teardrop of water falling down from that low, low ceiling. That's when I cried out: 'Don't shoot! Don't shoot!'

"It was all over the radio, the television, the newspaper. 'Kidnapping,' in capital letters. But I was in jail only overnight. They released me the next morning without charges."

Madison, Wisconsin, is one hundred sixty-three miles from the South Side of Chicago and nearly two thousand miles from Seattle. The road trip, the kidnapping, my father's dream—whatever you call it—it was over almost as soon as it had started.

Can a story you've only overheard somehow still give shape to your life? Can other people's stories also be your own? Hearing this was like discovering a lost piece of my past, like having my life told as legend. Could it have really happened? Part of me figured that when I asked my parents about it, they'd deny it. But when I asked each of them, they confirmed it—even if they told their stories in a different key.

They say trauma always accompanies birth, the beginning of new life. When I think about my parents and me driving toward my father's dream, I think about what it means to bear the legacy of these two people who were estranged from each other before I was born but remain tied together because I was born. It speaks to me about connections, willing and not. It speaks to the fact that when you try to tell your own story, you can't help but tell someone else's along the way. This is my life, my story, but it's their story too.

I think of my mother, a young woman with a child at the time threatened by a man she still loves. Maybe that's why she's always loved me so hard, like she could lose me at any moment. Today she is a mother, a grandmother, my best friend.

I think about my father and how his inner pains and self-doubt sometimes expressed themselves in ways he couldn't control. What possesses a man to aim a gun at the woman he loves and the child he helped conceive? If not the gun, then what possesses him to pursue a dream past all consequence? Today he is a thinker, a dreamer, a complex soul.

Who knows the truth of the story? My truth is this: I inherited love and trouble, joy and fear. I experienced all of these things before I could even put them into words. The story I have to tell you is one of inheritance and identity, of the values my mother passed on to me that I hope to pass on to my daughter, Omoye. The story is of making myself into the man that I want to be: an artist, a father, a child of God.

When I was given the opportunity to write this book, I had some misgivings. Had I lived enough? Would anyone want to hear my story? When I think of memorable life stories, I think of great men and women looking back over the decades. I think of Malcolm X and Assata Shakur. I think of Maya Angelou and Nelson Mandela. What story does a kid from the South Side of Chicago have to tell?

So I talked with friends. I talked with my mother, my father, my grandmother, my daughter. We laughed, we reminisced, we even shed a few tears. At a certain moment, I took in a breath, I breathed it out, and I knew that I had lived a life I wished to share. I knew that if I dedicated myself to writing about my life, it might all start to make sense.

I've always loved to write. It must have started with my mother. She still has a note I wrote to her when I was six or seven years old about leaving the key so she could get in the house and how I didn't want to get a whippin'. She tells me that's my first letter.

In school, I'd write love letters to cute girls in class. When I first started rapping, I'd write my lyrics in a composition book. As I grew older, I'd write my hopes, fears, and dreams in a journal. I still write to this day, even to people who are part of my everyday life—my mother, my daughter, my friends. I may be a talker just like my dad, but I love to express myself through letters. Maybe I write because I've learned to show certain parts of my heart on the page that I still struggle to capture in speech.

That's why I've decided to begin each chapter of this book with a letter. In these pages, I've written to my mother and to my daughter and to many others—to you, to lost friends, to distant lovers, to future generations. Each letter offers a way into the stories of my life that follow. Together they tell a story of their own, of a life still very much in the making.

I have loved and lost and given and failed and fallen and prayed and believed and worked and sexed and proved and listened and traveled and healed and grown and watched and journeyed and loved again and grown some more. I've done all of these things and all of these things have created the man that I am today.

I also realize that my life is an expression of all those I have known and all who have known me. They are people in and out of the public eye. They are friends and fans and lovers and mentors. They are people like my mother and my grandmother and the guy I only ever knew as Duck, who was on the street but used to say that one day I'd be a star. People like Yusef and Ajile and the bellman at the House of Blues Hotel in Chicago who always had a kind word when I arrived.

My life is people like Omoye, Murray, Kanye, Reverend Jeremiah Wright, Minister Louis Farrakhan, Maya Angelou, my father, Mike Jolicoeur, Dion, Dart, Ron, Rasaan, Monard, and the memory of another South Side son named Emmett Till. All of these people are a part of me as I am a part of them. Their souls have joined with mine. In fact, sometimes when I'm writing songs I find myself looking through their eyes, expressing what I believe they might see and feel.

You'll hear some of these other voices threading in and out of the pages that follow. Other than my own, the voice you'll most often hear is that of my mother. It's only right given that my mother has been—and remains—the most influential person in my life. Throughout the chapters, you'll find her speaking in her own words directly to you through italicized text, offering perspectives on my past that complement and occasionally even contradict the view of my life as I see it.

I'm writing you now because I know I have something to say to you. I believe we can forge a connection that will help us to recognize the other in the self. I know I can enlighten. I know I can inspire. And I know that this journey is not just about what I think about myself. It's not about how many records I've made or how many films I've done. It's about what has happened in my life that can spark you to be better in yours. What have I said and done, what have I failed to say and failed to do, that will give you insight as you strive to reach your full potential and serve your purpose on this earth?

So I hope this letter finds you in the place where you are willing and ready to progress in your life. I hope this book not only entertains you but also helps you grow in a spirit of openness. I write to you wishing, praying, and sending the best love to you. This is my story, the story of an uncommon life.

Love,

Common

1 "LOVE IS . . ."

Hey, Ma:

I woke up this morning thinking about you and how much you mean to my life. I thank God so much for you, Ma. I know I would not have been able to pursue my dreams—or even see them—I would not have been able to love so freely and purely if you had not been there for me.

Ma, you showed me what true love is, what God-like love feels like, by loving me uncondi- tionally and with such fierce strength. You have always been the most important love in my life. I don't know what I would be without your caring and your teaching and your listening and your nurturing—and your being bossy!

Growing up, I just knew that you would al- ways be there for me. I would look at my friends and see that they didn't have that same support. I saw how hard it was for them not to have a mother who could care the way you did. I knew then it was you who gave me a chance. I love getting to pray with you, Ma. Thank you so much for making me go to church, even when I tried to get out of it. Thank you for being my mother before you became my best friend.

I have always felt loved, Ma, and if you know it or not, that has made me a better person and a better man, a man who can love. Because you loved me, I was able to love myself, and because I can love myself, I can love others. I know I wouldn't be doing the things I am doing if you hadn't given me that foundation. You showed me strength and sacrifice and caring and hard work. You showed me hustle.

I know you tried to get me to appreciate things earlier on that I didn't get until late—and I do wish you had taught me how to cook! But just learning from you to care for others has been the most important lesson in my life.

Lately I've been stepping out, saying I gotta make my own decisions. "Ma, stay out of this one!" I have to live my life with all its ups and downs. I know you want the best for me. I know you try to keep your hold on me because you love me so much and don't want to see me hurt. But, Ma, I have to experience life to become the child of God that He wants me to be, to become the man I want and need to be.

I will make more mistakes on my own than I would if I followed your every word, but know that God has blessed me with a supreme mama. You have taught me to love wholeheartedly, to think beyond limits, to make others better, to up my father game, to handle my money, to give to others, to enjoy life, to seek God, to be still, to have faith, to be joyful even in the pain, and to let my leadership radiate.

Yeah, Ma, I know that sometimes you haven't agreed with me if I'm giving some money to one of my guys or splurging on my girl. But what's funny is that I learned that giving spirit from you. You know I'm not going to let anyone take advantage of me. I still remember that day you told me that God put us here to help others. "That's our purpose," you said. I needed to hear that because I can get so caught up in my work and in my goals.

Even when we don't agree, I know you want what's best for me. I'm growing up, Ma. I am a child of God, but I am a man, and I want you to know that if it's one gift I thank God for most, it is you. You have been the beginning to me sharing my gifts. And you have helped me develop into a gift giver who can love life and love myself and be in love with others.

I know you always tell me you want me to be with the right woman. When you're gone, you want to know that I will have someone to care for me, someone to be there to share my life. Well, Ma, no one will replace my mama, but know I will choose wisely and the woman I marry will undoubtedly have some of the beautiful things I see in you.

Know this: I am a man, and I will be wonderful in a relationship, and I will be a great father, and I will fulfill my purpose on this earth doing what God wants me to do. I thank you for holding me up to take the first steps on my path and I know you will always be there watching, loving, and praying as I walk it.

I love you, Ma.

Rashid

• • •

THE FIRST EMOTION I EVER FELT WAS LOVE. THE SECOND WAS fear. The love I felt was for my mother and her love for me. This love draws you into open arms and holds you close. It's the love of certainty.

The fear I felt was the unshakable awareness that her love could be taken away from me. It's the fear of loss.

I've felt this same combination of love and fear whenever I've felt something so deeply that I couldn't imagine living in its absence—the way I love God, the way I love my daughter.

My mother showed her love for me every day, not just in words but also in deeds. Insisting that we go to church on Sunday, no matter what—that was love. Making sure that I had new clothes for school and new equipment for sports—that was love. Making me catfish and cornbread—that was love. Reading books to me and, later, having me read to her—that was love. All of these things, both great and small, combined to envelop me in a warm embrace that stayed with me throughout the day and throughout my life.

So I loved my mother and I knew she loved me, but I feared that somehow that love might leave. Those two emotions—love and fear—motivate me to this very day.

I often marvel at the strength of my mother's will. With all the responsibilities that she had to take on, where did she find the strength to love so hard? Where does a love like that come from? Part of it comes from growing up around poverty, loving the little you have with everything you've got. Part of it is just a testament to her character. She was afraid too, intent on protecting her son from the dangers of the streets without sheltering him too much and making him even more vulnerable. How could she raise a young man who would be tough enough to take the weight and sensitive enough to love with his whole heart?

I raised Rashid in such a way that if anything ever happened to me, someone would say, "I'll take that child." I wanted him to be well behaved, well groomed, well nourished. I wanted him to be the kind of boy that would be a joy to raise, not just for me but for someone else if I was taken from him.

Why was I so concerned about him losing me? I don't know. I suppose there was the fear of his father that still gripped me from time to time like a spasm. But it was more than that. It must have been the remnants of a feeling I had as a child. We all are a product of our histories. I know I'm a product of mine.

Growing up in Chicago, you learn how to survive—some people call it hustle. Rich or poor, educated or uneducated, black or white, you'll find hustlers of all kinds in Chicago. For me hustling meant that even as I grew older and got more education, I was still able to relate to people on the streets. It meant that I could make a way out of no way, even if it meant bending or even breaking the rules sometimes.

As a school principal, they said I was "creatively insubordinate," which is just a clever way of saying that I took care of my kids—and myself. I was successful because I always did what I thought was best for the students while at the same time doing what was best for me and my family. They'd say, "Aren't you scared of losing your job?" I'd say, "No, because I'm willing to wait tables, work at a checkout stand, whatever I need to do." I know how to get money, and I mean legally. I'll take another job before I'll work in a place where I have to do something I don't believe in.

As a child, I saw that my mother always had two or three jobs at a time. We lived in a working-class black neighborhood. Most people had nine-to-fives, but there were a lot of street hustlers too. You had those who made their money running numbers—our street version of the lottery. I saw men who might have made their money on the wrong side of the law save up that money and buy Laundromats and corner stores and apartment buildings. So even though my mother always stressed education and pushed me to succeed, I also received a separate education in how to survive. Now I can sit down with someone from the street or someone from a university or corporation and be able to gain respect either way.

Here's my definition of hustling: knowing how to survive in a world that's set up for you to fail. That's why, as black people, we've had to strive so hard to develop a hustler's instinct and pass it on to our children. You have a door closed in your face? You have to learn how pick the lock or maybe just knock it off the hinges.

THIS IS MY LIFE IN EIGHT BLOCKS—the people and the places I love. This is where I had my first kiss and felt my first heartbreak. This is where I took my first sip of beer and got into my first fistfight. This is where I learned to breakdance and where I drove my first car. I grew up on the South Side of Chicago: Eighty-eighth Street and Dorchester Avenue, Eighty-sixth and Blackstone, Eighty-ninth and Bennett, Eighty-seventh and Stony Isle in a black middle-class neighborhood rubbing up against poverty. You had hardworking families with plenty of kids, but then you had gangbangers, too. That's just the culture in Chicago, I guess. It's a city of hustlers, legal and illegal.

I was born on March 13, 1972, at Chicago Osteopathic Hospital. My mother said it snowed that day. My father said it rained. I guess we can agree that some meteorological disturbance announced my arrival here on earth.

My grandmother likes to tell the story of how she rushed to the hospital as soon as she heard her first grandchild was born. She arrived at the incubators and started searching through the glass, looking for the beautiful little baby she knew she would find. When the nurse came up to her, my grandmother had already picked out a couple prime grandchild candidates.

"Which one is yours, Grandma?"

"Oh, I'm looking for the Lynn baby, ma'am."

The nurse scanned her chart, glanced through the glass, and pointed me out to her.

"Is that him?"

"Yes, ma'am."

"Are you sure?"

"Yes, ma'am. Lonnie Rashid Lynn."

My grandmother rushed to the recovery room where my mother was resting.

"Did you see the baby?"

"Yes, Mama. Isn't he beautiful?"

"Beautiful? Have you *seen* him? That little old red, long, dry-looking baby. He's so . . . ugly!"

My mother just shook her head and smiled.

"I need some sleep, Mama."

A couple days later, after my mother had brought me home, she called up my grandmother.

"He *is* kinda ugly, isn't he?"

THEY STILL TEASE ME about it to this day.

"Boy," my grandmother says now, "you were the ugliest little baby, all red and scrawny with a patch of hair up at the front of your head. But you know what? You've just gotten better and better every day, praise God!"

I may have been scrawny in the beginning, but I already carried a heavy legacy. I took my father's name, Lonnie Lynn. He and my mother also gave me another name, Rashid, the name I now go by to my friends and family. Rashid means "guide to the right path" in Arabic. I've always believed that our names hold our fate. I've tried to live up to the higher purpose hidden in my name. Early on, my mother noticed I had a spiritual side to me. I guess they say that all children are close to God.

His first babysitter was the trees. When he was no more than six months old, I'd lay him down underneath the large picture window in the front room and let him watch the trees sway in the breeze. You should have seen his face! He'd grin from ear to ear and just giggle like it was the greatest of jokes. Whenever I needed some time to myself, some time to my thoughts, I'd just set him under the window near the trees, and he was content. An hour or more would pass, and he would never cry. What a child I had!

LOOKING BACK, I can't recall much about my first years of life. My earliest memory was of a birthday party, maybe my fourth. It was on a party bus and there were different things to see and do. They had clowns. There was this little toy jail that you could get behind. That's the first thing I remember in my life: people having a good time on that party bus. I remember looking at the grownups, and they were having fun, too. It was my party and I was enjoying myself, but there was something missing. Even in my joy, I felt a certain sadness. I had on one of those little hats, the kind that looks like a cone on top of your head. I can still remember that jail, too. I had a picture of it at one point—little hands clutching at the cardboard bars.

The next thing I remember from childhood is playing around at my babysitter's house. Her name was Sheree, and she babysat me from birth until I was eleven years old. I loved staying with her because she used to play music. We'd dance and sing. I didn't know the names at the time, of course, but she would play Donny Hathaway and Roberta Flack and Marvin Gaye and the Commodores.

One night there was a knock at the door, and she went to

answer it. I followed close behind. When she opened it up, there stood a man, impossibly tall, that I knew was my father but somehow not my father. He was wearing a mask. Was it Halloween? Then again, maybe he wasn't wearing a mask at all. All I know is that I felt the warmth of recognition followed by the chill of fear. I was scared, but I wanted to see my dad, too. That's all that I can remember of that night. It's only a little glimpse, like glancing through the crack of a door while running past.

These early memories come at you in pieces, scraps of sight and sound, color and light. But even if the pieces don't fit together just right, you feel the truth of them in the emotions.

One of the strongest early emotions I felt outside of my family was for a place, for Chicago. Chicago is in my blood. My family has lived there for several generations on my father's side and three generations on my mother's side. Grandma Elva, my mother's mother, was born in Yazoo City, Mississippi, in 1927, the year of the Great Mississippi Flood, the most devastating river flood in the history of the United States. That spring the Mississippi River broke through the levees, covering an area fifty miles wide and a hundred miles long. People were still cleaning up from the wreckage that fall when my grandmother was born in the home of her grandparents. The day after my Grandma Elva's birth, her mother, Emma Donelson, went back to work as the cook at a private high school for whites only.

Like so many black folks around that time, my family was drawn to the North by the promise of greater opportunity. Historians would later call this mass exodus of blacks from the rural south to the urban north the Great Migration, but for the people themselves it was something more specific: it was a chance at a better life. Grandma Elva, after all, was only two generations removed from slavery. She can still recall meeting her great-grandmother Melinda, or Linda, who was born a slave. "All I remember," she once told me, "is that when I sat on her lap, she would always pinch me, and I would holler!" My great-great-great-grandma Linda was 103 when she died.

My grandmother's grandparents, Mahalia and Simpson Stubblefield, owned a store and farmed a small plot of land down in Mississippi. They had carved out a life for themselves and their family, but they wanted something more. Not long after my grandmother's birth, the family decided to move to Chicago, including their daughter and their new grandchild. My grandmother's mother, Emma, however, wanted to stay down south and continue working. She knew, though, that her daughter would have a better life in the north so she asked her parents to take her child with them. It was the hardest decision she ever made. It might have been the best one, too.

That's how my mother's family ended up in Chicago. My grandmother along with her grandparents took the train north from Mississippi bound for possibility, but prepared for uncertainty. The Chicago they found wasn't exactly to their liking. After arriving on the South Side, my great-great-grandparents found that the hustle and bustle was just too much for them to handle. So they packed up again and kept moving, this time farther north to South Haven, Michigan.

South Haven was a rural community, almost entirely white. For my grandmother and her grandparents, it was like moving to another planet; they were the first black family to live in the town. My grandmother enrolled in the all-white school. "They treated me like a paper doll," she said. "But I didn't feel prejudice. There was no color bearing that I can remember." My grandmother and her white classmates went to school together, they went to church together, they made a life. From time to time, her mother would visit from Mississippi, but she was raised almost entirely by her grandparents up north. "I loved those old people," she told me once. "They taught me common sense. My grandfather always said that an educated fool is the biggest fool going. So I never wanted to do anything that would make them ashamed of me."

WHEN MY GRANDMOTHER finished school, she went to live with her sister in Washington, DC, where she met her husband. When he went away to fight in World War II, he left her pregnant with my mother. My grandmother then went back to South Haven for her daughter to be born. My mother was the first black child ever delivered in South Haven hospital.

My grandmother ended up having three more children, getting divorced, and moving back to Chicago, becoming a single mother of four. She had little formal training but a great sense of hustle and ambition. She went to beauty school and worked on the South Side in a hair salon. Then one day she read an ad in the newspaper looking for a shampoo girl in a white salon on the North Side. She knew she could make more money there on tips alone than she could on the South Side, so she took the job. Her mother finally moved from Mississippi, motivated by her desire to help out, to take care of the four children during the day while my grandmother worked. All the while, my grandmother honed her skills. Before long, she had moved from shampoo girl to manicurist, then to owning her own shop. She started the first nail salon on the South Side, on Seventy-ninth and Champlain Avenue. She did nails for thirty-six years until her retirement, rarely missing a day of work.

Some of my earliest memories take place in my grandmother's salon. It's a place I associate with lots of love. My mother was working two jobs, so she asked my grandmother to drop me off and pick me up from day care. But my real day care was that nail shop.

"As soon as I would turn the corner to that day care you'd start crying and crying," Grandma told me years later. "So I'd just keep on driving." She secretly kept me out of day care for about a week before she confessed to my mom.

"Ann, I just can't stand to take him there. They're mistreating him."

"Mama, they aren't mistreating him. That's a good day care," Mom said.

"Then why does he start crying as soon as I get near the place?"

"You want to know why? Because he knows you can't stand to see him cry. He knows if he cries, you'll keep him with you. He's making a fool out of you!"

After that, they came to an agreement. My grandmother bought a playpen and set it up for me right there in her salon. The customers and workers loved me, and I loved them. Maybe that's why I've always been so comfortable around women. I've been surrounded by them my whole life. I thrive on their energy.

My grandmother loves to tell a story about me at age three. There was a young lady who worked at her nail shop who just couldn't get enough of me. So every day, she would take me out to lunch with her. We'd come back an hour later and I'd be as happy as can be. Well, one of those days, my grandmother and I were driving home from the salon, and I started pointing out the car window at a bar.

"Grandma! Grandma! I had cocktails in there."

"What did you say?"

"I had, I had kiddie cocktails there."

Little did she know that every lunch hour, my new girlfriend and I would head over to the bar and have a drink to go along with our lunch. I think my drink of choice was a Shirley Temple. For the next month, my grandmother tells me, every time we'd drive home along Seventy-ninth Street, I'd point to that bar and squeal, "Kiddie cocktails! Kiddie cocktails!"

ALL THE LOVE and happiness of my childhood exist side by side with a certain pain. When I think of my mother and my father together, I think of a pain that I don't know if I actually witnessed. Images flash before my eyes—my mother crying, the two of them fighting—but I don't know if these things actually happened or if they are simply my suppressed emotions made visible.

As long as I can remember, it's just been my mother and me. I can't recall ever living in the same house with my father. In fact,

I've only seen my parents around each other a handful of times. But the pain I associate with the two of them together has affected me emotionally in ways that I'm just now beginning to understand. It's certainly affected how I've dealt with women. They say the first lessons you learn about relationships come from your parents. Not all of those lessons are good ones.

"In the bottom of my heart," my father once told me, "I think your mother loves me so much she hates me." Somehow that made perfect sense. For the longest time, I would measure how a woman felt about me not just by the love she showed me but also by how upset she would get at me. Pain was as good as pleasure. They both told me that she cared enough to feel *something*. The worst thing was indifference, a flat line. I never wanted that, so I would do things and say things to provoke a strong emotion, regardless of what that emotion was. "I want to be the one to make you happiest and hurt you the most," I once said in a rhyme. Over time, though, I've come to understand myself well enough to know the difference between a healthy and an unhealthy love.

I don't think the love Rashid's father and I had for each other was good for either one of us. The good thing that came from it was our son. I met Lonnie in college. He was at Wilberforce University in Ohio, and I was at its sister college, Central State University. I had always loved basketball, so when I arrived on campus I got involved at Wilberforce working in the basketball office for the coaches. I got to know a lot of the players. That's how I met Lonnie. He was a big man on campus, in every way: a giant at six foot eight, a street-ball legend from our native Chicago. He walked around all the time like he had theme music playing. I was drawn to him from the start.

Lonnie and I had been seeing each other for several months when my mother came to visit for an event they had at Central called Mother's Day. They had a garden party with all the mothers and daughters. I asked Lonnie to come by so my mama could meet him. I was so excited because this was the first time I had ever really been in love.

"Mommy, you got to meet him," I said. "You'll love him!"

She talked with Lonnie for all of ten minutes.

"What do you think, Ma? What do you think?"

"He's not for you." She said it with a finality that brooked no dispute.

"But Mama, all he needs is just a little push."

She paused for a beat, then looked past me across the expanse of lawn to where it fell off in a steep ravine.

"You see over there?" she said. "If you push him off that cliff, that'll be your best bet."

Of course, I didn't understand what she was saying. I was in love and love is deaf, dumb, and blind sometimes. I stayed with Lonnie because I thought I could change him. I stayed with him because despite all that was difficult about loving him, I recognized the kindness in his heart. I stayed with him, too, I must admit, because I was a young girl and part of me dreamed that he would become a famous ballplayer.

My mother cried at the wedding, but not tears of joy. They were tears of fear and pain.

The trouble started soon after. Lonnie had always loved to party, but soon he got caught up in drugs. That's when I knew we were not going to stay together. I got pregnant, and I still had faith that we would find a way. But I had no idea just how bad things had gotten. I should have seen the signs. We were living in a small apartment together, and every morning I would wake up to go to work, and he would stay in bed. He had a hard time facing rejection. He had a hard time facing reality. He was Superman. He didn't feel like he could do a regular job.

Once Rashid was born, I thought for a while that things might get better, but they only seemed to get worse. It was horrible back in those days. I had to get a restraining order so Lonnie couldn't come near us. He would come to our apartment late at night and shoot at the windows. He kidnapped us when Rashid was only a baby, then kidnapped me again on my own just a few months later.

One day, though, I just got tired of being scared. He banged on the door, demanding to see Rashid. I opened it up with a gun in my hand.

"Come and get him, then," I said. "Come on. Come on. Why don't you try to come and get him?"

That was it. He turned around and walked away. Once he knew I wasn't scared of him anymore, it was over.

When he left to go to Denver, I was all alone with my son. I had to pay every bill. I was teaching school by day and working at Walgreens by night, but we made it work. I always thank God for those experiences—maybe not in the moment that I was in them, but when I found my way through to the other side. That's what shapes you. Now I look back and think, "Did I really go through all of that? People shooting at me, pulling me over, and jumping on me in the middle of the street, kidnapping me and my son at gunpoint?" It doesn't even seem real.

But I don't hate Lonnie for any of those things. And I never wanted Rashid to think less of his father. Honestly, I take pride in the fact that I never uttered a bad word to him about his father. No matter what went on between Lonnie and me, it had nothing to do with Rashid. He didn't choose his father; I did. He should not have to pay because his parents' relationship didn't work. A son needs his father, and Lonnie always loved Rashid. When it came to the two of us, though, Lonnie and I were just too different. I think I knew that from the start. I was always into changing people, though, into saving people. I tried to change Lonnie. I tried to save him. But you can't change anyone; you can't save them from themselves. In the end, the best thing you can do is to change yourself, to save yourself.

MY MOTHER WAS STRICT and she was protective, but there are certain things that you have to experience on your own. Growing up on the South Side of Chicago, you have very few opportunities to interact with someone who isn't black. Yeah, you might buy an ice-cream cone from a white store clerk or see Latinos or Asians when you went downtown, but in most of the places where you spent your time, you really didn't cross paths with other types of folk. That shapes you. It wasn't until I started high school that I had any significant contact with people who weren't black.

Think about it: in my community, the richest person and the

poorest person were black. You had black bankers and lawyers and businesspeople, but you also had black bums and hustlers and junkies. You had my mother, who was a teacher, a business-woman, and later a principal. And you had my uncle, who was struggling with addiction. The point is, never in my life did I think that being black would help or hinder me in a way that I couldn't address with hard work. It just was.

I first experienced racism when I was six years old. My mother and her sister had taken me and my cousin with them on a shopping trip. They wanted to go to T. J. Maxx and Marshalls, stores that were available only out in the lily-white suburbs. So we made the trip. It was so exciting for us because they also had a SportsMart. I remember I got a baseball glove and a new hat. It was nice.

I wasn't even thinking about race, about the fact that we were black and almost everyone else was white. It didn't cross my mind, that is, until we entered the last store of the night. There was an-other mother, a white woman, with a kid about our age. She was busy pulling clothes from the rack and checking labels and he was just kind of wandering in and out of the rows of clothes. Every now and then he would peek his head out and stare at us with a strange kind of smile on his face. It was strange because it was a smile, but it wasn't really friendly. It wasn't the kind of smile that made you smile too, in spite of yourself. It just made you wonder.

We inched closer to him, though, drawn in by the possibility of a new playmate. As we got closer, it sounded like he was sing-ing or something but I couldn't make out the words at first. When we got to within about six feet of him, I could hear what he was saying, but I still didn't understand it at first. In a singsong voice, he kept saying over and over again, "B-L-A-C-K . . . B-L-A-C-K . . ."

When it finally sank in, I just looked over at my cousin and then down at the ground. I don't know why I felt ashamed, but I did. Something started crawling under my skin and suddenly it didn't matter as much that I had a new baseball glove or a cap. Suddenly I felt like something very small. I didn't tell my mom. I didn't tell anybody. As a matter of fact, as I'm writing this, I realize that I've never told anyone before now.

I know a lot of people went through a lot more than I did that day. A few years later, I would learn about Emmett Till, the boy who wasn't much older than I was who was tortured and killed back in the 1950s for whistling at a white girl. He was from Chicago just like me. No, what I went through was nothing like that, but it put me in touch with feelings I had never felt before and would never want to feel again.

We all have moments like this in our childhood, when we suddenly become aware that for all the love our parents showered on us, we're finally on our own. How do you respond to this awareness? I guess that's one measure of your independence. Those early reactions go a long way toward shaping your personality. I know that's been the case with me.

I was a disciplinarian. I was strict because I had to be. It's not easy to discipline a child. But if you're a parent, that's your job. Rashid was a good boy, but he still was punished. I remember when he was first in the public eye, some news program came over to the house to do an interview. They had the two of us sitting on the couch, and the reporter asked, "So, Common, what do you most remember about your mother?" His little smart ass said, "She used to whip me."

I suppose I did. I knew that raising a son without his father meant that I had to be strict at times. Nowadays, I often speak to groups of young mothers. They ask me, "Well, how were you able to raise your son the way you did?" To begin with, I never liked him more than I liked me. I don't mean love—I loved him more than anything. But I always liked me best. If you don't like yourself, it makes it very hard to like and to love your child. So when I was raising Rashid, there's no way that he could have three pair of shoes if I only had two. And I'm the one working? That's not reasonable, mothers. How in the world do these young mothers go buy their child a designer something that costs a hundred dollars and you don't have a savings account? You don't have a house. You live in an apartment.

Being the parent of a child brings with it certain responsibilities. You are not their friend. You are their parent. You can be friendly, but you're not their friend. I'd tell Rashid in a minute. I'd say something, and he'd get ready to say something back—"We are not in a conversation. I didn't ask you a question. There is no reason to answer."

A lot of people think that's bad, I guess, because they want their kids to talk to them. Rashid and I talked. But he knew I could give him a look and not only would he be quiet, but he would stand at attention. I can give my granddaughter, Omoye, that same look.

They both understood the difference between conversation and di-
rection. When Rashid was growing up, if I told him we need to
talk, or if he came to me wanting to talk, then we would have a
conversation. We'd often end up talking about any and everything.
But if I told him to go get me a glass of water, then he'd get the glass
of water. There is no conversation.

WHEN I WAS EIGHT YEARS OLD, my mother bought me a bicycle. It was the first one I had ever owned. It was a blue Schwinn with racing tires, and I was sure that it was the best bike on the planet. It meant so much to me that for the first two weeks, I hardly even rode it and if I did, I'd spend a half an hour polishing it back up to a shine. The beginning of its third week, I took it on the longest ride yet—about eight blocks, down to the 7-Eleven. I drove it all the way onto the sidewalk right in front of the store window so that it would never be out of my sight. I bought myself a Slurpee and went back to my beloved bike. That's when they surrounded me: two older kids from the neighborhood—one fat and one skinny—that I didn't know by name but knew by sight.

"I ride the rhythm like a Schwinn bike when in dim light . . ."
—"RESURRECTION"

"Nice bike," the bigger one said.
I was silent.
"I *said*, nice bike."
"Thanks," I finally responded.

"I wish I had a nice bike like that."

"Yeah, me too," piped in the skinny kid.

"You want to give me your bike," he said.

It wasn't a question, so I didn't answer.

"Give me the bike, kid, or I'm going to take it from you."

What did I do at this moment of challenge? Did I fight the two kids off and ride away in triumph? Did I make a quick getaway, pedaling fast just past their reach? Did I take a beating but hold my own? No. I simply gave them the bike.

"Take it, then," I said.

They didn't even steal it; I just gave it away. The fat kid straddled the seat and started pedaling, his knees rising up almost to his chest. Before long, they had turned the corner and were out of sight.

It took me more than an hour to walk home. I don't think I ever walked so slowly. I could imagine the shame I was going to feel when I told my mother what had happened. But more than that, I kept feeling a churning sensation in my stomach from knowing that I had let myself down most of all. How could I give up so easily on something that mattered so much to me? How could I just surrender without a fight? Had I been scared? That was part of it. But fear alone had never stopped me before. It was something more: it was the suspicion that maybe I didn't deserve that bike in the first place. Maybe giving it up was the right thing to do. Maybe it was easier to be passive and just do nothing at all.

I've lived with this memory all of my life. It's a source of private shame, a fear of my own fundamental weakness, a hidden flaw buried deep in my character. My knowledge of it has driven me to react at times with extreme violence in the face of even the slightest provocation. At other times, it has led me to give in yet again, just like I did that day. I think we all carry with us these hidden shames, these deep-seated weaknesses. It's how you confront them that counts. From that moment on, I would try to live my life without shame.

On the face of it, my childhood was spent wrapped in love. Certainly, I was loved as much as any child could be. My mother made sure of that. But that love lived next to other emotions, ones that would find definition as I stepped outside of the protections of home.

2 "G.O.D. (GAINING ONE'S DEFINITION)"

Dear Emmett Till:

It may seem funny writing to a stranger, but, then again, I feel like I know you. My grade school English teacher Mrs. Lynn first introduced me to you and your story. When I heard about your short life and your tragic death, it scared me. It scared me that a little boy like you—a little boy like me—from the South Side of Chicago could be the victim of such hatred and such violence.

I used to stare at your picture: black and white, you in your suit, smile as wide as can be. I'd look deep into your eyes to see what type of person you might have been. I saw somebody who could have been my classmate, could have been my friend. I saw your innocence and your mischief and the goodness within you and that made it hurt even more to think of how you suffered.

Then there's the other picture of you. It's the

one that your mother had the courage to share. "Let the world see what I've seen," she said. Your face is bloated, almost unrecognizable. Your soft, handsome features have melted into a death mask. That face haunted my dreams. Could this even be the same boy?

Your story stayed with me. I could feel your spirit—like you were right there, telling me to do the things there wasn't time for you to do. When I was a ball boy for the Bulls basketball team, I would travel in this tunnel under the old Chicago Stadium. I would always get scared, thinking you were there in the darkness.

I remember finally talking to you, and I know you told me to be strong and do something with my life. "Do something that will have purpose, do something that will be powerful," I heard you say. I know I met you and I felt, I still feel, that responsibility to be something in my life. I looked at it like I have to live for you, and for all the other sons and daughters who lost their lives in the struggle for black liberation.

Here I was a young black boy from the South Side of Chicago, just like you. Emmett, you gave my life more value. You lost your life to senseless violence. You made me appreciate my life and want to be a greater human being.

I always thought your mother was so courageous, so strong to have demanded that they have an open casket at your funeral. She was determined to show the world what hatred could do. It taught us, it showed us. I always thought, "Why did this young kid have to give up his life? Even if his death helped birth the civil rights revolution, is it fair?" I still can't answer whether your sacrifice was just.

But, Emmett, I know that your life will never be forgotten. We *will remember. I will remember. I will continue to turn your death into a source of life. I will continue to live my life knowing yours was valuable and knowing I have to deliver something that will enhance the lives of others—especially children. Before I met you, all I knew was that I wanted to be a star. After that night, I knew that being a star would have to mean more than people knowing my name. It would mean a commitment to greatness, a commitment to memory.*

I know you told me that I had something greater to do on this earth. And I will do that, Emmett, in your spirit and in the spirit of all of those who paved the way for me. I just want you to know your life means something to me and to many others. Your spirit lives on in us.

Love,

Rashid

FOR AS LONG AS I CAN REMEMBER, I'VE WANTED TO BE A STAR. I still want to be. But now my purpose has more purpose. Now I want to use my fame to provide more exposure for my art so that I can influence people's lives for the better. I've come to realize that being a star means illuminating God's light.

> A little boy from Chicago had dreams to be a star
> And make a way and get some pay and drive a fancy car
> Though his mama used to say to him, "Hey, boy, just go to school"
> But whether it was old or new, in school he broke the rules
> —"WHAT A WORLD"

Back when it all started, as a little boy dreaming in the den on Bennett Street on the South Side of Chicago, all I knew was that I wanted to be famous. I wanted to be Michael Jackson, so I practiced my moonwalk and lip-synched along to "Billie Jean." I wanted to be Magic Johnson, or the hometown hero Isiah Thomas, so I dribbled a basketball wherever it would bounce and cradled it in my arms at night until I fell asleep. I wanted people to recognize me for my talents. I wanted them to honor my gifts. These were my dreams.

I always knew that Rashid was a dreamer. I always knew he had potential for great things. I thought it might be in music at first so I enrolled him in piano lessons. He went a few times, but he just wasn't interested.

"Mama, I want to play the drums," he said.

So I got him a drum set. He'd be down in the den banging on that thing for hours—at least it felt like hours! Then one afternoon, I didn't hear the drums at all. I went in to check on him and he had knocked a hole in the drum and made it into a basketball hoop. He had somehow balanced it on the doorjamb and was lofting a pair of balled-up gym socks at it.

"Well, like father like son," I thought. From that day, I really thought he might become a basketball player.

THE FIRST SPORT I PLAYED was Little League. What I noticed about playing baseball was the competition. I loved being around other young guys and being able to go up against them. You could get your neighborhood publicity—this dude got heat, or this dude can hit. You would gain a certain amount of respect from people in the neighborhood because your athletic success symbolized that you may have the potential to do something great.

I played shortstop and second base for the Red Sox. I liked being around the grown men—fathers, uncles—who coached us. They were teaching us, telling us what to do, but you could tell they cared for us, too. They'd give you fatherly guidance. For me, baseball was about fun, but at a certain point, I started getting tired of it.

When I was eight years old, I started playing basketball in a neighborhood league. It was in South Central Chicago, at a place called Avalon Park. My uncle was the coach. I started making friends with kids from all walks of life—from the projects and Sixtythird Street. I started learning how to mesh with different personalities, being able to connect and flow with everyone.

The way the games worked, the good players would play the first and fourth quarters and the scrubs would play the second and the third. My friend Dion and I played the second and the third, and, believe me, neither of us liked it. Don't get me wrong, we were still cool with the other guys, but I couldn't help feeling like I was second rate. I would get in the game at the start of the second quarter and, instead of playing my best and proving that I should be a starter, I just disappeared. I was on the court, I was running up and down with everybody, but I wasn't really in the game. I was just . . . invisible.

It got so bad at one point that I decided that I didn't want to play at all. Of course, I couldn't tell my uncle that, so I tried a more indirect approach. For the next week, every time the first quarter started running down, I suddenly fell victim to a terrible stomachache. I would be writhing around on the bench, trying to fake some tears. Then, before I knew it, the tears would be real as I thought about how I must be letting down the team, disappointing my uncle, and even disappointing myself. The first few times, my uncle bought it—or at least let on that he did. But when the next week rolled around and I tried the same thing, he had finally had enough.

My uncle Steve was a fun-loving guy, but he didn't take any mess. When he saw me warming up to do my little act on the bench, he pulled me to the side and laid me out.

"Quit your whining, boy, and get your ass in the game."

"But—"

"But nothing. I've had just about enough of this. Maybe your mama will baby you, but I won't. I told you to get in that game, so you better get in the goddamn game."

So I got in the game, but instead of going through the motions, I played with an attitude, a chip on my shoulder. I'm not saying I messed around and had a triple double—it wasn't that easy—only that I got myself in the right frame of mind to succeed. Over the next several weeks and months, I practiced every day. I'd dribble a basketball as I walked to school to improve my handle. I'd take extra jump shots. I was determined not to be invisible.

Before long, Dion and I were dominating the second and third quarters. Just hurting them! Soon enough we were running with the first team. I'm not sure if I realized it at the time—in fact, I'm sure I didn't—but that moment was laying some of the foundation for my future success.

How do you deal with being overlooked or underestimated? How do you deal with being raw and unprepared? Do you sulk on the bench, or do you force yourself to confront your weaknesses, to confront your self-doubts and the doubts of others and persevere? Time and again in my life, I've had to face these situations, whether it was somebody in the music industry telling me that a "conscious" artist would never sell records or a casting director telling me that I wasn't going to be any good as an actor. These are the moments that call upon your faith in God—and, through God, in yourself. These are the moments when you gain your definition.

Of course, the light of your greatness only shines if you work hard to cultivate it. You have to hustle. That hustler's spirit is one of my birthrights. I learned my hustle at home, watching my mother work two or three jobs, seeing how she made a way out of no way. That was my example and my inspiration.

_____

Raising Rashid, I sometimes think I neglected the hustle in favor of education. He grew up in a comfortable middle-class household. He never wanted for anything. I don't think he's ever held a job a day in his life. Don't get me wrong, he's always had a strong work ethic. He worked so hard as a student that he got straight As from elementary school all the way up through college. He's worked very hard on his career—first in hip-hop and now in film as well.

But the one thing I notice is that he has a hard time focusing on more than one thing at a time. "I can't be creative at the drop of a hat," he'll tell me. "I can't work on this thing and that thing all at the same time." I always say to him, "If you only do one thing at a time, then you'll only ever do one thing." It's the same as eating a balanced diet. Nobody sits down to dinner and only has grains on his plate. You have to have some protein, some vegetables, a few starches, some fruit. It's the mixture that makes things work for your body. It's the same thing for your life as a whole.

I remember one time when Rashid was maybe eight years old, he overheard me on the telephone talking to a professor from the University of Illinois at Urbana-Champaign, where I was studying for my doctorate in education. When I got off the phone, Rashid was giving me a funny look.

"Mama, how come you talking white?"

It took all of my composure not to bust out laughing. He was giving me that little-boy serious look, like he was deeply concerned.

"I'm not 'talking white,' honey. I'm talking with someone from the university, and when I do that I change up my vocabulary."

He still looked confused.

"Look, Rashid, do you talk to me the same way you talk to your cousin?"

He shook his head.

"Do you talk to your cousin the same way you talk to God when you pray?"

He shook his head again.

"Well, see, that's what I'm talking about. You change the way you speak depending on whom you're addressing."

Since he's been grown, he's mentioned that moment to me several times.

"Now I understand," he says. "The words you choose matter. That's exactly what I've been dealing with out here in LA. Talking to another artist in the rap game is a whole different thing from talking to directors or movie producers."

That was an important lesson for him to learn in order for him to be a man of the world. You've got to speak the language— and I'm not talking about French or Chinese or German. I'm talking about the languages you speak to different people right here depending on context and circumstance.

I learned these lessons because I had to. Sometimes I wonder whether I could have done more to teach Rashid how to move between multiple worlds. For all of Rashid's gifts, he doesn't really have that hustler's mentality. Perhaps it's because he never really had to hustle; he never had to face not knowing where he might get his next meal or where he was going to sleep. Maybe that's a good thing. Maybe that's progress. But I can't help thinking that it's left him without a certain kind of equipment for living.

In the last couple years, Rashid's gotten better at balancing several things at once. He's had to. But I don't think he understands or even defines hustling in the same way that I do. He's one of the hardest workers I know. But a hustler? I'm not so sure. He's still got room to grow. He still has years and years to go.

MY MOTHER EXPOSED ME to a world beyond my neighborhood, beyond Chicago. She did it through education, but she also did it through travel. Whenever she took a trip, I'd take a trip—to Atlanta, to Orlando, Florida, even to the Caribbean. But her greatest gift to me was faith. She probably thought that the sense of security I felt growing up came from knowing that she had my back. That was part of it; I knew I always had somebody there who loved me.

I'm going to tell you something else: for as long as I can remember, I always felt that God was going to bless me and take care of me. I felt in my spirit that God had great things in store for me. I had a sense of destiny. That has been my foundation. It's the reason I've never stopped believing in myself or my path, the reason I'm never afraid. I gained my self-definition through love of family, but also through the journey of faith.

I found that faith at Trinity United Church of Christ on Ninety-fifth Street. Reverend Jeremiah Wright Jr., the pastor there at the time, gave sermons the way Muhammad Ali fought a title bout. He would dance around with words, dazzling you with his rhetorical bobs and weaves, then he'd knock you out with his spiritual message. He preached the Gospels, of course, but he also preached black pride and black community and black heritage.

Reverend Wright would become my spiritual father: a teacher, a challenger, a source of inspiration to this day. His sermons are music. He is one of the greatest instruments I've ever heard playing in the key of God's word. "Unapologetically black, unashamedly Christian" was the motto, and we all came to live by it. I took that up as a challenge: to wear my blackness and my faith with pride, but not conceit. These were precisely the words I needed to hear as a black boy growing up in a society that often looked at me with fear and distrust.

Many people will know Reverend Wright's name only because of the controversy that surrounded him near the end of his career as pastor of Trinity. Back in 2008, a member of his congregation named Barack Obama was running for president. Reporters looking for any shred of controversy combed over thousands of hours of tape of Reverend Wright's sermons and broadcast a couple minutes of his preaching, taken completely out of context. They said he was angry. They said he was racist. They said, how could our future president sit in the pews and listen to such hatred? But they weren't talking about the Jeremiah Wright that I knew. They weren't talking about the wise, funny, thoughtful, and loving man who influenced me, and so many others, over his long career.

No one could listen to an entire sermon from Reverend Wright and say that he was hateful. He preached the Gospels. He preached love. To know that I was loved, to know that I was the descendant of African kings, to know that I was a child of the Most High—these things gave my life affirmation. As fortunate as I was to have a mother who loved me and believed in me, it was also important to know that I was valued outside of my family. So many things can chip away at a young person's self-esteem. So many things can lead to self-doubt. But hearing the message that God was around me, that He was alive in me and could act through me, inspired me to live with purpose, passion, and perception.

"WE HAVE BROTHER COMMON in the house with us this morning. Brother, won't you come up and bless us with some of your raps?"

It's New Year's Eve 2003 at Trinity United Church of Christ, and I've come to service with my mother. The Reverend Jeremiah Wright is at his usual place on the pulpit. We locked eyes sometime during his sermon, so this invitation isn't completely unexpected.

"Give it up, y'all. Let's bring brother Common to the stage!"

I've given hundreds of concerts all around the world, performed in front of thousands of people, but this is just about as nervous as I've ever been with a mic in my hand. The main thing going through my mind is, "Don't curse! Don't curse!" I can just imagine myself in front of all these God-fearing Christians dressed in their Sunday best, here to hear the Word, and in the end they hear the S-word, the F-word, whatever. That's the last thing I want to do.

So I grasp the mic, and the church band lays down a thick bass line, punctuated by African drums. That's when it takes over. It's the feeling one gets—call it divine inspiration, call it the spirit. The times when I'm closest to God are when I'm praying, when I'm reading the Bible, and when I'm creating. And so I find that link, that power, and I'm not worried anymore. I just . . . flow.

When I'm doing a freestyle, my mind is working faster than my mouth, and my memory is all but shut down. You can ask me what I said three minutes after I finish, and I won't be able to tell you the first thing about it. Sometimes you create for posterity; you create with that sense of timelessness. But sometimes you create something that's so delicate—so fleeting—that it can last only for a moment. To me, that kind of creation is no less beautiful, no less miraculous. It's just its own thing.

"Brother Common is playing with me now. He just took my whole sermon and rapped it in two sentences!"

As long as I can remember, Trinity United has been a big part of my life. My mother started taking me there when I was about six years old. Every Sunday, we'd be there. You'd have to arrive early to make sure you got a seat. At the time, Revered Wright was making his name and building a large congregation. In the years that followed, that congregation would help build a new church, more than twice the size of the old one, and would help fill that church with nearly four thousand worshipers every week. People weren't coming there because it was popular, though, they were coming there for the message, the affirmation. From the Ethiopian crosses that adorned the structure to the African scenes depicted in the stained glass, this was a house of worship dedicated to sustaining the community and connecting it with its Christian roots.

As a young black boy sitting in those pews, I didn't even realize at first what kind of an education Revered Wright was giving me. He instilled me with pride, but also with humility. He gave me wisdom, but also understanding. His sermons had political texture. He was learned, even erudite, but also hip. More than that, he introduced me to a Jesus who was cool and relatable. Listening to Reverend Wright's sermons made me want to read—the Bible, of course, but other books as well. And so as I grew up in the church, he would send me to Carter G. Woodson's *The Mis-Education of the Negro* and Malcolm X's *The Autobiography of Malcolm X as Told to Alex Haley.* He did all of this without even knowing who I was.

Of course, like every child, going to church was also something I did simply because *it was something we did.* I didn't always want to go. One Sunday morning when I was ten or eleven years old, I'd had just about enough of this churchgoing stuff. Getting up early, getting dressed in my Sunday best while some of the other kids were on the basketball courts. Sitting for hours surrounded by mostly old folks while the preacher went on and on. I'd had enough.

"Mama, why we have to go to church every Sunday?"

"Boy, it's not even a question. Get your butt dressed. It's almost time to go."

"I don't wanna go."

"You better get dressed and get in the car, Rashid. We'll be late."

"I'm not going. I'm not going. I don't even want to live here anymore. I want to move to Denver with my dad."

That sounded like a good thing to say at the time. I was going to try every angle. But she called my bluff. Before I knew it, she had every scrap of clothes I owned packed up in a suitcase and sitting near the front door.

What was I to do? Back down and show my true weakness—and end up going to church to boot? Or should I stick to my guns, even if it meant heading off into an uncertain future sure to include many of my father's peanut butter and banana sandwiches and those cold Colorado nights? So, I walked. And I walked—an entire block and a half, before I turned around and headed back home. And got dressed just in time for church.

As a child, it seemed like I spent most of my waking hours in one of two places: church or school. When it was time for me to start kindergarten, my mother enrolled me in the neighborhood school,

McDowell Elementary. It was a little yellow and blue schoolhouse with a big window in the front. McDowell was a public school on the South Side of Chicago, which is to say that it brought together the poor and the middle class. Kids who went to McDowell almost always went on to Caldwell Middle School. And as much as I tried to say I wanted to go to Caldwell when I was old enough, I was scared to death of it. That was one of those 'hood schools. If you went there, you'd better be able to handle your business.

> Gettin' green on acres, these broads were our mules
> That's when we used to serve in front of Caldwell School
> Fuel for cars and jewels, chains and tools
> It was organized crime, but we remained konfused
> Mom in the pews singin', "Lord, protect 'em"
> You might not agree with our views, but you had to
>   respect 'em
> Diamonds in the rough, but what were we reflectin'
> A system that's abrupt, the streets, and oppression
> —"DO THE RIGHT THANG"

I was still a little baby in my own way. McDowell was about as much as I could handle. I had some really good times there. We'd play hill dill and dodgeball. I remember dudes used to climb up onto McDowell's roof on the weekends just to say they did it. There were definitely kids who fell to the ground and kids who started up, then turned back around. Me? I never tried it.

I didn't want to leave McDowell. But halfway through second grade, my mother decided that it was time for a change. That's when she settled on the Faulkner School, where I'd stay until high school. Going from McDowell to Faulkner was like going from *Good Times* to *The Cosby Show*. Almost all the kids at Faulkner were from middle-class homes with parents who could afford private school tuition (a whopping two thousand dollars a year, I think!). Faulkner was located on Seventy-first and Coles. It was a comfortable place, sort of like a home learning center. We had only around fifteen kids per class. Everybody knew one another.

Not surprisingly, the kids at Faulkner weren't nearly as streetwise as my McDowell classmates. My first day at my new school, I was understandably apprehensive, but by the second day, I was walking the halls like I owned the place. I felt confident in my street sensibility. I knew when somebody was about to try something. I could gauge people's strengths and weaknesses—and I could exploit those weaknesses when I had to—all at the age of seven.

I made friends for life at Faulkner. Two of my best friends started out as enemies. First, there was Murray. I met him the last week of class before summer vacation in my first year at the school. Somehow we had both ended up in detention. I was in second grade; he was in third. I remember Murray teasing me, calling me "Rashit, Rashit." I hated that. Somehow, before that hour was over, we had developed a bond. The next year, I skipped from second to fourth grade, so we ended up being classmates. We've been friends now for thirty years.

Derek Dudley started at Faulkner soon after me. Nobody liked him at first. He had a few strikes against him: (1) he was the new kid, (2) he was vertically challenged, (3) he was way too confident.

His father owned a software company, so Derek always seemed to have a lot of nice things. To us, he was rich. He once came to school with this piece of jewelry for a girl he liked. For some reason, that set me off.

"Man, this little Richie Rich dude thinks he's real tough, don't he?" I fumed to Dion.

Later that night, I called Derek and threatened him. He hung up, but I kept calling him back. He was just a little too big for his britches as far as I was concerned. The next time I called, it went to the answering machine, so I left a bunch of threats on there for him to hear later on. For some reason it didn't cross my mind that his parents might hear them first. The next morning, his father came to the school—with a copy of the tape! I caught some heat for that one.

Before long, Derek would become my guy—and now he's been my manager for many years. Even then, he was really smart at science and math, so I made sure that I was always his partner when it came to school projects. Derek was really advanced. He was into technology, dealing with computers before most of us even knew what a computer was. One year he and I made it to the state science fair—fourth grade, I think. We did this project on fiber optics. First we won the school science fair, then the district science fair, and then on to state. Trouble for me was, the competition fell on the exact same day as my championship basketball game. Around my house, though, there was no discussion. I was going to the science fair or else.

There we were, dressed up in our church clothes, pressed shirts and slacks. We did our demonstration and the judges started peppering us with questions. One judge asked me, "What's faster: sound or light?" I had no idea. I just hoped it didn't show on my face. Meanwhile Derek was thinking, "This fool . . . I know he doesn't know this!"

So I just guessed: "Light."

"Yes!" Derek blurted.

We didn't win, but we got a nice little certificate, maybe a ribbon too. Meanwhile, my basketball team won the championship and I wasn't there. But I was given a special award for choosing academics over sports. Cold comfort.

My other good friend from Faulkner was Dion. The first thing I noticed about him was his comb. Faulkner had a strict dress code, so on Monday through Thursday we had to wear green-and-white uniforms. On Friday we could wear whatever we wanted. Those Fridays were important. You had to come with some style. I remember Dion used to sport this bejeweled comb in his back pocket. He thought he was slick. Dion, better known as No ID, would go on to produce most of the songs on my first three albums as well as hits for Jay-Z, Kanye, and many others. I'm working with him again right now as I write.

Faulkner was so small and homey that we even got to know the teachers.

There was Mr. Brown, who taught us math but would also come to school early to play basketball with us. We thought he was cool because he didn't get mad if you cussed around him, on the court and even in class sometimes. When it came to teaching math, he was no-nonsense. I thought I was the class clown, so any time it got too quiet, I'd do something crazy like fart or belch real loud. I'd just wait for things to get quiet and then let them rip. But every time you acted out, he'd put your name on the board. If you kept acting the fool, he might add a check or two after it.

"Okay," he'd say, scrawling your name out in chalk, "you got something else to say?"

For every mark you got on the board, you had to bring five copies of whatever mathematical formula we were learning at the time. Thanks to Mr. Brown, I still know the Pythagorean theorem, the area of a square, cosine, sine, all of that. At one point, after another bout of my foolishness, Mr. Brown pulled me aside.

"Rashid, stop being a bumbler all your life and do something great."

That resonated with me. He really taught me well in math—and in life. It's funny how a small moment like that can stay with you forever. If you asked Mr. Brown about it now, he probably wouldn't even remember saying that. But for me, the moment is indelible. In that moment, too, I was gaining my definition.

Many other teachers at Faulkner influenced my direction. We had an English teacher named Miss Scott. Dion swears she was deaf in at least one ear. Dion and I would be talking to each other in the middle of class, and she would look at us and say, "What? What did you say?" I always did well in her classes, though. She inspired me with my writing. I still see her from time to time at church when I'm back in Chicago. She'll come up to me without fail and say, "I'm so proud of you, boy! I always knew you were something special."

One year, maybe around sixth grade, we got a new science teacher. He was Jamaican, and when you stressed him out, he'd start speaking in such a thick patois that you couldn't really understand what he was saying. The first day of class, he went around the room and asked everyone to introduce themselves. When he got to me, I decided to put a little flavor into mine.

"And who are you, young man?"

"I'm the Cool Chief Rocka, I don't drink vodka / But keep a bag of cheeba inside my locker."

He was not amused by my homage to Run-D.M.C. He looked at me like, "What is this imbecile saying?" The other kids were impressed, though.

THE THING THAT REALLY impressed my classmates was when I became friends with a rookie guard for the Chicago Bulls named Michael Jordan. When I was twelve years old, my father helped me get a job as a ball boy for the Bulls. I started working the year before Jordan came into the League and stayed until the year after. Talk about a difference. I got to meet a lot of the players on the opposing teams too, because I worked the visitors' bench. Magic. Bird. Dr. J. I used to get them to give me their sneakers. Most kids would have collected them and hoarded them. Me? I started my own black-market shoe economy. My biggest customer was my math teacher, Mr. Brown. He'd pay me a few dollars every now and then, but mostly we'd barter. A pair of lightly worn Wes Matthews Pumas, size 12? He'd knock off a few demerits and keep me out of detention.

My first encounter with fame was being around the Bulls. I used to see Isiah Thomas, Julius Erving, Magic Johnson, walking around with furs on. I saw how just because my mother's friend's husband knew Isiah Thomas we all looked up to him. Fame was contagious, it seemed. Someone might say, "I heard Vanessa on *The Cosby Show* used to live up on Pill Hill!" Now everyone on Pill Hill would walk around with their chest puffed out just a little bit more. We definitely were starstruck.

With Michael Jordan, I got to see a star come to life. Sometimes it's the smallest things that let you know someone's a star. During one of his first exhibition games, Jordan brought a little red radio into the locker room, blasting Whodini. The general manager, Rod Thorn, came in and said, "Sorry, Michael. You can't play that in here." Jordan went out that night and dropped thirty points on somebody, and from then on, he could play whatever he wanted.

Michael was a big kid. He related to the ball boys because we had the same loves: music and basketball. He was a prankster, too. I remember one time I was working a game and this fan sitting courtside asked me to get Michael's autograph for him. I said I could get it for five dollars. So I went into the locker room and took the piece of paper for Mike to sign.

"Rashid, you sign it."

Well, why not? So I signed the paper and took it back to the man. He handed me the five-dollar bill and I handed him the forged autograph. He gave it one look and started shaking his head.

"This isn't Michael Jordan's autograph!"

"Yeah, it is."

"No. No, it's not."

"How do you know?"

"Because 'Michael' is spelled wrong!"

I used to run some other hustles, too. On game days, I'd sneak Murray into the stadium and he'd serve as an honorary ball boy. I remember one game was Jordan poster night. They gave out five thousand. Murray and I got a couple hundred for ourselves and got Mike to sign a bunch of them. We asked him if we could sell them, and he said, "Nah, you gotta give 'em away." But, you know, we took twenty or thirty of them and sold them right there in the stadium. In that year alone, I probably had thousands and thousands of dollars in Jordan paraphernalia go through my hands. I got two tickets for the 1985 NBA All-Star Game, including the slam-dunk contest when Jordan and Dominique Wilkins clashed in one of the greatest dunking displays of all time. Murray and I went down to the stadium and scalped our tickets for twice the face value. We were little hustlers like that.

My main responsibility as a ball boy was taking all the used towels after games from the visitors' locker room to the home locker room on the other side of old Chicago Stadium. I didn't know it at the time, but Chicago Stadium had been built way back in 1929. It was state of the art, bigger than Madison Square Garden, better than any stadium around at the time of its construction. Over the years, it hosted everything from the Blackhawks and the Bulls, to football games, concerts, and prizefights. Joe Louis fought there. So did Muhammad Ali. The Jackson 5 performed there. So did Bob Marley. You could feel that history in the building, the echoes across the decades. Kids can sense those things.

Once the game was over, I'd stack my arms high with as many towels as I could carry. I wasn't allowed to cross the court, so

I had to take this underground tunnel that snaked below the arena to reach the other side. Running down that corridor made you feel like you were the last person left in the whole world. The lights would flicker sometimes, from dim to almost dark. The sound of your sneakers hitting the concrete would echo through the emptiness. I was always a little scared so I would run as fast as I could. That's when I saw the ghost.

In Ms. Lynn's English class, we'd read something about Emmett Till, the black boy from Chicago who'd traveled down South to Mississippi in the summer of 1955 to visit relatives. While there, he allegedly whistled at a white woman who was working as a store clerk. That night white men came and pulled him out of the house. They beat him to death and threw his body over the bridge into the Tallahatchie River, a seventy-pound cotton gin fan tied around his neck with barbed wire to keep his body from floating to the top. Three days later, his body washed up on the banks. His features were so distorted, his family could identify him only by a ring he wore that once belonged to his father.

Rather than mourn her lost son in private, Emmett's mother made his death public, even allowing *Jet* magazine to publish pictures of his body in an open casket. She wanted people to see the brutality some people were capable of inflicting. For what? A whistle? The color of his skin? They say his death helped launch the civil rights movement. Ms. Lynn showed the pictures to us. His face was bloated, masklike, mangled beyond recognition. Then she showed a picture of him alive just before that summer: smiling, his hat cocked a little to the side. He looked like us. He was just a fourteen-year-old kid—cocky but insecure too. A little like me.

His story and face stuck with me. I remember reading about him and being scared and angry all at the same time. How could this happen? The pictures haunted me. When I was all alone in the tunnel underneath the stadium, I could feel Emmet Till near. When I ran, he was right behind me. The faster I went, the closer he came. But I always remained just beyond his grasp. I just knew that he—that his ghost—was down there. That's when I decided to stop running and confront him.

"What do you want?" I asked out loud.

There he was before me, his smiling face, hat cocked to the side. He didn't speak, but all at once, I knew why he was there. He wanted me to do more. He wanted me to *be*. *You have a purpose that's greater than just yourself.* He was a kid like me, and they took his life. Others had lost their lives so that I could live mine in freedom. I had every opportunity. Now I just had to be great: for my family, for my mother, for my people, for me. From then on, I wasn't scared of the dark.

Ever since that night, I've felt the spirit of Emmett Till driving me, pushing me past all sorts of challenges, inspiring me to achieve. I believe that still to this day. Gaining one's definition demands that we learn from others' experiences as well as our own. It means seeing yourself as part of a community—of family, of faith, and even of history.

3 "POP'S RAP"

Hey, Pops:

I was just thinking of you. We talked on the phone last night, but I just thought about you again today and what you mean to me. For as long as I can remember, you've always thanked me for choosing you and Ma as my parents. Well, I just have to tell you that I wouldn't have chosen any other parents but you, any other father but you.

If I had to describe you in a word, I'd call you a Seeker. I feel like I got my spiritual journey from you even before I knew that you believed in the Most High and that you didn't restrict your spiritual learning to any single religion. I thank you for that. I got it from you, Dad.

When you told me that you chose to call me Lonnie Rashid Lynn because you wanted me to have Christian and Muslim names together, that inspired me. Because of that, I walk in the way,

Dad, accepting people for who they are, knowing God is in them whether they are Buddhist or Muslim or Christian or Hindu or Yoruba. Becoming a Spiritual Seeker has been one of the most powerful lessons of my life. Because of it, I've found God all around me.

Now that I'm older, I have a whole new perspective on you. I see you not only as a father but also as a husband and a son and a friend and an imperfect person striving to do as much right as his will allows. It hasn't always been easy being your son. There were times as a child when I felt that you had abandoned me. What I see now are not excuses, but understanding. You had to move forward with your life, and your love for me was always there, no matter what you or Ma were going through. As a man, you loved me.

Growing up, I looked at you as both real and imagined. You were the man I knew, someone I would sometimes get on a plane to visit, but you were also a local legend. "My dad played in the ABA," I'd tell people. "My dad is from the 'hood, the low end in the Chi. My dad is real." And you are real, Pops. You are true to who you are and what you feel. That always gave me a sense of pride.

At the same time, I often felt like a piece of me had been broken off. Sometimes it was easier just to be angry than it was to remain confused. As I've grown older, I've learned more about you, more about life. I don't hold any of those pains or fears anymore. Once I built up a little bit of a name, it would fill me with pride when I'd hear you bragging on me to your friends—or even to strangers. "My son did this . . ." You remind me of the warrior that I am.

Dad, I always knew you were a smart man. To me, you are one of those rare people to walk this earth with more wisdom than is sometimes good for you. I hear it in our talks. I feel it when you *say certain things about our ancestors. I know that I tend to run around staying immersed in my career, but I'm stopping today to say thank you. Thank God you are my father.*

I think I inherited the long-winded talking from you—and the drinking, too. Aha. I remember Ma used to say I had a temper like yours. I've been working on it. Dad, I want you to know you are a special human being, spiritual and raw. You say some of the wisest things, and you say some of the craziest things. I know your heart is good even when things aren't good and you're saying some real crazy shit. Even then, I know that's you and your heart. You're always gonna speak your mind. You always reminded me to speak up for myself. I don't like doing it sometimes; sometimes I stay silent. But I admire that in you and strive to express it in me. When you believe in me, Dad, I feel even stronger.

I know you said I could have played in the League if I just had that killer instinct. Well, I know I'm getting that killer instinct in me now. I had to work on myself to get it. I realized I had some holes in my soul. I felt abandoned by you. Because you left, I never really realized until recently just how much that affected me. But I worked on it and dealt with it and struggled with it and acknowledged it and I forgave. I forgave you, myself, and anyone else who needed forgiveness. That's all part of my journey toward being a better child of the Most High. It's part of dealing with my demons and my fears.

Just the other day, there was a driver, an old-timer, waiting to pick me up at the airport. He held up a sign that read "Lonnie Lynn," your name and mine. "Man, I thought you were Lonnie Lynn the basketball player," he said when he met me. It made me so proud that he knew your name. It made me feel like I did when I was eight years old and one of the old heads on the block would stop me on the ball court and ask, "Aren't you Lonnie's son?"

Sometimes I get tired of hearing you complain or hearing you blame somebody else for your misfortune. "Dad, take responsibility," I say. "Look at you. Don't blame others for things you can do or change. You're focusing your energy in places where it won't help." At the same time, I understand. I do it, too. But some of that shit that you are in—the tough times, the loneliness, the not having money—you brought it on yourself. I want to take care of you, but sometimes I feel burdened. I feel the weight of you always needing something. But you do, and so do I. Sometimes that need is just the need to be heard. Pops, I hear you.

I look at you and see the ways you excelled as a father—being loving, being honest, being you—and I try to pass those same gifts on to Omoye. At the same time, I look at some of the things that you may not have done and I see myself repeating them now and then. The moment I do is the moment I strive to do better. I want you to know that you will never be forgotten—always loved, always celebrated, always heard. And even if no one else understands everything you do, know that I love you, and I thank God you are my pops.

Love,

Rashid

I WAS TEN YEARS OLD THE FIRST TIME I VISITED MY FATHER. UP TO that point, he was mostly a memory from what seemed like a long time ago and far away. My father was a local legend—"Oh, you're Lonnie's son. You shoot hoops?" people would say. I basked in the reflected admiration. I rarely saw my father, so I gathered what little of him that I could. My father was a Sunday voice on the telephone, a deep baritone that talked to me about jump shots and girls and how I was doing in school. He was what was left on my face when I took my features and subtracted my mother's features. He wasn't really real.

That changed with a plane ticket and a three-hour flight. One Sunday morning in 1982, my mother gave me the news over my bowl of Cheerios.

"You're going to visit your father."

"Huh?"

"Boy, don't say 'huh' to me. You're going to visit your father in Denver. You leave in two weeks, right after school ends."

"What's Denver?"

"It's in Colorado. You're going on a plane. Your cousin Ajile is coming with you."

I'd flown before, of course. Since I was little, my mother had put me on planes to visit relatives or go along with her on her annual vacations—to Florida, Puerto Rico, wherever. But this time was going to be different. I'd be visiting my father. Of course, the fact that my cousin Ajile was coming along made it all right. Having Ajile around turned just about anything into an adventure.

On that first trip, I can remember Dad driving us around in his Buick, him in the front and us in the back. One day we were headed to an amusement park—one of those temporary parks that they set up in a church parking lot or an empty field. Aj and I were whispering schemes and insults like boys do, rivals at one moment, best friends always. We'd taken to listening to the radio when I visited Ajile in Ohio. Records were something else, though; neither of us had ever owned one. My father, on the other hand, had what we thought of as the world's greatest collection of record albums. Flipping through them, we'd come across a whole new universe of names that seemed written in another language and images that recombined reality before our very eyes.

"Dad, who's Theolopolous Muck?"

"Huh?"

"Theolopolous Muck? Who's Theolopolous Muck?"

He walked in from the bedroom to see what in the world I could possibly be talking about.

"Thelonious Monk. Thelonious is one of the great geniuses of jazz. He'd be playing his piano onstage, get up in the middle of a song and turn around in circles, then sit back down and finish what he started. Here, let me play you some."

Dad played me Earth, Wind & Fire, Marvin Gaye, Al Green, as well as musicians from back in Chicago like Eddie Harris who had a song called "More Soulful Than Soul." I liked that. Before long, I was asking him if I could borrow a few albums to take back and dub in Chicago. Every visit thereafter, I'd take a couple more. I don't know if I ever got around to recording them—or returning them. My father would later joke, "You were cleaning me out, one trip at a time. You got some of my heaviest stuff!"

So on a drive out to the amusement park, I screwed up the courage to ask my father for a gift.

"Dad, would you buy me an album?"

I could see his eyes glance back at me from the rearview mirror before he responded.

"What album you want?"

I mumbled my response.

"What was that?"

"Soul Sonic Force."

The car filled with his low chuckle.

"You hip to that? Yeah, I think that can be arranged."

Because of those visits, I started getting closer to my father. Life with him in Denver was so different from life back home. We never went to church. "I pray through the ancestors," he'd tell me, and we'd try doing it together. We rarely sat down to dinner; we ate our meals on the run from one place to another. He'd tell me about black history, about leaders like Malcolm X and Medgar Evers. And, of course, we'd talk about basketball.

Over the next several years, I'd make more trips to Denver. Each time would mark some sort of growth spurt into manhood. On one trip—I think I was eleven years old—Murray came along. Pops piled Murray and me into the car and drove us over to visit a friend of his. He didn't warn us that his friend was David Thompson—one of the most famous basketball players alive. David Thompson was Michael Jordan before Michael Jordan; even Jordan seemed to admit as much when he asked Thompson to introduce him at his Hall of Fame induction. Thompson had smooth, silky moves and a power game to match. He could throw down a dunk and stick his whole arm through the hoop before landing lightly on the ground. He was a Superman, but he was also Dad's friend.

David Thompson's house was like nothing I had ever seen. He had a swimming pool like the kind you'd see at the YMCA, except there was none of the chaos of skinny kids peeing in the water. Instead there was an expanse of calm and glassy surface, a deep aqua blue. He had what felt to me like a regulation basketball court, too. We played two on two, me with my pops and Murray with David Thompson. I don't know who won, but I know that the afternoon was joyous and surreal.

My father could be playful—almost like a friend who happened to be six foot eight—but he could also be stern. He never held back his honesty. He always told his truth. When it came time to send me back home to Chicago, I could tell it wasn't easy for him to see me go, but he knew what had to be done. He wanted what was best for me, and he knew that wasn't him. "It's hard living a thousand miles away from your son just because you need to be a thousand miles away from his mother," he'd tell me years later. He had made his decisions. He had made his mistakes. But he was moving on the best way that he knew how. As far apart as we were in miles, I always knew he loved me and that I could count on him for advice, for assistance, and every now and then, for some sweet soul music.

Once I was grown, or at least when I thought I was, I remember feeling angry with my father. Why hadn't he been there? Why did he leave? I just couldn't understand it.

I remember him saying, "Your mother and I got divorced, but I never divorced you. A parent can never divorce a child."

"Then what happened? Why weren't you there?"

"Son, can you understand what it's like to live so far away

from your child and know that he has a life that doesn't involve you? I'm not saying it's an excuse, but can you understand?"

I couldn't or I wouldn't. It took having my own child to understand. It took breaking up with her mother. It took living a thousand miles away from my child at times, too. I fight with myself knowing that I haven't always been the father I wanted to be. It was never for lack of love, but for lack of fight. I haven't fought at certain times to be around her.

My father was there and he wasn't. Instead of one male role model, I relied upon many. I had my Uncle Steve. He had his troubles, but I always knew he loved and supported me. And then there was my stepfather, Ralph, whom my mother married when I was seven years old.

Ralph was a hardworking guy and he never tried to take on the role of my father. I already had a father, after all. But he was a male presence in my daily life, and that mattered. Ralph was the man who worked hard every day as a plumber and came home at night in time for dinner. He enjoyed his football and a cold beer. He believed in churchgoing, discipline, and education. Beyond that, I never really got to know him as a man until I was a man myself.

I was thirty-four when I married Ralph. Rashid was seven. I met Ralph when he came by my nursery school to do some work. He mentioned that he was recently divorced and was interested in meeting a good woman. Did I know anybody? I told my mother that story and she said, "I'd keep him for myself if I were you."

"Oh, no," I said. "He's too young for me and, besides that, he's not my type." A few weeks later, I called my mother up: "I'm going out with Ralph. Will you keep Rashid?" On our fifth date, I called my mother: "Ma, I'm keeping him for myself." We've been married now for nearly thirty-three years. Whenever she can, my mother says, "I told you so!"

Ralph was an indirect influence on Rashid. If it wasn't for Ralph, I wouldn't have been able to provide for Rashid the way I have. Ralph never asked me what I made. All my money went to savings—I never had to pay rent, light, gas, nothing. That's a very good way to operate. When I was getting ready to marry Ralph, my best girlfriend, Barbara, said to me, "Do not split the bills. Wherever he lived, he'd have to pay rent, gas, light. Let him pay that. You take your check and you be the saver. If you do that, then you'll always be able to live off of one check."

And she was so right. I told Ralph, "I'm not going to pay any bills." And he said, "Okay, Ann." As a result, I was the saver. As a result, we live well today as retirees. Even if one of us had passed, the other one could make it. Even if one of us was sick, we could make it. I let Rashid know I could do what I wanted with my money because Ralph was the provider in our household. I could buy Rashid a car. We could take vacations.

Never did I get a dime from his father. Never ever. And Ralph was the reason mainly that Rashid went out to visit Lonnie. With all that I went through, I wasn't about to send my son out there— not so much fearing for Rashid's safety, but to punish Lonnie. But Ralph had gone through it with his ex-wife, and she didn't want him to see his son. So he said, "Do not keep Rashid from his father.

Make sure he can go." Ralph is one of the main reasons that I was
able not to be as bitter toward Lonnie. If he's not on drugs, let him
see his son. Rashid was ten or eleven when he first went out there.
He and Ajile went out there. He and Murray went out. I never
wanted him not to have a connection.

LOOKING BACK, I can see that Ralph did certain things to try to instill responsibility in me. My mother only asked me to do a few chores, so I know he must have thought she was coddling me. But he didn't say anything. He didn't protest. Whenever he could, though, he'd try to have me take on some small responsibilities. Ralph loves to tell the story of the time we had the painter coming over and he and my mother had to go to another appointment. He left me in charge of things. I was eight years old so he figured I could handle this much responsibility.

"Rashid, just wait here and make sure the painter gets the key to the front door," he said. "I'm trusting you to take care of this."

So there I was alone in the house, and I suddenly had a taste for a Slurpee. I went to the drawer where my mother kept her paper and pens and carefully scrawled out a note. Then I got some Scotch tape, took the key, and attached it directly to the front door along with a note that read, "Dear Painter, here is the key to the house." Then I hopped on my bike and went about my business.

When I got home, the painter was there and so was Ralph.

"Rashid," he said, "you might as well have left the door wide open. Why'd you do that?"

"You said to let him know where the key was. So that's what I did."

He shook his head and tried not to let his smile show.

I learned a lot of lessons in that house. I was shown a lot of love. I also learned a lot from my father, both from him directly and from his absence. At certain points, he'd be there for me with a voice and a philosophy. When I think of him not being around, part of it may have to do with his own failings. I don't think he was happy with himself for a long time. He had disappointed himself by not making the League, by struggling with addiction. It's the kind of thing where it snowballs, and you end up saying, "You know what? I'm not going to take care of that either because my life isn't right."

The summer of 1984 was a turning point in my life. I was twelve years old, not quite a child and not yet a teenager. Part of me was still a baby in some ways. On Saturday mornings, I'd whine to my mother if she didn't cook up enough bacon. I liked kid shows— *The Space Giants* and *Super Friends* were my favorites—and baseball cards. But I also liked girls and obsessed over the possibilities of sexual conquest. I looked up to the older dudes around the neighborhood, guys known for whooping niggas' asses or for being generals in the Four Corner Hustlers. I guess you'd call them ghetto celebrities, but to me they were stars. With all of that swirling in my head it should come as no surprise that in 1984 I discovered two lifelong passions: hip-hop and girls.

I was searching for the thing that would make me stand out,

that would help my star to shine. I found it in hip-hop. Hip-hop wasn't that big in Chicago in the mid-1980s. Sure, we'd heard of Run-D.M.C. and Kool Moe Dee, but the thought of becoming a rapper wasn't really in people's heads. It took leaving Chicago for it to get into mine.

I was born in Chicago, raised on Planet Rock.
—"MAINTAINING"

Growing up, I used to spend part of my summers in Cincinnati visiting my cousin Ajile. We would hang out with his crew, just talking and listening to music. Afrika Bambaataa and Soul Sonic Force. Kool Moe Dee. Egyptian Lover. The biggest group in Cincinnati at that time was the Bond Hill Crew. They were like Cincinnati's version of Run-D.M.C. Of course, I had heard hip-hop in Chicago, but the Bond Hill Crew was different. These dudes were right there. I could watch them with my own two eyes. They made an impression on me.

So one summer night in 1984, I sat in my cousin's room and tried to rap. Ajile wrote a rap about the eighth graders, and I wrote one about the Bond Hill Crew. I still remember some of it:

Well, let me tell you 'bout a trip, a time ago
I was going there to run a cold-blooded show
When I was there I saw some people jamming, too
They called themselves the Bond Hill Crew
Dr. Ice, Romeo, and Master E
All of the Bond Hill crew rappin' to a T
I asked them could they rock with me

That's all I can recall. As soon as I finished my verse, I noticed that my cousin and his friends were looking at me with their eyes all wide. "Man, that's cold!" They were repeating my lines back to me, memorizing what I had just written. That was deep to me. I don't know if I can say it was life changing, because I had no way of knowing just how much my life would change because of hip-hop, but let's just say that it brought the sunshine in.

Cincinnati was a place of discovery and adventure for me. Part of it was having a partner in crime like Ajile. Part of it was being in new surroundings. I felt like I could be bold. I was the big city guy from the Chi.

I remember one day Ajile and I were playing ball with a bunch of dudes from his neighborhood: AJ, Eric, Corey, Craig. My game was nice, so I was doing my thing. At one point, things got a little rough. Somebody pushed somebody else. Somehow I ended up in the middle of things. That's when I got into it with this kid named Keno.

"Let's take it down the block and fight," I said.

"Man, Rash is gonna smash Keno!" The other kids were saying. "Yeah, he's gonna bust Keno up!"

I had a rep simply because I was from Chicago, a place known for gangbanging. I'd burnished my reputation by teaching them how to throw up different signs, how to cock your hat just right, stuff like that. You come up with some tough city stories, make yourself out to look like Al Capone or something.

A kind of makeshift circle formed around the two of us and I started hopping up and down and shadowboxing like I was Rocky

Balboa. Before I could even get in a punch, dude was smashing on me. Ka-pow! Ka-pow! Like that. All I remember is my jaw going right, left, right, left. I didn't get in one blow.

Next thing I knew, Ajile came flying in with a karate kick and started beating Keno down. The fight was over in a matter of seconds: Ajile by technical knockout.

As we were walking away, the guys are laughing at me.

"Yo, Rash, what happened?"

I looked at the group with a cockeyed grin.

"Man, I thought we were gonna fight with *words* . . ."

I MIGHT NOT HAVE BEEN a fighter in my early days, but I was quickly becoming a lover. That's to say that the best thing about Cincinnati had to be the girls and being the new kid, the Chicago dude, was great. We'd hang out with Ajile's groups of friends and I'd meet girls of all types.

I'd always loved women. My first crush was probably my babysitter, Sheree. I'd cuddle up to her whenever I could, maybe even try to sneak a touch. I remember one time she put me to bed at her house, and I noticed this stiffness growing in my pants. It was my first erection, but I didn't know what was happening so I threaded my joint through my pajama bottoms and fell asleep. I was soon awakened by the strange sensation that it was raining—indoors! I was peeing all over myself, straight up in the air and down onto my chest in a perfect parabola.

No one ever sat me down and told me about the birds and

the bees. I learned what I learned about sex the old-fashioned way—through schoolyard speculation, whispered rumor, and a healthy dose of trial and error.

It wasn't long before I was putting some of my sexual theories to the test. When I was eight years old I went to see the Ice Capades. My mother and her friend were taking me, her friend's daughter, Melissa, and Ajile, who was visiting from Cincinnati. We all got back to the house around eight or nine. My mom and her friend were in the kitchen talking. Us kids were in the den. I needed to pee, so I went to use the bathroom. Midstream, I heard the door open and I looked around to see Melissa accidentally walking in on me. She shut the door quickly without saying a word. When I finished my business, I went and found her.

"I'ma tell your mama that you walked into the bathroom on me and saw my thing."

"Uh-uh. You better not."

"Well then you better give me a kiss."

I could see her running the calculations in her head. She didn't say anything, but she gave me a slight nod. So I took her into my room and she gave me a kiss. She turned ready to leave.

"I'ma tell your mama on you if you don't let me lay on top of you."

This time she gave me a glare, narrowing her eyes. But then she walked over to the bed and laid herself flat, not so much an invitation as a capitulation. I got on top and started grinding on her like I had seen grown folks do on TV. It felt good, but not *that* good, so after maybe a minute I got up. She was headed for the door again, when I decided to push my luck.

"I'ma tell your mama on you if you don't let my cousin do it, too."

She wrinkled up her nose and gave me a serious look.

"Uh-uh," she said. "He too dark. Nah, he too black for me."

That surprised me because I had never really stopped to think that being one shade or another could be better or worse. Ajile was darker, and I was lighter, but like I once rapped: "I was always told to act my age not my color / Not knowing that my color was out of the Original." It's sad to look back and realize that even little kids were color struck, not knowing that their blackness should be a source of pride. At the time, though, I was thinking only about sex—or if not sex, exactly, then that excited sensation I felt when I saw a pretty girl, even if I didn't know why.

I had to wait a couple more years before receiving my first kiss without coercion. It was a girl from Faulkner named Latrellia. I was in fifth grade, and she was a year older. We talked about it before we did it, even schemed on when we would ask for our hall passes. We met in this alcove that housed a water fountain. Boy, Latrellia could kiss. She really knew what she was doing.

Courtney was my first crush. Her father drove a Benz and wore an earring. He must have been a hustler or something because he had serious paper. Courtney was a cutie: real skinny, brown skinned. I was afraid even to talk to her. By the time she started liking me, though, I was already on to the next one.

Then there was Carla Green. Some dudes used to call her "Collard Greens." She was cute and experienced—definitely more than me. One time a bunch of us were all hanging out at Dion's house. Dion walked over to me, Carla by his side.

"Rashid, let me tell you something."

"Huh?"

"Man, Carla likes you. She wants to know if you like her."

I don't know what got into me, but I turned and started running.

"Where's he going?" I heard Carla say, as I sprinted off into the night.

Fortunately, my luck with girls improved. Murray and I used to head over to the Museum of Science and Industry on Fifty-fifth Street. We'd leave Faulkner after school and make our way along the lakefront. The museum was heated when it was cold outside, and cool when it was hot. It didn't close until seven, either. And, best of all, it was a great place to meet girls. Whole classes of girls would be there on field trips. Others would be there with a parent or two. Still others would be there in pairs or small groups, perhaps for the very same reason as us.

Little did we know it at the time, but we were learning things in spite of ourselves. Not every hour could be spent flirting with girls, so in the downtime, we were learning about the birth of aviation or the lunar landing. We were learning the difference between particles and quarks and how tornadoes form. While the rest of our homies just stayed on the block, we were chasing girls—all the way to the science museum.

My romantic education really took off on my trips to Ohio. There was Erin, a dark-skinned girl who wore glasses. She let me finger her—the first time I ever felt pussy. It was like a substance I couldn't quite determine: wet, but sticky; soft, but textured. Sliding my finger in between Erin's legs was . . . Let's say, I was just happy to be there. I had crossed a border into what I thought was manhood; more than that, it was something I'd be able to tell my homies.

The first time I ate some pussy I was in Cincinnati, too—with a white girl, to be specific. Given that I was coming from the South Side of Chicago, where I lived an almost all-black existence, that was a big deal. Ajile went to this private school that was really integrated, which meant that some of his friends were white. I met this girl, and one thing led to another, I guess. You know how you might be overseas and decide to try some exotic food you'd never think of trying at home? Try some snails or something? "Shit, I'm in Paris, after all . . ." That's basically what happened. I told a couple of my homies about it when I got back to Chicago. "Yo, you ate a white broad out?" They laughed about that for days.

My attitude toward girls at that point was pretty simple: they were lips to kiss, shapes to touch, mysteries to solve. I was driven by physical desires that I only vaguely understood. In the moment with a girl, I can't say it always felt that good, but I knew in the end that I'd have a story to tell. The story was key because it relieved the pressure you often felt as a young man among other young men, all pushing one another to get grown.

When I got back to Chicago after that summer in Cincinnati, a lot had changed. I had more confidence with girls. I had more confidence with my fists. And I had more confidence with my raps. I was rapping all the time—but I kept it to myself. Back in the mid-eighties, rap just wasn't that big in Chicago. I wasn't sure what my friends would think. So I wrote my rhymes in secret and performed them in my room or even in front of the bathroom mirror. All along,

I was honing my craft. I was probably about fourteen when I finally brought my raps out into the light. Even then, my mother didn't know.

Soon I was rapping everywhere: walking to school and walking home from school, sometimes even in class. People started noticing. They seemed to love it, and I loved the attention. Soon rap became something bigger than me. It started out as self-expression, but rap became a means of communication, of stepping outside myself and reaching others. My friends were the main reason I kept rapping. I used to love to freestyle to see if I could impress them. Even then, I wanted to be their voice. I wanted to speak with their tongues.

4 "REMINDING ME (OF SEF)"

Sef:

What up, brother? You know I miss you and think about you often. Lately I've been stepping up as a leader, as a boss, as a king. You always told me I was a leader, but back then, I wasn't ready to take on that responsibility. Well, now I'm ready.

It's been years since you left us. When they told me you had been shot, I couldn't believe it. You were so strong, I guess I thought you were indestructible. To find out you'd been gunned down just steps from your own front door—it seemed impossible.

Back when we were kids, who could have known the course our lives would take? Two little black boys from the South Side—so much the same, so different. We first met at McDowell, but it wasn't until high school that we started hanging for real. You were right there in the car when I heard them play my first single, "Take It EZ," on the radio. You were right there to challenge me when you thought I wasn't stepping up to my potential.

Back then, you were a shot caller. The only reason I could get away with calling myself a Four Corner Hustler in high school was because of you. Yes, you were in the streets but there was so much more in you. A thinker. A dreamer. A father. A friend.

Sef, you taught me so much. You did it by having faith in me, by calling me out, and by showing me how to do it yourself. I've learned that in being a leader, you have to inspire, teach, give, listen, learn, decide, rule, hurt people's feelings sometimes, and help others develop. That's what leadership is about.

When you were here, Sef, I didn't know how to help others develop. Maybe I just hadn't experienced enough myself. It's in part because of you that I embraced the challenge of leading, using my experiences to empower others. Sometimes I don't feel like it, but I do it. I have to. It might have taken thirteen years, but I'm on it.

Speaking of thirteen, my daughter, Omoye, just became a teenager. She and your daughter, Aliah, are about the same age. When Omoye lived in Chicago, they would hang out a lot. Aliah and your son, Abdullah, came to Omoye's thirteenth birthday party. They were so mature. Dullah is smart and focused. I was out shooting hoops with him on the mini–basketball game, and he talked like a little man. He was stocky and built like a football player, and really doing well in school, too. I see him and can't help but see you. Both of your kids are an inspiration. They're looking in the right direction, focused on the right things.

Man, Sef, I've had dreams about you over the years. I think about how you were really taking care of your business when you made your transition. I never knew the true story of what happened, but I know those were dark days. But even in the darkness, you still shined your light.

Man, Chief, I feel like I'm getting stronger, becoming a warrior when necessary. I always looked at you as a warrior. Those days we used to kick it, it seemed like we didn't have a care in the world. Times have changed for me, though, as I know they would have changed for you. I have a lot more on my mind, a lot more responsibility, but I know how to handle it now. I'm enjoying life, brother. Even with the moments of pain and hurt, I appreciate life in a new way. That's thanks in part to you.

I want you to know, Sef, that I carry you with me—that when I lead, you're leading, too.

Love,

Rashid

HIGH SCHOOL MEANT SEVERAL THINGS FOR ME. IT MEANT LEAVing Faulkner, where I had spent most of my waking hours since the age of seven. It meant stepping into a new phase of life, leaving some old friends and making some new ones. It meant Luther High School South.

Luther South was located on 3130 West Eighty-seventh Street. Being able to say you were a student there meant something. Luther South meant that you were smart, that you likely came from a good family, that you had a future. If I got hassled by the police, simply pulling out my Luther South ID card went a long way toward getting me out of trouble.

Playing ball at Luther South, I bonded with a new set of friends. Some of them had come from Lutheran grammar schools, and some of them were from the hard-knock neighborhood on the South Side that we called the Wild Hundreds (or sometimes just the Wild, Wild). But most of them were middle-class guys from other parts of the city. Playing sports prepares you for life. There's a discipline, there's a force to it. An athlete's energy is at a higher level. I don't know if I was as disciplined then as I am now, but it created certain habits that I still follow today. I had to go to practice. I had to run suicides. I'm not going to let myself get tired. When you challenge your mind and your body like that, it tends to bring out the warrior.

In my prime, my game was like a poor man's Derrick Rose or Rajon Rondo. I made dudes around me better, but when I had to take over, I took over. I could be fancy, but I was always in control. I used to like putting on a show. Once I got to high school and started playing organized basketball for real, I had to learn how to tone down my game a little bit. But the flash was still there.

My pops tells the story about the time he took me to Larry Brown's basketball camp at the University of Kansas. "Larry was basically recruiting you," he says, maybe with a little bit of fatherly embellishment. "One day," he recalls, "y'all were scrimmaging for Coach Brown, and I turned my back to talk to somebody, and all I could hear from the court was Larry saying to you, 'Way to go, Lonnie. Way to go.'"

The big knock my dad had on my game, though, was that he

said I lacked that killer instinct. "When I played," he'd tell me, "I wanted to put a devastating move on somebody early in the game so that they didn't even want to guard me. You? You never wanted to embarrass anybody." I guess I didn't. To me, I'd rather have eight points and seventeen assists than score thirty. I was a true point guard, not only in my height, build, and skills but also in my mentality. Still am today.

My sophomore year, I suffered a serious injury. I was killing it in this game, dishing out assists, cutting hard to the hoop. I was going for a rebound and this white kid on the opposing team accidentally poked me in the eye. It cut my cornea or something. My godbrother Skeet swears that when it happened, I yelled, "Oh, he detached my retina!" I know I didn't say that. All I can remember is writhing in pain and pressing my palm against my eye like I thought it might fall out of the socket.

I was out of commission for a month and a half. I couldn't play at all. That's when I started getting more into rapping. When I rejoined the team, the coach's son had taken my starting spot. The coach said I had to work my way back into the rotation. By the time I got to varsity, I was finally getting some ticks—but yet again, I wasn't the starting point guard. It felt just like it did when I was eight years old, but this time I wasn't even given the chance to prove my worth to the team. One game the coach put in everybody but me. My guys were yelling from the stands, "Man, put Rash in the game!" That hurt my pride, but more than that, it redirected my attention.

I quit the team in my junior year. I told my pops that the reason was that I knew I would never be a pro like he was. That was part of it. I also quit because I had discovered a new passion in rap. Why not go pro in that? I still think back on my hoop dreams from time to time. When I was training for my role as a professional point guard in the movie *Just Wright*, I got to see at least part of my potential. I was scrimmaging with NBA cats like Baron Davis. I wasn't dominating, but I was holding my own. After one session, Baron came up to me and said, "Man, you got a little game." I'll take that.

One of the most memorable days of high school basketball had nothing at all to do with the game itself. It happened during practice on November 25, 1987—the day that we learned Mayor Harold Washington had died. Being black in Chicago in the 1980s meant a lot of things, both good and bad. The greatest thing it meant, though, could be summed up in two words: Harold Washington.

Just imagine what effect it had on black boys and girls when he was elected as the first black mayor of Chicago. Back in 1983, Harold Washington and his campaign organizers would canvass the South Side handing out buttons that read "Brother Harold." It was a source of pride to know that a black man from our community could achieve such success. It inspired me to dream about what I could do. Man, even as a kid I wanted to thrust my fist up in the air and shout like James Brown, "Say it loud—I'm black and I'm proud!"

I remember it was a Wednesday and we were in the middle of a scrimmage when someone rushed into the gym with the news of Mayor Washington's death. There were six-footers in tears about it. But there was one kid on the team, a white kid named Ed, who started clapping at the news. I'll never forget that. Where does that kind of hatred come from? How could he have built up so much bitterness when he wasn't any older than fifteen, sixteen? The coach had to excuse him from practice to keep him from getting beat down by the rest of the team. He played out the rest of the season, but my relationship with him was never the same.

My sense of racial identity really started taking shape in high school, in part because of moments like these—moments when your sense of self rubs up against something. Living on the South Side of Chicago, it was almost all black people. I never really had social experiences with people of other races and nationalities until high school at Luther South.

That Chicago blackness gave me understanding, awareness, street sense, and a rhythm. I learned the way that soulful people move, act, and talk. We all think differently, but there are certain common ways that we maneuver through life, through struggle. We have survival tactics. I learned a little about African history, but I also learned that black people in America have developed differently than our African family did. Hitting the shores of America as slaves, we cultivated a distinct culture. And though certain practices of our culture in Africa were taken from us, we developed a new way of living and being here. It is a birthright I inherited. It's organically in my system, but I also had to learn more, too, and live it. Doing so allowed me to meet people of other backgrounds and maintain pride in my own heritage. I never wanted to be white. I have always been grateful to be black.

As grateful as I was to be black, though, I had an eye for girls of every race, creed, or color. My freshman year of high school I messed with this white girl named Erica. My mother caught me out there kissing her one time. "Okay, wait until you try to go home with her," she told me later on. I liked Erica a lot, but there was always another girl for me around the corner. In school I was known for taking niggas' girls, I guess you could say. I didn't do it out of spite or disrespect. I'd just fall in love hard. I'd fall out of love just as hard too.

But I was a gentleman, respectful. My mother had taught me to open doors and pull out chairs. And I've always had a romantic side to me, so I'd write girls long love letters or stay up on the phone with some girl until dawn. Maybe I could relate to women because I was so close with my mom. I'm not saying I was an angel—I was still trying to get the drawers like every other boy my age—but even then I enjoyed talking to women and hearing their stories.

I lost my virginity with this girl named Kamiko. I said to her, "You wanna come through and hang out? What you doing later?" You think you're slick, but she knows exactly what you have in mind. She came over to my boy Dave's basement and we just started messing around. She had a funny smell, like cheap perfume or strong deodorant. I don't know. But I was committed. We got naked, and she told me to put it in. I got inside of her and was just happy, you know? I'm not sure how long I lasted, but now I could at least say that I had done the deed.

Me and my boys were sex fanatics in high school. We'd go on sexual excursions looking for new girls. We were walking around hot from all that pent-up energy, all those hormones coursing through our veins. We'd find girls who felt the same and just fuck like rabbits—behind a bush, in a car, on the floor, standing up, whatever. I might be with four or five girls a week. And this is all before I had a record deal. This is just on the strength of Rashid, not Common. When my guys would complain about all the groupie love thrown my way on the road, I'd remind them: "Shit, I got more ass back in high school!"

> I don't wanna be a freak, but it's the dog in me
> I don't pretend to be the open-door, roses type
> I open the door for myself and I close it right
> In your face. Now you wanna taste my food? What?
> You got your own food—get a attitude
> —"PUPPY CHOW"

The only steady girlfriend I had was Kiva, in my senior year of high school. Even as a shorty, I was captivated by the art of seduction. I loved that spark of romance. I would sit in class and write her long notes. She later told me that she knew back then that I was going to be a good writer. Kiva was a ride-or-die type girl. She was good people.

Luther South marked another turning point in my life: it was the time when my life outside the home began to loom as large as my life within the home. By the time I became a teen, I was living two lives: one with my family and one with my friends. Home was my mother, my stepfather—sometimes my stepsister, Rachelle—and my grandmother. We had church on Sundays, and I had homework every day. I spent afternoons helping my mother at her day care centers and spent free time dreaming about becoming a star. I was a good son, a hard worker, an athlete, and a little bit of a mama's boy.

Away from home, my crew—Murray, Rasaan, Ron, Monard, Marlon—was my life. We spent our time on pick-up games until dusk, fighting, and chasing girls. To my boys, I was the little dude—until my growth spurt late senior year. But I was also a leader. When I first started hanging out, I was definitely softer than the rest of my friends. After all, I had essentially been raised by women.

I often wonder what the definition of a mama's boy is. What does that mean? I know that we're close, we're really good friends. I know that he'll listen, but does he do everything I say? No. No. I'm trying to figure out what that term means. If it means that you're close to your mother and you honor your mother and you feel that your mother is responsible, then, yeah, he's a mama's boy. If it means that you're going to seek your mother's advice, then he's a mama's boy. But if it means that you are going to do whatever your mother says and you depend on your mother for your livelihood or for the important decisions in your life, that's not him. I would have to have it defined.

It was always important for me to know who Rashid's friends were. I wanted him to have good friends—people who would look out for him as much as he'd look out for them, people with similar goals and values. Ever since he was little, I taught Rashid that the people around you help shape who you are and who you'll become. I told him never look down on anyone or think that you're better than anyone, but you can be different.

It was easy for me to oversee who his friends would be when he was young. But around the time of middle school it started getting harder for me to exert control. Those are the years your children's peers can become the most important thing in their lives—even more important than their parents if you let it happen. I wasn't about to let that happen with Rashid. No. I couldn't control who his friends were anymore. But I made sure of two things: that I got into his head and into his heart. I kept our relationship close so that he could talk to me and I made sure that he feared my disapproval of his behavior more than he wanted the approval of his friends. He wouldn't want to disappoint me, and when he did, I made sure I let him know how I felt.

By the time high school came around, Rashid had friends from all walks of life. Some, I'd later find out, were involved in gangs. But even if I knew then what I know now about some of those boys, I wouldn't have told him not to socialize with them. I never told Rashid he shouldn't hang with this person or that person—that would have been the quickest way to get him to want to be with them. I believe in having lots of friends of all types, but you need to know where they belong as you go through life. I simply told him to think carefully about where people fit into your life. "You may have lots of friends in the audience of your life, but not everyone can sit in the front row," I'd tell him. There are some friends that you need to move to the balcony, and some that you need to move out of the building altogether. You will try to change

them because you care, but in most cases you can't change people.
You can still love them, though, but only from a distance.

ONCE I GOT AROUND BOYS MY AGE and older, things changed.
You get a bunch of adolescent boys together and you can pretty
much predict what's going to happen. They're going to talk shit to
one another, they're going to fight—other crews and sometimes
one another. That's how I grew up. That's how I got tough. It was
our way of showing love. Maybe we were toughening each other
up because we all had the foreboding sense that the world would
be even tougher on us. We didn't know it at that time, but we were
helping to shape one another into men.

> *Simple motherfuckers tellin' me hard is criminal*
> *Niggas you thought was hard, you pouring out your liquor fo'*
> *Years ago, I thought I was hard, in high school fightin'*
> *Now I'm the hardest man workin' in show business*
> —"1'2 MANY . . ."

I can honestly say that my friends have shaped me just as much as
my mother and my family. My mother was a constant force, a con-
tinuous guide, always a voice in my head. But like most kids, the
majority of my time was spent among friends—in school and after
school, at work and at play.

My friends helped teach me how to be a leader and Chicago
helped cultivate an authenticity in me like no other place I could
imagine. You gain a certain street sensibility and a certain aware-

ness of your surroundings growing up there. I think that comes from being around so many slick people. You don't let yourself be easily guided. As we say, you don't let others put cables on you, or, rather, finagle you into doing something dumb. My homies embraced a think-for-yourself mentality. If one of my guys came up to me with a gun and said, "Yo, go shoot that nigga," I would have looked him in the eye and said, "Man, you crazy!"

As I think back on it now, we were quite a crew. And we grew up to become surgeons, community organizers, real estate agents, gangbangers, and ex-gangbangers. We'd have children and wives and lives both in and out of Chicago.

I met Monard through Murray. Moe was this big, tall, fun-loving dude. But he would get into some scrapes—a little bit of trouble here and there. He's a Pisces, so we related. We're sensitive people. Monard was very talented as well. When he was in high school, he wanted to be a chef. But he always had issues with pleasing his parents. He'd blame a lot of things on the way his father treated him. He'd fall in love easy, too, kind of like me.

When I met Marlon during freshman year, he already knew he wanted to be a doctor. He was always very practical—a Virgo. He was that practical side of me: focused, hardworking. But he could fight, too. (Monard learned that the hard way one day.) Marlon would drink and have fun, but he wasn't out there starting fights with us.

Ron was the hothead. He had lost his mother when he was young and his father was dealing with drugs. Ron and I used to start a lot of the fights. "Yo, stud!" he'd say. He could get real hype. We used to call him 4CH Ron. He used to lead the Four Corner

Hustlers for a minute. Ron was that guy who was doing work in the streets, but he went to college for a while, too. His evolution actually mirrors mine. Ron's a new person now. He's had a rebirth and sees things from a lighter perspective, not so hype as before.

Murray, who was from the hard-knock neighborhood of South Shore, liked to joke that Eighty-seventh Street niggas like me were soft. And, yes, maybe there weren't as many shootings and stabbings where I lived. Maybe you had two parents raising their children in single-family homes with a hoop out front and a lawn in back. But if you got caught slipping, if you let your guard down at all, Eighty-seventh Street niggas would rob you blind.

Sometimes, though, Eighty-seventh Street would eat its own. My crew and I would fight. We'd fight South Side niggas just for practice. For us, the entire South Side was a warm-up for the West and North. We'd tune our fists up around our own block, then take the bus, hop the L, or once we got cars, drive outside our neighborhood for the main event.

We'd fight West Side dudes for talking to the wrong girl in front of us. We'd fight North Side white boys for looking at us wrong, or for not looking at us at all. And when we were done with all of them, we'd fight each other to avenge some perceived insult or maybe just for fun. At the time, it was what we did. I didn't give it much thought. If I gave it any thought at all, I suppose I believed fighting was a good way to build my rep. I always wanted to be known. In sports, I wanted to be the shortstop who could turn a double play or the point guard with the cold handle. In the neighborhood, I wanted to be the dude who got the girls or the cat who was nice with his fists. "Yo, Rashid and them is crazy!" I wanted a calling card. I wanted my reputation to precede me.

Back in high school, me and my partners would hit Kenwood Liquors on Eighty-eighth and Stony Island and buy a case or two of beer. We'd get a big bucket and fill it with ice and put the beers in there. After a couple hours, we'd be drunk and want to fight. Sometimes we would just roam the streets looking to start something. Other times we'd just stay around the crib and fight one another.

Looking back, I think there was something more going on when we fought. The fights were more than just rites of passage. My friends and I were making one another into men. We were toughening one another up in anticipation of the difficulties that undoubtedly awaited us. As hard as we were on one another, we knew life would be tougher. With few exceptions, we were coming from fatherless homes. We were boys being raised by single women who worked hard to support us and harder to be both our mother and our father. That meant they were protective, often overprotective. Even with Ralph in the house, my mother raised me like she was a single mother. She loved me so hard that I risked becoming soft. Something instinctive within me must have known this, so when I left home, I always seemed to seek out danger. Not true danger—at least, not by choice—but situations that were far enough out of my control, or anyone's control, to test what I was made of.

I didn't want Rashid kept away from the streets. By the time he started getting exposed to street things, he had a foundation. I be-

lieve that a child's foundation is built between birth and ten or eleven. By then a child should know right from wrong. Did I go out and say I want him involved in street things? No. But in Chicago, the streets come to you. My brother was street. He was a loving uncle, but his struggles with drugs put him in constant touch with a street element. Some of the families of Rashid's friends were street, but I wasn't about to tell my son he couldn't play with another boy because of who his father was or who his mother was. Rashid was going to be around the street regardless. The goal was for him to be street smart.

I intentionally put up a basketball hoop in our backyard for Rashid and his friends. I did this not just so that he would play close to home but also so that he would bring his friends around the house, too. His first introduction to the street was on that court. All the boys in the neighborhood started coming to play. And I let them all come because I knew that they would be the ones to protect him if something went down. I wasn't worried, because Rashid was more afraid of me than he was of them. Believe me.

There was no protecting a child all the time. You couldn't stop them from walking to the corner store. Not at fourteen or fifteen. That's how he actually ended up getting a car early. Because right up on Eighty-seventh Street across from the high school there was some kind of burger place, and one day Rashid walked in, and they snatched the designer glasses right off his face. So I said, "Oh, no. I'm getting him a car so he doesn't have to do that kind of walking." Needless to say, that car gets you into more stuff. But it still was protection from some things.

The gang culture didn't touch his life too much. Even though *gangs were around during that time, they usually kept to their own. They weren't like they are now. If you were hanging with them or opposing them, then you made yourself a target. And they weren't trying to recruit you if you were sort of nerdy. And Rashid was really sort of nerdy.*

I never worried about Rashid because he had a foundation that was spiritual and moral. He knew the right thing to do. Yes, I heard that he liked to fight. But I figured that's just what boys do. They didn't fight with guns, just fists. He would tell me that sometimes he would be walking through the park, and someone would start saying something to him, and someone else who had been over to play ball would say, "Uh-uh. Don't say nothing to him." Because they'd come over. I'd fed them. I knew which ones were street, but I knew that he needed to know them, being a black boy in Chicago.

That's just how it was. It was giving him the foundation. It was also letting him have his freedom to make his mistakes. My philosophy was to protect him by putting him in the environment so that he could know about it and, number two, not to put him in there until he had the proper foundation. I think about it like little lion cubs. The mother protects them until they're old enough. But if you don't put them in the wilderness, they'll never survive by themselves.

WE CALLED OURSELVES Four Corner Hustlers. It was our birthright. If you were from around Eighty-seventh and Stony Island, that was 4CH territory. In those days, the South Side of Chicago was a patchwork of warring territories, the borders of which could be plotted on a map in lines that snaked across streets and bisected neighborhoods.

Chicago has always had a gangster culture. After all, we brought the world Al Capone and Sam Giancana and Jeff Fort. We developed a mean political machine, too. Is it any wonder that we gave the world two pimps like Iceberg Slim and Rod Blagojevich?

It was like this. You had these two groups—two families really: Brothers and Folks. Under the Brothers umbrella, you had Blackstone Rangers, you had Vice Lords, you had Four Corner Hustlers. You had different types of Stones: Cobra Stones, Black P. Stones, Titanic Stones. You had Conservative Vice Lords. Back in the 1960s, Jeff Fort and Eugene Hairston turned what had begun as a community organization for black youth into one of the most powerful criminal syndicates in the city.

Both Hairston and Fort went to prison, and Fort emerged in the 1980s with a new vision for the Brothers based on Islam. He introduced the five-point star: Love, Peace, Truth, Freedom, and Justice. It had a lot of knowledge in it. They started with community and political presence, but, of course, the Brothers started adapting to street things. Eventually, they say Fort became so powerful that he was invited to the White House. In 1986 Fort, now renamed Adbullah-Malik, was charged with conspiring to buy weapons to commit terrorists acts on behalf of Colonel Mu'ammar Gadhafi's Libyan government. Even as kids, we'd flash our gang signs, throwing down the pitchforks and throwing up a five or four, in emulation of the Four Corner Hustlers. We'd wear our black and red or black and gold and tilt our hat to the left, just like we saw the older kids do.

Then you had the Folks. They were Gangster Disciples, the Black Disciples. Disciples were the ones who threw up the pitchforks. They represented using a six-point-star symbol and tilted their hats to the right. I used to say it in my raps: the gangs are tribal. We're tribal. When you represent a certain gang, you're saying to the world, "These are the niggas I relate to. These are the niggas I'm connected to, and we're going to keep things true."

For us, Eighty-seventh Street was the land of Puda and Bebe. They were guys who were five or six years older, but they seemed generations apart. They set the standard. They were the generals. When we got to a certain age—maybe around fifteen—they said point-blank that if we were going to call ourselves Four Corner Hustlers, we were going to have to take some initiation.

So one night they came to whoop our asses. We knew we were going to have to catch it. A "bukin'," is what we called it. I remember getting chased into Bebe's yard and niggas beating me into the gate. It was one of those initiations. I remember that Bebe and Luther and them—all the niggas who were a little older and had ranking—they were whupping on us. They do have to know that you can take a beatdown, that you're going to thump, you're going to box with niggas. They need to know that you'll be there.

Now we're part of a regime, a family that is going to have your back. Now you can wear that star, you can throw up those signs. You've earned your stripes. You've earned a certain ranking. You can carry that with you.

Things changed, though, in the Crack Age. Crack hit the South Side of Chicago like a balled-up fist. Crack turned mothers into customers and sons into suppliers. It turned some neighborhoods into the *Night of the Living Dead*. If I had been born just a few years later, there's no telling what my life would have looked like.

Drugs touched every family, no matter how educated or how comfortably middle-class you might be. It certainly hit my own. My uncle Steve, the dude who coached my peewee basketball team and snuck us into the drive-in theater in the trunk of his car, caught a habit. Even when he was getting high, though, he'd still be around showing us love. He battled his addictions for close to a decade before beating them into submission. Ralph's first wife fell hard too, and soon one of their two daughters came to live with us. Every family has its own stories. Few families weren't touched by it at all.

THE THING THAT KEPT ME out of trouble—and got me into different trouble, I guess—was having a car. My first car was a Hyundai Excel, which my mom gave to me when I was fifteen years old. I felt really loved, that she and Ralph trusted me. I didn't even have my license yet, just my learner's permit. But I rolled that Hyundai, and I played a lot of good hip-hop along the way: BDP. Rakim. Run-D.M.C. Big Daddy Kane. We're bumping N.W.A., "Gangsta, Gangsta." "With six niggas in the car, are you crazy?!?" Getting charged.

I would freestyle in that Hyundai, too. Monard or Murray started a game where one of them would say a word, and I'd have to spit a freestyle around it. "Heineken!" or "Hyundai!" or "Chlamydia!" Just crazy shit that came to mind. Junior year, I'd drive over to pick up Twilite Tone, and we would go to Marlon's basement or Derek's basement and make demo tapes. I think that contributed to me not wanting to play on the hoop team. I had a car. We had a lot of good days, getting bubbly, going around doing dirt. The Hyundai represented youth and fun. It represented freedom, but also responsibility. I've got to drive the fellas around. Cats might be busting out my windows, shooting at cats. I'm gonna drink a little, but I'll have to drive.

Having the car allowed me to meet people I might not otherwise have met. My mother got me a job working at a summer program through Paul Robeson High School. While I was there, I met these dudes who played ball. They also sold dope. One day they asked me to hold some of their work in my trunk. This was the only time I decided to get involved in that street shit. I wasn't dealing dope, but I drove it for them. I had that dope in my trunk all day while I was at school. It was adventurous and fun, but it was frightening too. I was driving safe—I didn't want the law to get on me for anything. I stayed chill about it and did what I had to do. That's the only time that I ever dealt with any drugs.

Me, Murray, and Monard used to have this one gun we'd carry. In certain situations, we would get in a little bit of shooting sometimes. Nobody got killed or anything like that. But I've had guns pointed in my face. I've pulled a gun on someone else. That gun was a weapon of last resort for us, though. The first time I shot a gun was on my dude Dart's front porch. Dart was in the streets for real, but he was also a deep thinker. He liked the Ultramagnetic

MC's; he read Malcolm X. But he sold dope. He ended up getting shot five times. Most of my homies who were doing dirt, they came from hard situations. Dart's father was locked up. His mother had passed away. He was a kid doing the best that he could for himself.

I started hanging with the Abraham brothers—Rasaan and Deante—in high school. One time Rasaan got in a fight with this dude over some girl. He ran off in the middle of it, and little 'Te got knocked out by a girl. So we're pulling up in the car. Murray and I get out the car and start whoopin' niggas' asses. These dudes jump in their car, and the way they spin out, they jar the door open, and the girl's purse falls out. We didn't steal the purse, mind you; the purse fell out. Our dumb asses decide to go to the ATM and see how much we can get off her card. We're drunk. We're not thinking. One of our homies takes off his shirt and breaks the ATM glass so he can shatter the camera. Now, this is how stupid Murray and I are: we head home like nothing happened. By the time I get to the crib, the police have already called my mother.

> *Used to gangbang, ain't really thug that much*
> *Rather have some thick broads than the dutch to clutch*
> *Went to school in Baton Rouge for a couple of years*
> *My college career got downed with a couple of beers*
> *Came back home, now I gotta pay back loans*
> —"IT'S YOUR WORLD, PT. 1 & 2"

I've been arrested a couple times in my life, never for anything too heavy. I'm sure my mother stayed up many nights in those

years over things that I did. Another time Murray and I headed over to this school called Lindblom. We went to confront these dudes we had been getting into it with. I'm sure it was over a girl. We started fighting right in front of the police cars. So the police picked us up and took us down to the station. They didn't want to do too much to us, though, because they found out we went to Luther South. So they just handcuffed us to a bench in the hall and called our folks. My mother came down to the police station and started whaling on us, right there out in the open while we're handcuffed to the bench! I got off the hook that time, but the next I wasn't so lucky.

The scariest incident of all involved a dude named Chris. I used to fight with him a lot. He was kind of like my nemesis. He had a partner who was a known killer. You've seen the HBO series *The Wire*? Well, this dude was our Omar. He used to carry a shotgun through the city like he was in the Wild West or something. So this cat—let's call him Omar—was known for carrying a gun and being willing to use it. One day, I got into it with Chris. We were boxing, and Murray jumped into the melee. Next thing I knew, Omar had Murray on his back, cocking a gauge right at his chest. But somebody, I think it was Monard, knocked Omar down before he could pull the trigger. Omar was a bona fide killer, but like so many killers, he's dead now himself.

It was mostly fists with us. Every now and then someone would pick up a brick or pull out a knife. And once in a while someone would threaten to "go to my car," which was code for going for a gun. Occasionally dudes would get shot. This is just to give you

a sense of the silly shit we were doing at that time. We didn't start trouble, but we created a lot of chaos. In fact, in high school we used to go to jail so much that on Friday nights we'd call up girls and say we needed three hundred dollars for bail, even though we only wanted beer money. It said something—more about us than about them—that they often believed it.

We spent days on the basketball court and nights on Lake Shore Drive. We drove my red Hyundai until the tires went bald, day tripping to Six Flags to pick up girls and ride the rides or to the suburbs to pick some fights. We'd hang outside of Kenwood Liquors or at Harold's Chicken on Eighty-eighth and Stony Island, drinking beer and talking shit.

It's funny. As I write about this, I feel like I've almost denied certain parts of myself and my past. I wasn't a killer, but I guess I was out there doing certain things. Dion once told me that he thought he could easily have gone the wrong way and ended up hustling on the streets, in jail, or dead. I don't think I ever could have. I felt like I had too many things I wanted to achieve in life.

Maybe things could have gone wrong. I'm going out and niggas are shooting at us. I'm going out and niggas are getting stabbed. I'm going out and something jumps off. I could have gone the wrong way. But I never said, "Fuck it, I'm just going to hang on the corner and sell dope."

I sometimes think about what would happen if I hadn't been so driven and if I hadn't been so fortunate to avoid the heavy costs of my heedless actions. I think about Yusef Asad, and I wonder where he'd be today if he'd been as lucky as me.

I want to be as free as the spirits of those who left

I'm talking Malcolm, Coltrane, my man Yusef

—"BE"

Yusef was a friend of mine. We grew up together, but our lives couldn't have moved farther apart. Where I had a home with a loving mother and a stepfather to raise me, he had an apartment to come home to at night that was either empty or filled with strife. Early on, he got caught up in street life. By the time we were in high school, he was a shot caller. But to me he was just Sef.

Sef was one of those dudes Malcolm X was talking about when he marveled at how the hustlers he knew might have been doctors or lawyers or even president if given the right opportunities. Come to think of it, I think Sef could have been a psychologist. He could look at you and see all the way through, no matter what front you tried to put up.

Sef was a Gordon Gartrell. You remember that episode of *The Cosby Show* where Theo wants that expensive designer shirt, the Gordon Gartrell? He can't afford it, so he has Denise make him one from scratch. Sef was a Gordon Gartrell. He was one of a kind. He was a dominant personality. As Black, one of our mutual friends puts it, he was "lightning in a bottle."

Yusef was from a family of a lot of brothers—maybe twelve. The Asads were Muslim, but they were known for holding down the streets. Some fought. Some hustled. Yusef was my age. So was his brother Esau. I used to go to McDowell with Yusef. They lived on Dorchester when I lived on Blackstone. Those blocks seemed so big when we were young, but they're just some little blocks from my perspective now. Yusef talked a lot. He would speak his mind. And he had something real good about him inside. But he knew how to be tough when it was necessary. He and Esau were the coldest breakdancers. They could do windmills. But they'd get in trouble and do stuff while hanging out with their older brothers.

Sef had a certain strength about him. If he went to a party, he would drive. And when he got tired of being at the party, he would just leave you there. He was able to do what he wanted to do in many ways. He had his son before any of us had children, so he was growing up faster too.

One day when we were older and I already had a couple albums to my name, Sef and I were sitting out on the stoop, a couple Mich Drys in our hands, just watching the day go by.

"Why you always play the background, Rash?"

"What you mean?"

"I'm saying, why you always let these other knuckleheads take the lead? Rash, you the leader. You the center point. Don't you understand that?"

"Nah, nigga, not me."

"It's not a choice. You're the leader. You're going to have to lead."

I looked at him puzzled.

"That's crazy, Sef. If anybody's the leader, it's you. You got on the fresh new gear. You're the one making moves."

"This? Man, this ain't leading. I'm the biggest follower around. Let me put it this way: on the basketball court, who runs point?"

"Me."

"When we go to parties over on the West Side, who drives?"

"Me. I got the car."

"When Murray and Monard are beefing, who steps in the middle?"

"Me, I guess."

"Don't you see? You're the leader. You may not want to be, but that's just how it is. That's how it always will be. Just think of what can happen if you step up and own it."

Over time, I came to understand what Sef meant. He saw me better than I saw myself. He witnessed my potential. More than that, he had faith to believe that I would realize that potential. I wonder what he saw when he looked at himself?

Sef was shot and killed in 1997. I remember getting a call at three in the morning from my man Sean Lett. He couldn't contain his grief. Neither could I.

"Nah, Rash. Nah, Rash. They killed Sef. They killed him. Why they do that? He laid out. Laid out right here in the street."

Sef was shot right outside of the Godfather, the club where people would step, the place where we shot the "Resurrection" video in happier times. He left a daughter and a son. He got killed no more than a hundred feet from his front door, just a hundred feet from home.

FOR ALL THE DUMB STUFF I did, three things always brought me back: my dreams, my mother, and my faith in God. Don't get me wrong, I made more than my share of mistakes. But things never got too out of hand. Pretty soon I was pouring myself into music, into my dreams of becoming an MC. When people think of hip-hop, they rightfully think of New York City. Then LA. But Chicago was fertile soil for a new style of rap music—hard-edged but playful, eclectic but ultimately soulful.

To understand Chicago hip-hop, you first have to understand Chicago music as a whole. You have to start with the blues. When all those black folk started hopping trains and heading north from the Mississippi Delta, you know that some of them brought their guitars. Some of them brought their harmonicas. Some of them brought their voices that could holler just as well as they could coo. Some of them brought that sense of timing, that way of slipping in between the breaks and reaching the soul. When southern blues people got to Chicago, they must have thought: "Why not plug this guitar into an amplifier? Why not add some distortion and some sound?" The Chicago blues was born. The names read like legend: Muddy Waters, Willie Dixon, Howlin' Wolf, Buddy Guy, Jimmy Rogers, Bo Diddley, Elmore James, Big Walter Horton, Little Walter, Jimmy Reed, Junior Wells.

Out of that blues tradition, you get Chicago soul. Curtis Mayfield. Jackie Wilson. The Dells. Jerry Butler. And, later, the divine Chaka Khan and the incomparable Minnie Ripperton. We heard all this music growing up. It was a sonic birthright.

But the most popular music in 1980s Chicago was house. That house music was very influential for us, but it was soulful house music. It wasn't just *dunt, dunt, dunt, dunt, dunt*. It was some of that, but it was also *All I do . . . is think about you!* Michael Jackson's "Off the Wall" was a house song because it had the right tempo. So was Harold Melvin and the Blue Notes' "The Love I Lost (Part 1)." Ron Hardy, the famous Chicago house DJ, was a legend. That music was discovery, that house music. It had such a strong presence and influence in Chicago.

House music and culture endorsed individuality. Dudes would wear Chucks in different colors. They'd rock boufs, slanted haircuts. There was a uniqueness that was embraced by all. There were gay dudes who were kickin' it at the parties, bringing their own sense of style to the mix. Those house music parties were far more inclusive and accepting of individuality than any other part of the culture. Me and my boys might use gay slurs, but then we'd go to a party with gay cats who loved the same music we did. I don't think we understood the contradiction. In fact, it would take me years to realize that the words I might use in casual conversation could injure.

One of my greatest regrets about my music is that my early albums include lyrics that might be considered homophobic. I was just using the language we used growing up, I told myself. I really didn't give it a second thought. Then one time after a concert I gave in the Bay Area, a fan came up to me backstage and said, "Common, I love your music, but sometimes I hear you saying homophobic things in your rhymes, and it hurts me. I hear them, and I hear you talking about me."

That affected me. Here I was claiming the title of "conscious artist," and I had this huge blind spot in my consciousness. I never wanted to be guilty of mismeasuring someone else's humanity. I've had it done to me, and I know the pain it causes. Hearing from that fan opened my eyes.

Chicago's musical culture, in all its diversity, opened my ears. It gave me a foundation for the music I was drawn to and would want to make later. I was always a fan of good chords and strong melodies. That's why I love that "Take It EZ" sample. Soul. Jazz. Blues. Funk. House. I loved all that. In fact, I was kind of going against the norm by loving rap like I did. But I loved her, and pretty soon she started loving me back.

5 "TAKE IT EZ"

Dear Younger Me:

Man, you a cool little dude, but you got a lot to learn. I like your style, though. I can see that you want to be an individual, to be unique. At the same time, you're trying so hard to fit in. Which one is it gonna be? You're nineteen years old, caught somewhere between a boy and a man, between your shadow and yourself.

Well, Rash, you have to stand up for who you are. You have to know that fitting in is not your path. Don't diss the true you. You need to start speaking up for yourself. That same confidence you bring to your raps, you have to bring to everything that you do.

And what are you doing with that forty? You think you're N.W.A. or Ice Cube or something? Okay, I understand that you're reppin' the South Side—Eighty-seventh Street does tend to kick it a lot. But you're not going to find the answers to your questions at the end of a bottle.

Okay, damn, you're nineteen—you can still have fun. I've seen you at the parties, talking to girls, sipping your brew, busting your raps. College is a time to enjoy life and to act a little bit crazy. That shouldn't be hard to do with Murray and them around. That nigga's bound to stir up some shit! So cherish these times. Cherish your freedom from responsibility; it's the last taste of your child-hood.

But, little dude, things are about to get real. I know you're thinking about leaving college to pursue this rap thing. It's not gonna be an easy decision. Ever since you can remember, Ma's been telling you how important it is to finish school. College? That wasn't even a question. You'd get your degree—in business or economics—and then continue on for your master's.

It's gonna take a lot of courage to have that talk with her, to tell her that you want to leave school. So here's a little piece of advice: just blurt it out fast, as quick as you can—just like you used to rip off a Band-Aid when you were a kid. It's still gonna hurt, but the sting won't last as long. And besides, she wants what's best for you. She knows that the best thing you can do is to find your own path and to walk it.

At some point, you will have to start becoming a business-man, or at least focusing on the business side of the game. I know you are an artist at heart, but you can't have other people run-ning your career. They can work with you but you have to step up and lead. I know you are a mama's boy—I can appreciate that because I still am today—but you have to have a vision and a voice of your own.

This might not make sense to you now, but don't give up. I know you think you're destined to become an overnight celebrity. Find your voice. I know you love De La Soul, KRS-One, A Tribe Called Quest, Leaders of the New School, N.W.A., EPMD, but you have to find the voice that suits you. So be prepared to struggle, to doubt, and even to despair. Just stay resilient. Keep dreaming. Success rarely comes all at once.

A few years ago, I wrote this letter in song to an older you, to a younger me. Even fifteen years later, you'll still be getting to know who you are and who you want to be. It's a lifelong process. Maybe it'll help you to hear some of it now. The song goes like this:

> The world's seen me lookin' in the mirror
> Images of me gettin' much clearer
> Dear Self, I wrote a letter just to better my soul
> If I don't express it, then forever I'll hold
> Inside. I'm from a side where we out of control
> Rap music in the 'hood played a fatherly role
> My story like yours, yo, gotta be told
> Tryna make it from a gangsta to a godlier role

That's the journey: from gangster to godly. It's not too early to start reflecting on yourself and your actions. It's never too early to face yourself in the mirror. Be ready for evolution.

Now, as for your rap name, I know you've gone through a

few. The Black Poet Kadin. (What was that all about?) Nayshon.
Now it's Common Sense. The name fits you. I hate to break it to
you, though, but you're gonna have to lose the "Sense"! You'll be
all right, though. "Common" looks a whole lot better on a movie
marquee . . .

Love,

Rashid

PS: Oh, and one more thing. You know that little cutie who waits
tables at the diner that you've been trying to get the courage to ask
for her number? Just get the digits. She's feeling you. I promise!

THERE ARE AT LEAST THREE STORIES BEHIND HOW I CAME UP WITH
the name Common Sense. All of them are true. Here's the one I
don't tell in interviews.

I was going to school down at Florida A&M University but
spending a whole lot of time dreaming of being an MC. I started
with the name the Black Poet Kadin. It sounded cold to me at the
time. For a while after that, I went by Nayshon, which was my
younger half-brother's middle name.

Then one day I'm at the dining room table with one of my
guys, Joe. He liked to smoke, and he'd always try to get me—or
anybody, for that matter—to smoke with him. "Man, let's go smoke
that sensi," he'd say. He must have said that line a hundred times
before, but something about it caught my ear this time around.

Sensi. Sensi. Sense. Sense. Common Sense. Common Sense.

If this were a cartoon, the lightbulb would be illuminated just above my head.

"Common Sense!"

"What? What the hell you talking about, Rash?"

"Common Sense. That would be a fresh name for me."

"Common Sense? Man, you have just about the least common sense of anyone I know. You can't even boil water."

"But think about it: ain't nobody out there with a name like that. It's not some exotic shit, either. It's straight to the point. Common Sense—like everyday. That's what common sense means. Everyday logic."

"Yeah. Aight, man. I'm gonna go smoke that sensi."

But it stuck. The more I thought about it, the more it fit me. My mother always used to say things like, "Boy, you need to use some common sense." Or, "Common sense will tell you that." It just suited me. Here I was a boy from the Chi, a hardworking kid from a hardworking town. I needed a name that reflected that. I also thought it'd look fly on a sticker. I could imagine Redman or whoever on *Yo! MTV Raps* rocking a Common Sense sticker on his shirt. I wanted to be heard. I wanted to be seen. I wanted to be seen by my friends for what I truly was. Common Sense.

I loved the name so much, you can imagine how hard it was to lose it. In 1995 I was sued by this ska band from LA for rights to the name. My label pressed me to change my name rather than to fight it out in court. I had no choice. I didn't have a good lawyer to represent me. There wasn't much I could do. It was a bitter pill to swallow. This was the name I'd chosen. I'd been building it for three or four years. Common Sense meant something in the rap game. So when my next album came out, I decided I'd get the "Sense" back one way or another. That's why I named it *One Day It'll All Make Sense*. I wanted to use the word *Sense* with *Common* again. It was just a clever way of getting some get back.

At first I didn't like Common without the Sense. Common? I'm not everyday. I'm extraordinary, not *extra* ordinary. But the more I lived with it, the more I heard the name coming out of the mouths of my fans, the better I felt about it. I started thinking about what the name represents. Common. The everyday person. The everyman. The common folk. The blue-collar worker. I strive to represent that in all that I do.

But that's getting ahead of the story. When it all began, I was just Rashid. I started getting serious about rap around my sophomore year of high school. By junior year, the word was out around the city that I was an MC. That summer, I decided to form a group with my boys Corey and Dion. Dion was the producer, and Corey was the other MC. I wrote almost all of the rhymes. We decided to name ourselves CDR.

What did CDR stand for? Compact Disc Recorders. Controllers of Devastating Rhymes. And, yeah, Corey, Dion, and Rashid. We started going to Marlon's basement to make tapes. He had a Roland TR-707 beat machine, so we put together these wack-ass beats—nothing but drums. Then we'd go to Derek's because he had an E-mu SP-1200 drum machine. We'd go to Steve's sometimes because he had a keyboard. But mostly we would be at Derek's.

Derek was promoting parties and using his extra money to buy music equipment. He wanted to be a DJ, so he was setting up a little home studio. He had a huge basement with linoleum floors so we could breakdance. We thought we were Hip-Hop 101 back then. By the end of high school, we'd be recording at Twilite Tone's spot and, later, at Dion's spot. We even had some female dancers who'd dress up in spandex biker shorts like Salt-N-Pepa.

One of our songs was called "CDR in Effect," and we made T-shirts for it that kind of bit this Public Enemy design. When PE came to town, we were front and center at the concert, with our T-shirts on, of course. Flavor Flav was onstage doing his thing, and he must have seen the shirts because he went over to our part of the stage and started pointing at us in rhythm to the beat. That was big.

We did anything and everything we could think of to build the group's buzz. Murray even pitched in to help promote. He and I would head over to Hyde Park to the campus of the University of Chicago, where they had their radio station, WHBK, 88.5 FM. WHBK was the first station I listened to that played the real hip-hop. That's where I got to hear "Milk is chillin', Giz is chillin'. What more can I say? Top billin'!" That's where I first heard De La Soul B-sides and live tracks from BDP. The DJs were these dudes J P Chill and Chilly Q. They played nothing but incredible hip-hop music.

My guys and I would sit outside the studio sometimes from seven in the evening to one in the morning, waiting for them to play a CDR song or to let us get on the live mic and spit a verse. They were the first station to play my demo tape. That meant something, because if you were wack, J P Chill would let you know. J P was this cool-ass white dude; they called him Chill because he had the calmest voice. He wouldn't play just anything. You had to be cold. So after several days of us going to the station, J P Chill finally listened to the demo and gave us the thumbs up. He said he was going to get it in. Not to leave anything to chance, we got all our friends to call in to request the song.

> Then 'HBK was the only station that would fuck with rap.
> —"NUTHIN' TO DO"

That night me, Murray, Monard, and Ron hung out right outside the radio station on Fifty-seventh Street, just waiting for the song to come on. We were drinking Gill's, a beer you could find only in Chicago. They advertised Gill's as "the beer that won't go flat," but none of us was letting it sit long enough to test that claim. We must have pounded through a couple six-packs when J P Chill finally played our song. That was the first time I ever heard my voice on the radio.

Looking back, it would be easy to say that this was a small moment—your song getting played on college radio. But to me, it felt as good as or better than seeing my video on MTV or BET. I was happy that my guys were proud of me. I wanted to make my family proud, too. I was MC-ing for all of them. Music gave me a way to relate to so many people.

Having your voice heard makes you a spokesman, whether you like it or not. It felt like I was becoming a spokesman for my neighborhood, my little slice on the South Side of Chicago. I had friends whose parents had died from drugs, I had others who were gangbanging, but I also had friends whose mothers and fathers were doctors and teachers and attorneys, who'd traveled to Africa and Europe and Asia. The beauty of representing the South Side was that I was representing all of these things at once. I'm connected to all of these people. I can be their voice.

Getting underground airplay is one thing. Standing onstage with hip-hop celebrities? That's something else. CDR's big break came in 1988. That summer N.W.A., Big Daddy Kane, and Too $hort were on the road together. They needed a local opening act that was willing to play for free. For us, the publicity was worth more than a paycheck. So we signed on. We'd be performing at the Regal Theater, a South Side landmark that had hosted concerts by everyone from the Jackson 5 to Smokey Robinson. This was rap for real.

The night of the show, we arrived at the theater and were ushered backstage to the green room. I'd never been in any kind of dressing room before, so that alone was amazing. As we walked in, there was Ice Cube lounging on the couch sipping on a brew.

"What up, cuz?" he said.

I don't know if I answered right away. I was dumbstruck, but trying to play it off, of course, like this was just an everyday thing for me. We kicked it for a minute, talking about music, hearing some of his stories from the road. Cube ended up asking Monard to give him a ride to the record store—they had left their albums at the last venue and needed to buy a copy of one of their records.

We did all of this without stepping foot outside of Chicago, but I knew early on that making it in the rap game meant making it in one place: New York City. They had this thing called the New Music Seminar in New York. It was the premier industry event. If you were a new artist, that's where you went to get discovered. If you were a known artist, that's where you went to showcase your latest work and reinforce your place in the industry. Derek was helping to manage another group at the time called 1213, which consisted of Omera, the MC, and Twilite Tone, the DJ.

The New Music Seminar had this compilation cassette tape for unsigned artists. They'd pick one or two artists from every genre, and the tape would go in the registration bag of all five thousand, six thousand participants. In 1988, 1213 got picked. I felt happy for them, and I also felt happy for what their success might mean for me. After all, I was kind of like their sixth man—a second-string player on the team. So we all went to New York for a gig at a place called Irving Plaza. I was going to do a song with 1213, but at the last minute, their stage time got cut in half, and my part of the show was lost. I was disappointed, of course, but it gave me a taste of what it was like to be in the mix of the industry. I couldn't wait to come back.

I didn't have to wait long. The next year, Derek submitted my demo, under the name Common Sense, and I was selected. In July of 1989 we headed to New York again so I could do my own show-case at the New Music Seminar. Chi Ali went on first; he was from New York, so everyone expected that he would kill it. I couldn't believe it when they started throwing pennies at him. Before I took the stage, I was petrified. If this crowd would throw pennies at a native New Yorker, what do you think they would do to me? I went out there and did my thing, and didn't get one penny thrown my way. That was a good night!

Back then, I rolled with my whole crew wherever I went. That meant that there were fifteen of us squeezed into two rooms at the Marriott Marquis hotel in Times Square. Derek was a big dog; he had his own room. The night after my showcase, Derek turned in early for the night, and me and my guys hung out in one of the rooms doing a little drinking and a little shit talking. Around one or so, the party had spilled out into the hall.

The way the Marriott Marquis is laid out, there's a huge opening that runs straight down the middle, with all the rooms running along the sides. We were up near the top floor, so you could look down from the balcony and see the hustle and bustle of people below. Some were checking in late, some were heading out for the night, some were enjoying a bite to eat or a cocktail at the lounge.

For one of my guys (who shall remain nameless), the temptation was too much. He went to the complimentary dispenser and filled a whole bucket with ice. That's when the fun began. Guys started dropping ice cubes down onto the people below. Luckily, no one was hurt, but a few people got quite a shock. Of course, security came. By two o'clock they had us all out on the street. Well, all of us except for Derek. Murray found a pay phone and gave him a call.

"Wake up, Derek. We're outside the hotel."

"Well come on in, fool!"

"Nah, you don't understand. They kicked us out."

"What? What are you talking about?"

"The police came and kicked us out. You gotta come handle this."

Derek went down and talked to the manager. Can't we keep some of the people? This is New York in the middle of convention season. All of the hotels are sold out. But they told him that the disruptive behavior, combined with the fact that we were way over capacity, meant that we had to go. It all sounds reasonable to me now, but at the time, I was heated. "Fuck that, it's because we're black!" That's how we looked at it. But, actually, it was because we were knuckleheads.

So now we were on the street, with nowhere to sleep. Fortunately, the Embassy Suites hotel was diagonally across the street from the Marriott, so Derek walked over there and pleaded with the guy at the front desk. He gave us two rooms. All of their rooms were suites, so we'd even be able to stretch out a little. We don't make the same mistake twice, so we didn't all go in at once. We staggered it—one of us every half hour. By six in the morning, we had everyone in the rooms. We must have slept until two, then sped to the airport to catch a flight by four.

When I was back in Tallahassee, Florida, New York seemed like a distant dream. I was in class again—no stage lights, no audience, no boom bap. It was college life for me. I never graduated, but I certainly got an education. Florida A&M University was a revelation when I arrived on campus with my mother just before the fall term of 1989. The first thing I noticed, I must admit, was the women. These were southern girls of all shapes, sizes, and skin tones. Beautiful girls who talked with just a touch of a drawl, like honey dripping from their lips. I loved my Chicago girls, but this was something new, and new is always exciting.

I learned to love other aspects of the school, too. Here was a place filled with black folk dedicated to the cause of learning and self-improvement. As my mother would always say, "A black boy can go to any school to get an education, but he goes to a black school to become a leader." There was a spirit of leadership instilled in all of us. I studied hard while I was there.

By the time I got down to FAMU, I knew I wanted to be an MC for real. But I still hadn't told my mother about it. I guess I knew that she would be skeptical—wait, that's not strong enough of a word. I guess I knew that she would be completely and utterly unconvinced by the wisdom of anything that would take me away from my studies. So I kept it quiet and went down to FAMU with two intentions, one stated and one unstated: to get good grades and to get a record deal.

I worked hard for the grades. My mother and Ralph bet me that I couldn't get straight As. For every A I got, they'd give me a hundred dollars. That first semester, I made some good dough, but that second semester, I cleaned them out. I took my studies seriously. My mother had encouraged me to pursue business administration, and that seemed like a good choice to me, particularly given my ulterior motive of moving into the music industry. Sometimes it's those small things that help forge your character—what you wear, how you speak to someone. I was learning all of those things from my professors at FAM.

Every day, I set aside a three-hour period just for homework. No matter what else was going on, I'd be at my desk for those three hours to make sure all my work was done. One time while I was living with Murray, he brought two fine-ass women by the house—one of them wanted to meet me. Problem was, it was right in the middle of my homework time.

"Yo, Rash, I got these two bad chicks in the other room waiting," he said. "Why don't you finish that later?"

"Nah, man," I said, "fuck that. I gotta work now."

"How many times . . . Man, I'm bringing it right to you. I'm like the pizza deliveryman. Nah, I'm the *pussy* deliveryman."

"Sorry. Some other time."

And that was that. Another time, I was in the middle of a problem set for my macroeconomics class, and the phone rang. Murray picked it up.

"It's your mother!" he said. "Pick up the phone."

"Tell her I'll talk to her later. I'm studying."

"Since when do you say no to your moms?"

"I'm studying."

I could hear him when he returned to the phone.

"Mrs. Hines?" he said. "You're going to have to call him back. He's in one of those moods . . ."

I was dedicated to my study sessions because I knew that the only way I was going to succeed was through discipline and hard work. No shortcuts. No compromises.

My motto back then was work hard, play hard. And, boy, did we ever play. House parties were the thing back then. Cats would fill a tub full of ice with forty-ounces. Maybe they'd mix up some spiked punch. And then there was the music. We'd play everything from New Jack Swing—Teddy Riley, Bobby Brown, Bel Biv Devoe— to hip-hop—Rakim, Public Enemy, 2 Live Crew. Sometime during the night, a freestyle session would break out. I'd always love that because it gave me the opportunity to test my skills. I'd freestyle forever, busting my raps.

I was still working on my demos, too. Dion was back in the Chi, which made it hard for us to collaborate the same way we had been doing before. But we came up with a clever alternative. Dion would record his beats to the outgoing message on his answering machine. I'd call in and compose my raps like that. Of course, I'd have to keep calling back over and over again so I could hear the track. It wasn't the perfect system, but it worked. That's how I composed "A Penny for My Thoughts."

After a while, Murray and I convinced Dion to come down to Tallahassee. He got in his car—an old Dodge Aries K—and drove the sixteen hours down Interstate 65 with his SP-1200 in the passenger seat. That's when we really started getting it in. Dion was producing, and I was rhyming, and we were creating the sound that would become *Can I Borrow a Dollar?* People always ask me about that title. Well, it comes from the fact that we'd go to campus and straight up ask people for money—sometimes because we were broke, but mostly just for the hell of it. "Say, bruh—say, sista, can I borrow a dollar?" Then we'd go get us six wings and a quart of beer. It's as simple as that.

> *I can remember times when for a forty I had to beg for bucks*
> *Nobody really gave a . . . so I had to beg for fucks*
> *Now what do niggas do when they got no food?*
> *Skibbidy-skap and busta-bust a rap*
> —"A PENNY FOR MY THOUGHTS"

FAMU was a playground for some kid from Chicago. I had never known that so many varieties of beautiful black women existed. Light-skinned lattes, mocha browns, deep chocolates, natural hair and perms. These were southern girls, and they seemed to want nothing more than to take good care of some midwestern city boys. They'd cook for us, buy us clothes, let us borrow their cars. You'd get their hearts for real. I never fell in love when I was down there, but I certainly came to appreciate the girls I got to know.

When we got down to Florida, it wasn't long before Murray was up to his old hustling tricks. His latest hustle involved calling cards. Somehow he got his hands on a bunch of prepaid AT&T calling cards that he could charge up with different amounts of time. This was back in the day before people had cell phones, so if you wanted to call your family out of state or your girlfriend or boyfriend at another college, you had to get yourself a calling card. If you needed to make a call but didn't want to pay full price, then Murray was your man. He was like the don of the calling card mafia. Say he saw some dude he didn't like. He might tell another dude, "Yo, go fuck him up, and I'll give you a calling card. Good for two weeks." Murray was straight putting out hits on niggas with those calling cards.

Here's another hustle: We'd buy some expensive clothing right before school let out for break. We'd head to the airport with two bags—one empty and the other filled with the new stuff. Well, at the airport, you'd check in both bags, but when you arrived at your destination, you'd pull the tag off the empty bag and throw that bag away. Then you'd claim it as lost and submit receipts— they'd reimburse you for up to two thousand dollars. It was a long con, and you could really do it only once, but, man, it was nice to have a couple grand in your pocket courtesy of TWA or Delta.

Our most elaborate hustle, though, went down near the end

of freshman year. It was like our *Ocean's Eleven*—well, maybe *Ocean's Ten and a Half*, given how it turned out. One of our boys had a roommate who looked exactly like him: a straight-laced cat who had a decent job, a couple credit cards, whatever. So we convinced our boy to get a hold of this guy's wallet and cop his ID and credit cards. He was reluctant at first but finally did it. Man, we went on an eight-hour spending spree. First thing we did was get a big-screen TV. The American Music Awards were coming on that night, and I wanted to see Michael Jackson do his thing. Then we got us a dining room table, some video games, some food. We went to a half dozen stores. Around six o'clock, we decided to make one final stop, so we pulled up at Macy's and, just like before, sent our dude in—this time, to get us a microwave. Ten minutes passed. Twenty. Thirty. We were starting to wonder what was taking so long. Then we saw him being led out of the store in handcuffs, a couple plainclothes detectives on either side.

We wanted to help him out, but what could we do? No use in us all getting popped. So we headed back home, set up the TV, opened some brews, and turned on the awards show. I remember what happened next like it was yesterday. They were just announcing Michael's performance when we heard pounding on the door. "Police!" Man, Murray was looking for a window to jump out of, a hole to climb into, whatever. Me, I just kept my eyes glued to the television screen. When someone finally let the cops in, they took us all into custody and dragged us down to the station. I had the nerve to ask if they'd wait until Michael was finished, but they weren't amused. How'd they get us? Our guy had ratted us out, but who could really blame him? It was only his first offense, so he got off pretty light. So did we. Let's just say that we never tried anything like that again.

Around the same time, I started developing a reputation on campus as an MC. I'd go to the house parties and kick freestyles. I'd have one of my boys or even people at the party shout out random words or point to things, and I'd spit them in my rhymes. That got a lot of the guys respecting me. Lots of these dudes were from the country, so seeing a city guy who could rhyme made them show deference. There were certain cats, mostly from Miami, who were hardheads. They didn't care a lick about Chicago. "I'm from the bottom, nigga. Opa-locka. Liberty City." They were up on game. Coming from a big city, coming from poverty, they had a street education. So they weren't going to be taken in, even by some niggas from the South Side.

Sometime in the fall of my junior year, things started to take off for me with the music. The legendary Jam Master Jay of Run-D.M.C. must have been at my New Music Seminar showcase or he had heard my tape somewhere, because he got a hold of Derek to say that he was interested in signing us to his JMJ imprint. One of the label's acts was Onyx, whose joint "Slam" was everywhere in the fall of 1993. So Derek and I flew to New York and went up to Jay's house. He was such a generous guy. It was like being in the presence of hip-hop royalty. The deal didn't work out, but it was a beautiful thing just to be in his presence.

Meeting Jam Master Jay was the beginning of a string of fortuitous events. As soon as I got back to Tallahassee, Derek was blowing up my telephone again. Back at Howard University, Derek had received a call from an editor at the *Source*, which in 1991 was the hip-hop bible. Earlier that summer, we had sent the magazine my demo for consideration in its Unsigned Hype competition. Derek called to say I had been chosen.

Unsigned Hype had helped to launch some major rap careers, such as the Notorious B.I.G. and Mobb Deep. It would go on in the years to follow to help discover DMX, Eminem, 50 Cent, and others. Now Derek was telling me they were going to feature me. When the October issue hit newsstands, I ran to the store to get my copy. The article read something like this: "He has a distinct, squeaky, but likable voice and impressive rhyme skills especially for an MC coming out of Chicago." *Squeaky?* Well, at least they spelled my name right and had a good picture of me.

Unsigned Hype was just the beginning of the good news. They also wanted to include my song on the Unsigned Hype mix tape to be released in conjunction with Relativity Records. That had me geeked. The news only got bigger, though. Derek called to say that Relativity had decided to scrap the mix tape and just sign me as a solo artist instead. Matty C (now Matt Life) had been executive producing the *Source* mix tape for Relativity and saw potential in me for greater things. "These Chicago niggas is dope. They got they own little style, they own little lingo." I had been influenced by Rakim, N.W.A., KRS-One, and Big Daddy Kane, but I would say it all in my Chicago way. Was this my chance? Was this what I had been dreaming about back when I was ten years old?

There's a distance, though, between dream and reality. It seemed like forever passed before I heard anything more from Relativity. Then we got the call in late September. The label bought me a ticket to fly up to Chicago, where they'd meet us from New York. They got me a budget ticket that had me making three or four connections, but I didn't care. I was going to meet with a label. Derek and I sat down with Peter Kana, and he said that I was a "good kid" and a "nice-looking guy."

"We want to sign you," he said. "What do you say?" I wanted to sign right then and there.

But first I had to get permission from my mother . . .

I was disappointed, but more than that, I was confused. A record deal? A rap career? No one believes me when I say this, but I never knew Rashid was into rap. I knew that he breakdanced, but I thought that was just a fad. Now here we are at the kitchen table, and he's telling me that a company named Relativity has offered him a contract.

"Ma, I want to do this. Can I do this?"

"I need to understand something," I said. "What is your plan?"

"I'm going to make a record with these people—"

"No, what is your plan? What will your life look like in three years? Five years? How will you support yourself?"

"I'm good at this, Ma. When the album comes out—"

"Son, there are no guarantees in life. The only guarantee is that if you work hard and finish school, go on and get your MBA, then maybe that's close to a guarantee. But this music thing? Rashid, I just don't know."

"Derek already told his parents that he's leaving Howard. He'll come with me. Dion, too. I think I can do this, Ma. And more than that, I want this. Can I please have your blessing?"

I could hear it in his voice and see it in his face. He was serious about this and he believed, rightly or not, that it was the best thing to do. I thought about regrets—my own, but also his father's. Lonnie dreamed all his life about playing professional basketball, and he did it. But he never played in the NBA. He never played at the highest level. That festered inside of him. He never got over it. Maybe that's what this was—or at least what it felt like—to Rashid: his chance to make it in the League. Who was I to get in the way?

"Okay, I'll support you—"

"Yes! Thanks, Ma!"

"I'll support you under the following conditions: that if in three years you aren't able to make enough of a living from rap to provide for yourself, you'll go back and finish school. Up until that point, you can count on Ralph and me to help you. But only for three years. After that, you return to school; you can't come back here. You're a man now, Rashid. And I won't have any man but my husband living in my house. You gotta be sick, dead, or dying before I can let you move back home. We'll always be here for you, but it's time for you to do for self."

He nodded his head at me—some but not all of the excitement drained away in his awareness of the moment. Then we embraced, and I held him in my arms like he was a little boy again before watching him walk out the door as a man with a passion and a plan.

AFTER GETTING MY MOTHER'S PERMISSION, I thought that was it. I went back to Tallahassee thinking the world was mine. This was my dream ever since I was a little kid: to become a star. I had no doubt that I would become a star—if not overnight, then certainly by the next afternoon.

It didn't quite work out that way. First, the contract negotiations took months. It wasn't ready to sign until December.

Then I had to sit in the hatchback.

Let me explain. When the contract was ready, I flew up to New York with Twilite Tone, Dion, and Derek. We walked into the label, and I sat down and signed my name. That was it. We got our advance check, and I said we should split it four ways. Peter Kana took us downstairs, and we headed to his car. It was a hatchback, and I remember deciding that I should be the one to sit in that hatchback, letting my guys take the seats. It was my way of saying, "I may be the artist, I might be the one in the limelight, but I'm going to make sure to let you all know that I'm not getting a big ego." I wanted them to know that we were in this together. I wanted them to know that it wasn't just about me. I was probably the happiest guy in history ever to sit in a hatchback. That was the beginning of my dream coming to fruition—the beginning of the beginning.

How much my life had changed really hit me the first day in the studio recording the album. Here I am in New York with twelve of my friends, Chicago niggas in the city. We're going into Calliope Studios where the Jungle Brothers, De La Soul, and A Tribe Called Quest have all recorded. We're staying in a New York hotel—a budget hotel, but a New York hotel—and it feels like a dream. You walk onto the street in midtown, and it's like entering the Grand Canyon, only remixed in steel and concrete. It gives you a sense of human scale.

When the album was finished, I felt good—not great. At times I felt like I was being rushed, that I wasn't being given a chance to perfect each song. I was constantly thinking, "Just one more take." But it was an album, and it was mine. It would bear my name—the name I chose. It would show my face. It would be the beginning of my journey into stardom.

But it didn't quite work out the way I dreamed it would. The label released three singles, "Take It EZ," "Breaker 1/9," and "Soul by the Pound." Together they brought me underground buzz but without moving major units. I went back home to Chicago to contemplate my future. I had to decide if this rap thing was the life for me.

When I listen to these early songs, I hear a young guy who's just full of . . . mucus. For real. I would always be stuffed up; that dairy will jack up your tone. But more than anything, I hear the heart of a raw, young dude. I would always be stuffed up, though.

Can I Borrow a Dollar? was me as a new, fresh, raw, little South Side dude who wanted the world to hear him and wanted to be recognized by hip-hop. First of all, I wanted to be known as a dope MC. But I didn't really have a sense of direction yet. I was like an artist who loves to paint but has never trained at it. I had that raw element, that passion for it, but I had a lot to learn in mastering my craft. My thing was pop culture references: commercial jingles, television references. You hear the rawness, the energy, the enthusiasm. It was an energy that was so innocent, and vibrant and excited and ignited.

I'd crack my voice on that early album; I guess that's what the *Source* meant by "squeaky." It was a style I'd picked up by listening to Charlie Brown from Leaders of the New School. That's the thing in hip-hop: you always wanted to find your voice and your distinctive style, presentation, and image, but, like all artists, you start by learning from others. Slick Rick had his presentation. Run-D.M.C. had their presentation. I was trying on a bunch of different presentations.

For all its flaws, I'm proud of what I did. I was able to offer a record of my experiences up to where I was at that moment. I was trying to step into the world and say: "I'm here, y'all. Come check me out. I'm Common Sense. I'm from Chicago. Listen to me. Chicago homies, I'm representing y'all." Drinking. Fucking with broads. Fighting still. Everything was so new. Basically, I was just out of high school.

Early on, that immaturity would show itself. For one, I'd always insist on bringing my guys with me to every show. I'm not talking about four or five, I'm talking about fifteen, twenty dudes! They'd get backstage and run amok. I remember one time, right after the release of *Can I Borrow a Dollar?* I was doing a big show in Chicago at the Regal with Redman and Keith Murray. This was major for me. These cats were some of the hottest artists out at that time. So I was back in my dressing room with my guys, basically in a utility closet. Ron, Rasaan, Murray, and a few others found Redman and Keith Murray's dressing room, a spacious spot with a lavish spread of food. We're talking little finger sandwiches, crab cakes, shrimp cocktail, all that shit. They didn't leave a morsel. I don't think I knew what was going on, but if I did, I wouldn't have minded. Derek did, though, especially when management came up to him and told him that we'd have to pay for everything they took! Meanwhile, I went out and rocked the show.

The first time I saw him onstage, it was just okay for me. He was supposed to come on at ten, but he didn't come out until one or two in the morning. I remember Barbara, my best friend, went with me. She said, "I am never going back to one of these things!" The first time, I wasn't as into it. I think later on, as rap began to change, I really felt proud and began to enjoy the music. I really like hip-hop now. I like real hip-hop.

The explicit content doesn't bother me. I didn't like to hear the word bitch *at all. I used to tell him, when you use that word, it's like you're calling me out my name. He didn't do that much anyway. The other language, it was cool. You had to learn how to switch it. It wasn't the language used around here; it was the language for that particular field of entertainment. A couple times, though, I'd think, "Ooh, Lord!"*

I'VE ALWAYS BEEN a seeker of knowledge. Yes, I left school but I've never stopped learning. Maybe it was my mother giving me books for Christmas and birthdays. Maybe it was Reverend Wright referring to so many works of literature in his sermons. Whatever it was, I've always looked to books for wisdom.

I remember one time I was at the airport, going to do the

video for "Soul by the Pound." I'd been reading *The Autobiography of Malcolm X*. Malcolm moved me more than anything. I was struck by the story of his transformation. As the preachers say, you start out Saul and end up Paul. You can remake yourself into an image of your own design. Most young men want to do that. I know I did. We're all works in progress, though. You have to feel your way to a new identity. Sometimes you stumble—like the time that Malcolm X got me arrested.

I headed to the airport, made it to the gate, and had some time before my flight, so I started making a few calls at the pay phone. I'm making my calls and then I notice a middle-aged white man staring at me from ten feet away. I mean, he's boring holes right through me with his eyes. He walks over until he's standing right in front of me, like he's about to confront me.

"Is that your bag over there?"

I had left my bag near my seat, several steps away from the pay phone. I didn't know at the time that there were rules about keeping your bags with you. I didn't see the need to answer the man's question, so I didn't.

He waited a beat or two, then asked again.

"Whose bag is that?"

"That's mine," I said finally.

"I'm going to have to ask you to get your bag," he said.

He spoke with authority, maybe even entitlement. I didn't like the sound of it. It pissed me off. Who the hell was he to tell me what to do? I just looked at him like he was crazy.

That's when he flashed the badge.

"I'm going to have to ask you to get your bag, sir. Regulations require that you have your belongings in your possession at all times."

"Man, get out of here."

"Okay," he said. "If that's how you want to play it, show me your ID."

This man had me heated, so I reached into my backpack and pulled out my copy of *The Autobiography of Malcolm X*. I'd been reading it for a week or so, and it had me fired up. I must have been still reading that hardcore Nation of Islam part, though, before Malcolm goes to Mecca, because I wasn't playing. Who was this white man to tell me what to do? So I pushed the book in his face and said, "This my ID!"

He looked like he wanted to punch me; I could see it in his eyes. But he didn't move, just looked at me with an icy calm.

"You're going to jail now."

That's all he said. He cuffed me, got my bag, and took me to jail. I don't know what they charged me for, but I spent the night in lockup. I sat in there just thinking up rhymes, trying to get my mind off things. I guess you could say I still had some growing up to do. The younger me might have been following a crooked path, but in the end, I guess it was pointing in the right direction.

6 "I USED TO LOVE H.E.R."

Dear Hip-hop:

I used to love u.

Matter of fact, I guess I always have. Probably always will. When I think of how beautiful you are, how much you mean to people, I can't help but believe you're a gift from above. For those of us who love you, you've always loved us back. You've taught us and brought us closer together, closer to God.

I met you when I was ten years old. People talk about love at first sight. Well, this was love at first sound. It was your beat. It was your kick and your snare. It was your flows on top of flows. It was your new school soul, even though we look back now and call you old school.

You went by many names. You were the Number One Chief Rocka. You were the Grandmaster Cuts Faster. You were the Microphone Fiend.

Where would I be—who would I be?—if I hadn't fallen in love with you? You gave me a sense of self and a voice for speaking it. You gave me a chance to express all that I am: the flaws, the fears, the fuckups, the creativity, the greatness, the discovery.

I can still remember my first tour with you, traveling around the country in a broke-down van, eating fast food, and barely sleeping at all. Just when I felt like giving up on you, you'd do something wonderful to bring me back.

When I wrote that song about loving you in the past tense, I guess you could call it tough love. You see, it was just so hard watching you change, especially when some of those changes didn't seem for the better. Some dudes took offense because they thought I was pointing fingers at this coast or that, this clique or the other. But what I was trying to say is: Find yourself. Know who you really are. By saying that to you, I was really saying it to me, too.

We've been through some dark times. Times of death. Times of doubt. When you lost two of your greatest, Tupac and Biggie, I thought you might self-destruct. I even thought about leaving you because I didn't want to fall victim to your collateral damage. But I stayed with you, and many others did too, and together we made our way through it all back into the light.

Listen, I know you have to grow, and everything you do is not going to please me. It shouldn't, because you're not only mine to keep. I'm not gonna front: I've never been good at sharing. I never wanted to drive the same car as somebody else. I never wanted to date the same girl. But I know you're something that must be shared. So I guess what I want from you is not exclusivity but creativity—a way for us to relate in sound and sense.

So, yeah, I love you. I love you so much that if I see you doing something I don't like, I'll tell you. I just want you to be true to you, to the core. I want you to be true to your purpose. I don't know all of what you were sent here to do; only you know that. But I do know that you are here to inspire and to enlighten. You are here to provide a voice for the voiceless, hope for the hopeless, life for the lifeless. Love for us all.

As I write to you today, you're just about the same age as me. It's nice to reminisce. But the things I love about you aren't just what you used to be, they're what you're now becoming. You're opening yourself up to the world, allowing different people from different backgrounds and different parts of the globe to get to know you. I see you expressing yourself in different ways, speaking with new accents and flowing to new beats.

I can tell some of these younger MCs out there are really serious about you, too. There's that kid I know from the Chi with a heart as big as his ego. There's a young lady from the islands who's taking you in all sorts of wild directions. There's even a dude from up there in Canada who's fitting you with new metaphors and similes. They care. That's all I want for you.

Hip-hop, you're so much more than a music. You're a culture. You're a way of life. We can see you in a Jean-Michel Basquiat canvas, in a Michael Jordan fadeaway, in a presidential speech. You come in black and white and brown and red and yellow. You speak every language, and every language speaks you.

I see greatness ahead as you embark on the new pages and stages of your life. Do you know how much you mean to us? I don't know if you understand just how influential, how monumental you are. Let me tell you, then, from me to you: You made me who I am. You introduced Rashid to Common and Common to the world. You've blessed so many of my friends, too, so many millions of people around the globe. You've changed the world, and I just want you to recognize your value and continue to grow in loving yourself. Remember your purpose—and oh, yeah, have fun, because you were always the life of the party.

Maybe you think I've neglected you since I've started making movies. "I've been through relationships like this before," you tell me. "Acting and rapping . . . It doesn't usually work out. Once you all get a taste of the silver screen, you tend to drop me like a bad habit."

But I can't let you go. That's why I'm in the studio at three in the morning, laying down a fresh verse. That's why I'm driving up the Pacific Coast Highway in the middle of the day with my iPhone off, bumping new beats in search of rhymes. That's why you'll still catch me in the cipher, spitting poems off the dome like it's 1991 and I'm at a house party back at FAMU.

I love you more than I can describe. And I will always hold a high place for you in my heart. You are part of me forever.

Love,

Rashid

WHOEVER SAID THAT LIFE ON THE ROAD IS GLAMOROUS WAS never on tour with the Beatnuts and the Black Eyed Peas in the early nineties. Don't get me wrong, this was my first tour—a big deal for me. This was my first time seeing the country, from New

York to Cali to all points in between. But we were on a budget, so instead of a jumbo tour bus with a driver, a big-screen TV, and a PlayStation in the back, we had a simple panel van with some room for equipment in the back. It comfortably sat eight; there were nine of us.

We took turns at the wheel, though Derek claims that he drove most of the way. You might have just stepped off stage to rousing applause, then have to hop in the driver's seat and knock out three hundred miles of highway driving. You'd better be sure you weren't too drunk or too tired, or you might catch white line fever.

One night it was Psycho Les's turn to drive. We set off from somewhere in the Southwest—maybe Amarillo—bound for somewhere else in the Southwest. Maybe Albuquerque, maybe Flagstaff. The motion and the monotony of the drive lulled me to sleep quickly. I don't know how long I was out; all I can remember is the van coming to a stop, with the tires clattering against the warning strip on the side of the road.

"Why we stop?" I called from the back through the darkness.

"Man, hold on a second," Derek said from the front passenger seat.

Everyone else was still asleep.

"Yo, B, I forgot to look at the gas tank, B," Les said.

"You what?" Derek said. "Hell, no!"

"I guess I forgot to look at the gas."

"What are we supposed to do now?"

I looked out the windows, and all I could see was an expanse of inky black on all sides.

"Ain't nobody gonna come along this road at this hour," Derek said, the voice of reason once again. "And if they do, they're not stopping for a vanload of niggas."

"Yo, what about that burnout?" Les asked.

This was in the days before everyone had cell phones. All I had was a pager. But one of the other dudes had one of those pay-as-you-go cell phones. We called them burnouts. He pulled it out and tried to dial the operator. No signal.

Derek looked back at me and said, "Come on, man. Let's go see if we can find a gas station or something."

I didn't really want to go, but what else were we supposed to do? I got out of the van, and we started walking along the side of the road into the night. We made it about twenty feet before the howling started. Coyotes? Wolves? I don't know, but I wasn't about to stand around and find out. I'm not sure which one of us got back inside the van the fastest.

So now we're back in the van and back to the burnout plan. After another ten minutes of trying, we finally get through and get connected to AAA. (Derek had a membership.) An hour or two later, the tow truck arrives and gives us just enough gas to make it to the next exit.

"It ain't much of a town," the tow truck driver said. "But they got a gas station, a diner, and a motel, too, I think."

When we reached the place that the tow truck driver had generously referred to as a "town," it was three in the morning. The gas station was closed. So was the diner. So we stopped at the motel. Derek got us a room, and all nine of us piled into it. We were sleeping on beds, in bathtubs, wherever there was space. Three hours later we were at the gas station and on the road again.

I did a lot of touring back then, playing small towns and smaller venues, trying to make my name. There were no concert riders banning red M&M's from the dressing room. It was hip-hop delivered direct to the consumer. Sometimes, though, my delivery wasn't the smoothest. For a 1993 show in Indianapolis, Derek, Dart, one of Dart's partners, and I drove down from Chicago. We found our way to this little club on the outskirts of town to do a show in the middle of the day. Whoever heard of a hip-hop concert in the middle of the day? But, hey, we made the drive. We gotta get paid.

I'm performing for maybe forty people, and most of them are talking or drinking or doing something other than watching the show. But I'm rocking regardless, doing my thing. In the middle of "Take It EZ," this dude comes up and throws something at me, spins on his heels, and starts walking away! I flinch to absorb the hit, but instead of a handful of pennies pelting me in the chest, a shower of confetti rains down nice and easy right on top of my head. For some reason, that makes me madder. It is the equivalent of him coming up and saying, "Get the fuck off the stage! Please."

As he's walking away all proud of himself, I throw the mic right into the back of his head. The next thing I know, security's yanking me off the stage by the collar of my jacket. The next thing after that, I'm toe to toe, fighting the security guard. I mean, we're trading blows. That's when Dart jumps in, throwing haymakers. Before we know it, the whole club has turned against us. We're black. Most of them are not. We're from Chicago. They're from Indy. It's four against forty. We're fighting all comers. After what feels like an hour, but must have been only a few minutes, we fight our way out of the club. You should have seen us running to the car. Talking shit the whole way, too. That's when they start chanting, "We fucked Chicago up! We fucked Chicago up!"

I look back now at my younger self, and I see a kid with great potential but a lot of rough edges. I was in the studio with No I.D. the other day, and for fun, one of the engineers pulled up an old YouTube clip of the two of us. It was from a 1993 appearance on *BET's Video LP* with Madelyne Woods. I was dressed in these baggy jeans, a hoodie, a jacket, and a black stocking cap. I was probably a little bubbly too.

Madelyne: "Nothing should confuse you about my guest today. This brother is all about using a little common sense. He's a swingin' rapper from the South Side of Chicago, one of the most hardcore 'hoods in the country. But he's not a gangsta nor a pimp, he's Common Sense, rapping about life as he sees it. And welcome to *Video LP*."

Over the course of the next ten minutes, I proceeded to explain the meaning of a two-piece dark with mild sauce from Harold's Chicken. And to describe the meaning of a hardcore artist: "I am a hardcore artist. Because to me *hardcore* means coming from the heart, putting your heart on that paper and being true to the streets." Let's just say that I had some room to grow.

Treach from Naughty by Nature was one of the first artists in the industry to really embrace me. When I was visiting New York, he picked me up from my hotel and drove me to New Jersey in his white big-body Benz. I remember that really impressing me. He and Vinnie took me to the Naughty store, to the skating rink, all over Jersey. It was inspirational to see how they were doing their thing as entrepreneurs. They had all their people working.

I had my first celebrity crush on Ladybug Mecca from Digable Planets. I was definitely digging her. She was sexy, had that sexy voice. She had star power, too. Digable was really big right about then. She was a little more advanced in her style of talk than most of the girls I was dealing with at the time. She kept that intrigue going. She even made me a mix tape. I knew it was love! I was goofied out. I didn't know what tantric sex was at the time, but I had this inclination that I could get some real special sex like that from her.

Digable was doing a show at Northwestern University, so I headed down there to check her out, knowing for sure I was gonna get some of that next-level love from her. I went up to her, and we were talking, but somehow we got separated. I found her again a little bit later, and we got separated again. I found her a third time, walked over to her, and she said, "Quit being a pest!" That wasn't exactly what I was hoping to hear from her. Come to find out she was dating Butterfly, her bandmate, and the dude was watching the whole time. She was probably trying to make sure that I wasn't messing up her game. At least that's how I massaged my bruised ego on the long drive home.

In those years, being "Common Sense" wasn't all I thought it would be. It didn't make me a celebrity overnight. I didn't see my face all over MTV, on the cover of the *Source* or *Rap Pages*. That's just not how it worked. *Can I Borrow a Dollar?* was a turning point. It was a moment to show and prove. I didn't get the recognition I wanted, so I had two choices: go hard or go home.

I did both. I went hard by honing my skills. But I also went home, to Chicago, to family, to where it all began. I wasn't sick, dead, or dying—my mother's three criteria for her adult son to move back into his room—so I was renting an apartment with one of my guys, Rasaan. We were kind of living the college life but without having to go to class—different girls coming around, just having fun. That was my first time out on my own, paying my own rent and utility bills. That's the first time I felt real responsibility.

For a while, I even thought about giving up on rap and going back to school in Chicago to finish my degree. But dreams of stardom still hovered in front of me, just beyond my grasp. Sometimes they would be clear; other times they would seem to fade away. That's when I decided that I'd forget about the fame and focus on the things I could control. That's when I decided to dedicate myself completely to the art.

Those months after *Can I Borrow a Dollar?* were a turning point not just in my music but also in my life. I started getting better with the raps and learning more about songwriting. I had to go deeper. I had to get better. I was developing, getting more concepts. We'd be freestyling in my room every day with these brothers from Indiana. It was like training. Like *Fight Club* or something. I'd go jogging on the lake, saying my raps so that my breath control would be good.

Rasaan would always clown me, "Nigga, what you running from?"

"I'm not running *from* nothing. I'm running *to* something."

The quality of my voice was starting to change, too—figuratively and literally. I started stripping down some of what I'd been before. I stopped eating dairy. I stopped eating pork. I moved from drinking Old Gold, Cisco, and Bud Drys to drinking Heineken. It was a time when I said, "I really can be a rap artist, and I have to embrace that and believe in it, regardless of whatever else is going on around me." I was unlearning some things, discovering others. Around that time, I started reading the Koran. I had what I call a resurrection, awakening a place within myself that I had never really explored, that I didn't even know existed.

One day I was over at Dion's laying down some vocals for a new song for my second album. I had my Bible and my Koran with me because I'd always read from them before a recording session. Dion, who had spent years as a member of the Nation of Islam, picked up the Koran and flipped it open to a random page. He opened right up to the book of Resurrection. We took that as a sign. It let us know we were on the right path with this new album. *Resurrection* was the perfect title.

Resurrection (re-zə-'rek-shən) n.
1. The act of rising from the dead or returning to life.
2. The state of one who has returned to life.
3. The act of bringing back to practice, notice, or use; revival.

Resurrection meant all of these to me: a return, an advance, and a change in the way that I composed my raps. With *Can I Borrow a Dollar?* I wrote down almost every lyric on the page. I've composed in my head ever since, not out of principle or of art at first, but rather as a matter of necessity.

When I was living with Rasaan, he always used to ask me to drive him places. There was this girl he was kicking it to who lived on the North Side. So a lot of times, that would be the destination.

He'd be doing what he'd do with her, while I sat in my car, drinking a beer and thinking up rhymes. I didn't have anything to write on, so I'd repeat them to myself over and over until they stuck. The practice became a habit. All that fall and into the winter, I'd write my raps for *Resurrection* from the driver's seat of my red Toyota Celica.

Fall moves fast in Chicago. As soon as it's here, it seems like it's gone. Winters are long. Chicago winters are clouds draped low from the sky, promising storms. They are snowstorms blanketing cars and buildings and anything else in their path, covering everything in a coat of white that fades to gray that fades to black. Many winter days, I'd find myself driving along Lake Shore, tracing the borders of Lake Michigan, rubbing my sleeve against the windshield to clear the glass. Driving along, I'd think up rhymes. Something about the motion made it easier for me to create. It was cold enough that I could see my breath, but still I'd drive and write, drive and write.

Cruising through the city, making my way toward Lake Shore, I'd just freestyle about what I saw. Even when the rhyme I was thinking up had nothing to do with what I was seeing, the city was still present in the cadence. Even now, as I drive along the Pacific Coast Highway with a new beat vibing the truck, I think back on those earlier times, those earlier rhymes. I was breathing in the city, exhaling it back out in my verses.

I've never really advertised the fact that I don't write down my raps. Sometimes I'll spend weeks just trying to find the right word, the right sound. I compose orally in the same deliberate way as when I'm writing down the words, but minus the crumpled-up

My mother, Mahalia Ann Brown, at age sixteen at her junior dance.

My pops, Lonnie Lynn, flexing his skills on the court.

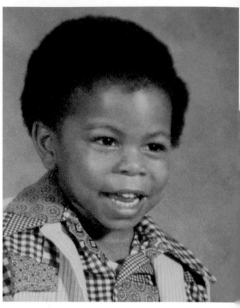

Me as an "ugly baby."

I had my own style, even at age three.

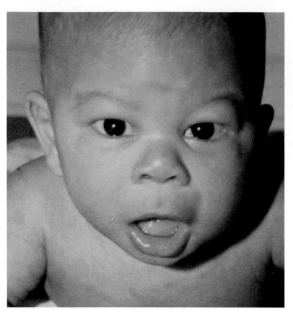

Me and Mom on a trip to Jamaica.

My school photo from Faulkner Elementary.

Breakdancing was my first taste of hip-hop culture.

Derek (with the headphones) and I dropping knowledge at the state science fair.

Skying to the (Nerf) hoop for a reverse jam.

My cousin Ajile and I play-driving a Kawasaki.

My mother bought me this red Hyundai, my first car, when I was fifteen.

My graduation photo from Luther High School South, class of 1989.

Thanksgiving 1997 with family in Cincinnati, from left to right—kneeling: Uncle Steve and my stepsister Rachelle; first row: my cousin Bianca, Grandma, and my stepfather, Ralph; back row: Mama, me, my cousin John-John, Ajile, and Aunt Mattie.

To Common,
You are not
common, you
are a rare
and exquisite
gift from Allah.
Peace & Love
Louis Farrakhan

Meeting Minister Farrakhan at his Hip-Hop Summit back in 1997.

One of my first promotional posters—old-school-style.

RELATIVITY PRESENTS:

DEM DARE

DISLEXSICK

COMMON sense

8$ ALL NITE 17 N OLDAH IDz PLEEZ 8 TA 2 AM

ALBUM RELEASE PARTY!

DEE SAYIN: TWILITE TONE AND X RAY

THURSDAY AUGUST 20 1992

the VIC

3145 N. SHEFFIELD CORNER OF BELMONT & SHEFFIELD

Rocking a show in the early days.

In the vocal booth.

On tour for *Like Water for Chocolate*.

Erykah and me in our bohemian days.

A snapshot from the famous photo shoot with the Soulquarians, from left to right: Talib Kweli, me, Mos Def, James Poyser, Erykah Badu, ?uestlove, D'Angelo, Q-Tip, Bilal, and Jay Dee.

Daddy with his little girl,
Omoye Assata Lynn.

Posing with the After-School All-Stars, one of the groups I reach through my Common Ground Foundation.

My manager and childhood friend, Derek Dudley.

With my cousin Ajile at his birthday party on August 17, 2009— the last photo of us together before his death later that year.

Thugged out on the set of *Street Kings* (that's me on the left if you didn't know!).

My mother and Kanye's mother, Dr. Donda West, at Ye's thirtieth birthday party in New York.

Me and Ye at my birthday party in 2011 in Los Angeles.

Seeing eye to eye with President Barack Obama at Chicago Midterm Election Rally on October 30, 2010.

Expressing myself onstage at the Lincoln Theatre
in Washington, DC, on November 16, 2010.
[Courtesy of Jati Lindsay]

pages and scribbled-out lines. The beats are kind of like the lines on the page; they're a form of necessary limitation and order. They give me something to play off of. They put me in the right mood. They set the vibe.

I compose the way a painter paints. Jean-Michel Basquiat once said about his approach: "I start a picture, and I finish it. I don't think about art while I work; I try to think about life." Learning about Basquiat's process was like unearthing a kindred artistic spirit. Just like I do with my rhymes, he'd begin his creative process using free association. Improvisation. His colors and forms hit the canvas like a Charlie Parker riff, a Charles Mingus bass line. He rejected precision, not for lack of ability to be precise but out of his belief that nothing human ever is.

One of my best-known lines is actually a line I never finished. I was in the studio putting down the lyrics for "The Light," and I was having trouble figuring out how to finish this line, so I just did it like this. It just kind of stuck, so I kept it.

> I know the sex ain't gon' keep you, but as my equal
> Is how I must treat you, as my reflection
> In light I'ma lead you. And whatever's right
> I'ma feed you digga-da, digga-da, digga-da, digga-digga-da-da
> Yo, I'll tell you the rest when I see you.
> —"THE LIGHT"

What I do when I rhyme is like throwing a riot of color and line, shape and shadow on canvas. I let my mind roam unfettered, to play with sound and meaning as it will. Only afterward do I step back and look at what I have. At that point, maybe I can see that the work needs a dash of color here, a brushstroke there. Or maybe I'll just set the whole thing aside and start again. I never throw it away, though.

Basquiat's canvases captured his soul and the soul of the streets. He made art that provokes raw emotions. His paintings display everything from savage cruelty to playful tenderness. It's impossible not to be moved by his work.

Over the years, I've gained a reputation as a relentless worker in the studio. I'll do dozens of takes of a single song until I'm satisfied. Some MCs boast about going into the booth and knocking out their verse in one take. That may work for them, but it's never worked for me. I always want to have options. I love to hear how I could make the same line sound different with a slight dip in my inflection, or a subtle shift of emphasis or tone.

Freestyling, which I've always been known for, is something else entirely. Back in Chicago, one of my guys—maybe Monard or Murray—would throw out words for me to shape my flows around. I still do it from time to time. A little while ago in Atlanta, a woman in the crowd gave me the word *Destiny*. I was almost tripped up. But I rhymed with that word for close to six minutes.

Performing freestyle is liberating because I don't feel compelled to perfectionism like I do when I'm recording for an album. For one thing you're not making art for posterity—you spit it, and it's gone. And for another, there's something wonderful in the rawness of someone extemporizing lines right before your eyes. Listeners judge it on a different scale, too—not a lower scale, just different. To me, a true MC has the capacity to freestyle *and* to formally write a song.

When I listen now to *Resurrection*, I hear a voice in transition —from raw energy to controlled power, from straight freestyling to songwriting. One of the first songs that I really felt was successful is still one of my best known, "I Used to Love H.E.R." The idea came to me one night while I was hanging with my guys, Murray and 'Te, in this apartment we had in Hyde Park. They were smoking weed. I don't recall if I was smoking with them or just high from the contact smoke. We sat there for a while, then they left me alone listening to a beat that Dion had made. He had found a jazz guitar riff from George Benson's "The Changing World" and built this soulful track around it. A concept kept floating through my mind. What if rap were a woman? How could I tell that story?

I met this girl when I was ten years old . . . I thought about those trips to Cincinnati. I thought about listening to Run-D.M.C. and Afrika Bambaataa with my cousin Ajile. I thought of that first rhyme I ever wrote.

And what I loved most, she had so much soul . . . Rap was soul music for us. It was the same thing we loved about house music. I always wanted my music to have harmony and melody, even if my raps didn't. That sweet soul music.

She was old school when I was just a shorty . . . I remembered the feeling of being twelve years old, spitting my first rap. Hip-hop is what it feels like for other people to know your words. Hip-hop is representing more than just yourself.

Never knew throughout my life she would be there for me . . . Through my highs and my lows, hip-hop has been my constant. I play it when I'm up or when I'm down. It's my universal language, my universal beat.

Composing "I Used to Love H.E.R." was a lightbulb moment for me. I wrote it more quickly than I've written almost anything I've ever done. The words flowed. The feeling was divine—one of the most heavenly experiences you can have in life. Divine inspiration is better than good food and even better than sex most of the time. I'm in an altered state, without chemical intervention. Call it a divine high.

My whole crew was in the studio when I recorded "I Used to Love H.E.R.," and in the recording booth, I could see them while I rapped. I liked that because I'd draw from their energy. So I'm laying down my lyrics, and the deeper I get into the song, the more I see them—especially Ron—looking disappointed. All the while I'm thinking, "What's wrong? I thought this was one of my coldest raps ever." I'm nearing the end of the final verse, and now Ron looks like he wants to punch me. Then something strange happens, just as I'm delivering the final lines: " 'But I'ma take her back hopin' that the shit stop / 'Cause who I'm talking 'bout, y'all, is hip-hop." All of a sudden, Ron was nodding his head with a broad smile on his face.

I stepped out of the booth, and he was the first to greet me.

"Yo, Rash, you had me worried there for a minute."

"What you mean?"

"I thought you were on some old punk smooth shit. Some old Teddy P. turn-off-the-lights lover-man shit. Now I know you was talking about hip-hop."

I laughed at the time, but it had me thinking. What if I had been just rapping about loving a woman? Would there have been something wrong with that? Apparently so. Unfortunately, I don't think I had the courage at the time to face the rejection of my brothers and write a love song about a woman. Expressing all the love I had in my heart would take time, maturity, and my own expansion as an artist.

"I Used to Love H.E.R." was a love story but also an ode to hip-hop. I think that's why it captured so many people's attention. For those of us who love hip-hop, we each have our own story. We remember when we met her and when we had beef with her. We know that no matter how much she does us wrong, we're most likely coming back to her.

The song became controversial, and that blindsided me. There's a line in there where I say, "Then she broke to the West Coast, and that was cool." In my mind, it was purely descriptive. I was talking about hip-hop's life cycle and how the West Coast cats had really taken over by the early 1990s.

Back when I was in high school, we used to cruise the South Side streets bumping N.W.A., "Gangsta, Gangsta," and "Straight Outta Compton." They had that raw energy that got us hyped, made us want to get a little bubbly, made us want to fight. After all, my first big concert with CDR, we were opening for N.W.A. We hung out with the dudes after the show, too. I had the ultimate respect for them as lyricists—especially Ice Cube. Being from Chicago, we were kind of neutral in the whole East Coast–West Coast beef, so I was influenced just as much by Cube as I was by KRS-One or Rakim.

But I guess Ice Cube heard my song different. I was in New York, hanging out backstage at an Alkaholiks show, when King T said, "Yo, Com, you heard that Cube verse? He's talking about you. It ain't really that bad, though." The way he was saying "It ain't really that bad," I knew it had to be precisely that bad. So I went ahead and listened to the song, "Westside Slaughterhouse" by the Westside Connection. It was Mack 10, WC, and Cube. And Cube was spitting these lines right at me, talking about "Pussy-whipped bitch, with no Common Sense."

I just kind of smiled, like, "Okay, I see how it is." I probably wouldn't even have reacted further if Cube and his people hadn't kept talking about it. Westside Connection went on BET's *Rap City* talking trash about me. That brought my Chicago up. So I decided I needed to bust back with a track. That's how "The Bitch in Yoo" was born.

The first time I performed the song was down in Atlanta at this music festival. Cube and his people were also on the bill. I didn't know who else was out in that crowd, but I didn't really care. "Man, fuck Ice Cube!" I was thinking. So I had them turn down the beats, and I spat that first verse a cappella. The crowd went wild. A few weeks later, I performed the song at the House of Blues—the House of Blues on the Sunset Strip in LA! They loved it too. That made me write another verse talking about "even in your town, they be loving my shit!"

All of this was going on in front of a backdrop of far deeper tensions between East Coast and West Coast. The weapons went from being diss tracks to bullets. Then came the day in 1996 that Tupac was murdered. I was in shock. What was happening was scary. Eerie. Who did that? Something evil was going on to suck genius from the world like that, somebody so important to a generation. Tupac was headed toward greatness. He had so much influence. I don't think there will be an artist of this generation who will have that much influence.

I met Pac only once, and he gave me a lot of love. I went to see him at this place called the China Club back in 1993. He greeted me backstage and embraced me like, "Yo, Common! That nigga Common. What's up?" He was giving love. I always thought on "I Get Around" that he was giving me a shout-out when he says "Baby, take it EZ." I was happy that Pac never dissed me, because he didn't hesitate to come out and just get at cats.

Then I met Biggie at a Howard University homecoming. He was telling Puff, "Man, we gotta do a song with Common Sense." We had both come through the Source's Unsigned Hype. That's how Biggie got heard; that's how I got heard. Then one time Biggie came to Chicago, and we sat and chilled and got drunk with him and Cease and a couple other people. He treated my guys so well. Biggie was one of the nicest cats in the game. I didn't know him well, but each time I would see him, he was always throwing love. He did a shout-out for me in one of my promos, and he said, "I wish Common was from Brooklyn." Coming from him, that's love indeed.

When Biggie was killed just six months after Tupac, I remember getting the call late at night, right before I was supposed to head into the studio with Erykah Badu. We were recording that song "All Night Long," but we just couldn't get into the spirit of it. We couldn't find the vibe. We were at Battery Studios. That was the moment when I was thinking, "Do I want to be part of this rap thing anymore?" Recent developments were discouraging, draining. I wasn't enjoying myself. "I love hip-hop. I love the culture. But with this kind of thing going on?" It reminded me of how I felt after a while going to parties, getting drunk, and acting up. Do I really need to be doing this? In that moment, hip-hop was hurting my soul. I didn't want to be a part of that.

By July 1997, hip-hop was on the verge of self-destruction. Pac and Biggie had been killed. A bicoastal war was on, and even the Midwest was on fire. I thought the world had gone topsy-turvy. "This hip-hop shit is crazy. Cats are dying. This isn't why I got into hip-hop to begin with." I needed to make a change. I needed to help change hip-hop.

That's when Minister Louis Farrakhan stepped in and held a summit. When Farrakhan called, all of us came. I was there. Ice Cube was too. Maybe here we could squash our beef. Farrakhan was talking to us about how we as a people have been divided against one another for far too long. It was time to unify. "All this turf you fighting for—East Coast, West Coast—who owns it? Not you." He really got through to us.

The only time I ever feared for my son's life was after he started rapping. Rapping was real different back then. Especially when they started doing that rivalry thing and when Rashid had that thing with Ice Cube. That was about the only time. It was the rap scene. Then when some of the boys here had gotten jealous of him, I didn't like for him to come back here too much.

You'd hear things about one of his friends who he put on the album, but he didn't feel Rashid did enough to help him. I felt a little concerned about that. I basically called some of them in. That's when the street came back in. And they would say, "Oh, Mama, it's not me." And I said, "Okay, that's cool. But you better let whoever it is know nothing better not go down. Nothing. Not even a hint of that." That's one thing about street folks: they simply know when you're serious. That quashed it. A couple came and apologized. That's the only time I felt any fear. And it was only here.

SO AS FAR AS I WAS CONCERNED, I was cool with Cube now. Some of my people didn't let bygones be bygones quite so easily, though. Later that year, I was in LA shooting a commercial for Sprite with a bunch of artists from the East, the West, the South, and the Midwest: Fat Joe, Mack 10, Goodie Mob, Bambaataa. It was all love. But one of my guys was still beefing over the Cube thing. When he crossed paths with Mack 10, he grilled him so hard that Mack stopped and confronted him.

"What you looking at, nigga?"

"I'm looking you in the eye. Chicago niggas look you in the eye."

> *Raised in the temple of Chi, taught to look into the eye*
> *I identify with bobs and weaves*
> *And niggas makin' moves that bob and weave*
> *And niggas with jobs on the side sell weed*
> —"HEAT"

Even Cee Lo was like, "Damn, he went in kinda hard right there." Mack 10 was heated, so he sent one of his boys out to the car, and he came back with a mag. That's when Fat Joe intervened, kinda like a Mafia don. He pulled me aside and said, "Com, ain't nothing gonna happen to you out here, but you gotta check your man. He's out of pocket." I was a little mad at my guy 'cause he was messing with my money at that point. We stayed around and shot the video, and it was all good from there.

In the years since, I've crossed paths with Cube every so often. Now that I'm in the film industry too, it seems only natural that we should connect. That whole thing really got blown out of proportion. I'm just lucky that no one got hurt. Much worse things happened around that time. I'm glad neither one of us became a martyr.

When it came down to it, what mattered was making good music. Those recording sessions for *Resurrection* were full of adventures. We were in New York finishing up the album, mixing the tracks down and writing some last-minute lyrics for a few songs. It was an exhausting process, and I needed to unwind, so I decided I could use some herbal inspiration.

Mind you, I've always been scared of drugs. Maybe it has something to do with having seen at a young age just what kind of damage drugs can do. My father was a loving man when he was sober; when he was high, he became a stranger. My uncle Steve was the most reliable, most loving person, but when he was on drugs, sometimes he would just disappear.

My own experiences with drugs were limited. When I got to high school, my boys and I would drink beer all the time, of course. We might smoke some weed occasionally. I even knew some dudes, not close members of my crew, who would ski every now and then—that's what we called snorting blow. The idea of cocaine just never appealed to me. I had a hard enough time with weed.

When I was eight or nine years old, my boy Andre and I rolled up some weed and tried to smoke it. I mean we literally rolled up some grass—like, from the lawn! Dried up leaves, whatever. We called ourselves getting high. We got some scraps of paper and put all these leaves in there then lit our little joint with a match. We even knew to puff-puff-pass, handing our improvised spliff back and forth until we smoked it all the way to the roach. I don't know if I got high, but I sure got sick.

So here we were in the studio. Dion was there and maybe a half a dozen other folks.

"Yo, who's got a j?" I asked.

To my surprise, not one person in the studio was holding any weed. This had to be the first time in the history of hip-hop studio sessions that no weed was on the premises.

"I'm gonna go find me some trees."

My engineer said he had a cousin in Queens who sold weed, so I got in a cab and drove all the way out to this neighborhood in South Jamaica. Whatever he sold me must have been laced or something because when I got back to the studio and sparked it up, I almost immediately started tripping. I can remember sitting on the edge of the couch thinking, "I'm about to die. I'm about to die." I got so desperate that I ended up calling my mom.

"Ma, I don't know what's going to happen, but I love you."

"Rashid, what are you talking about?"

"I love you, Ma. I smoked this weed, and I think it was poisoned or something."

"Boy, you shouldn't have been smoking that weed! How long have you been smoking it?"

"Ma, that's not the point! I'm dying over here!"

"Go get some castor oil."

Not even my mother could help me. So there I was, rubbing my knees and praying to God that I would make it through. "Lord, please, take this off of me. I know you don't usually step in during moments like these, but I need you right now. I promise I won't smoke that weed again." I guess that's the point in the process they call bargaining. But even God didn't see fit to release me from my artificially induced struggles.

So I called my pops. After all, he knew a thing or two about coming off a bad trip. He talked me through. "Son, what you're going through, it's all in your head. Just focus on something in your immediate vicinity." So I fixed my eyes on the gold album hanging on the studio wall—until it started spinning and spinning and spinning right off the wall.

Finally, Peter Kana, my A&R man at Relativity, decided that the best thing to do was to take me on a drive, let the cool air blow in my face. We got in his car and when I didn't move, he reached over and fastened my seatbelt for me. "Let's just take a little drive," he said. "This should fix you right up." But something in that phrase "fix you right up" set off alarm bells in my paranoid mind. Fix me right up. Fix me right up. That's the sort of shit that the mob guy in the movie says before fitting some sucker for cement shoes.

I dismissed the thought from my mind. "Man, I must really be tripping! This weed got me paranoid."

Peter put on some jazz—Miles Davis's *Kind of Blue*—and we drove toward the ocean. I can remember the window rolled down halfway and the cool air tickling my face from my cheekbones to the top of my head. I don't know what it was about the wind, the weed, and Miles's silky horn, but I was now completely certain that Peter Kana was going to kill me and dump my body in the river. For some reason, the thought left me completely frozen, incapable of acting or even moving. So I just let my mind fall into the music. When we arrived back at the studio after what must have been thirty or forty minutes, I was mildly surprised to still be alive.

It seemed like it took me days to come out of it, but it was really just overnight. They finally had to send me home from the studio. When I woke up the next morning, my head was still foggy, but my thoughts were clear. There's a silver lining to all of this: when I made it into the studio that day, Dion had come up with two new tracks. They ended up being two of the coldest on the album: "Nuthin' to Do" and "In My Own World (Check the Method)." Every time I hear those songs, I think back on that weed. Writing about it now, I can feel the paranoia creeping in all over again.

Since I've been out in Hollywood, I've had friends and family members ask me about the celebrity drug culture in the entertainment industry. To be honest, I don't see it. I know it exists, but it's just not something people bring around me. If I know people who do coke, I'm not aware of it because they don't do it around me. People look at me at this point in my life, and they know my image and my lifestyle. I'm not judging anyone; I just know how I choose to live my life, and I stand firm on that. Those around me usually respect that.

Put it this way: you have to know who you are before you get to where you want to be. It must be tough for these teenage stars who have grown up right before our eyes and been exposed to all there is in the adult world. We have to take some responsibility as a culture. You have to have a strong foundation to go through all the things that celebrity brings and come out a well-adjusted human being. When you know yourself and know who you are already, you're not going to get pressured into doing something that you just don't believe in doing. Even as a shorty, I couldn't get influenced to do something I knew would harm me. And I'm generally an impressionable person, but my foundation was strong enough that no one could talk me into just anything.

Resurrection came out in late 1994, but I always associate the album with 1995. Maybe that's because it had such a slow burn. It got decent critical buzz, but nowhere near the commercial attention I had hoped. At least, not at first. Maybe it was the sound, maybe it was the rhymes, maybe it was the fact that we were from Chicago, but it took a little while for people to warm to it. The *Source* gave it only 3.5 out of 5 mics when it dropped, but four years later, the magazine put it on its "100 Best Rap Albums" list.

I think I most associate *Resurrection* with 1995, though, because '95 was such a big year. Not just for me, but for the whole country. The stock market was booming. Timothy McVeigh and Terry Nichols bombed the Federal Building in Oklahoma City, killing 168 people, including nineteen children, in what was at the time the deadliest act of terrorism in the United States. The Unabomber continued his killing spree. O. J. Simpson stood trial for murdering his wife and her male friend and was found not guilty. And two weeks later, black men from all over the country converged on Washington for the Million Man March.

The contrast between O. J. and the Million Man March is so dramatic when you think about it. They send such different messages about the nation's racial health. O. J. was contention, it was tribalism, it was pain. Whether you believe he did it or not, you didn't feel good about it either way. The Million Man March was about love and unity and redemption. It was about the present acknowledging the past and making way for the future.

That tension between these two historic moments was played out within me as well. Here I was, a young man full of contradictions. I was a rapper with two albums who had built a name, but wasn't exactly a superstar. I was still a knucklehead doing what knuckleheads do, but I had a dawning sense of my greater purpose. It's no surprise, then, that these moments outside of me offered opportunities for me to reevaluate what was going on within. One of these turning points revolved around the Simpson case, the other around the Million Man March.

It was a Friday night, June 17, 1994, and I was at my godbrother Skeet's house watching game five of the NBA finals between the New York Knicks and the Houston Rockets. Of course, we were drinking some beers. I lost count, but I had at least four or five. The Knicks pulled out a 91–84 victory, led by Patrick Ewing's 25 points and 12 rebounds. But the thing I remember—the thing everyone remembers—is watching a white Ford Bronco in an impossibly slow-speed chase across the freeways of Los Angeles. We all know how it ended—O. J. Simpson in police custody, accused of the brutal murder of his wife, Nicole Brown Simpson, and another man.

It was around ten or eleven o'clock when I got in my car to drive home. I still had a buzz, but I felt like I was more than good to drive. I was driving down a side street when I came to a stop sign. Anxious to get home and get to bed, I did a tap stop and continued through the intersection—running into the side of another car.

Neither of us could have been going more than fifteen miles an hour; it was a residential neighborhood, and we collided in the intersection after a four-way stop. But it was jarring nonetheless. After the initial shock of the collision had worn off and I could tell that I wasn't hurt, I got out of the car to see about the other driver. He was out of the car now, too, and we exchanged bewildered glances. He was maybe in his midforties, and he looked like he was coming home from work. He was wearing a gray shirt with gray pants, like a uniform.

"You all right?" I asked.

"Yeah. How about you?"

"I'm fine."

"You're Common Sense, right? The rapper?"

For a second, I didn't know how to answer. I didn't feel much like Common Sense right about then. I felt 100 percent Rashid.

"Yeah. Yeah, man."

"Well, I'm glad to meet you. Maybe it's not the best of circumstances, though."

"I just—I don't know what happened."

"Don't worry about it," he said. "I don't think we need to call the police. Just give me your information."

We exchanged information and drove our separate ways. I felt so fortunate. This man didn't need to show me love like that. I imagined what would have happened had the police shown up. I imagined them putting me through all the tests—touching my index finger to the tip of my nose, putting one foot in front of the other and walking in a straight line, balancing on one leg. I thought of how ashamed my mother would be. Worst of all, I thought of what might have happened under different circumstances—a different road, a different intersection. I paid for the man's repairs and gave him tickets to my next show, too.

I didn't stop drinking all at once. I wasn't scared straight or anything. There were times in the months that followed when I would drink so much that I'd wake up the next morning and couldn't quite remember what I had done the night before. There were times when I would act the fool and embarrass myself. "I can't keep doing this," I'd say. Then the next weekend would come, and I'd end up doing some of the same things. I have an addictive personality. I know that.

What saved me from myself, though, was my sense of purpose. If I needed to stop getting drunk in order to achieve my dreams, then I would do it. Whenever I need to remove something from my life so that I can succeed, I do it. That holds for people, too. It was around the same time as the accident that I started really paying attention to my health. That meant drinking in moderation or not at all and eating a more healthful diet. Those two things brought discipline to my life. Cutting out certain foods actually helped me stop drinking so much, and both of them helped me in my career.

The next year, after the O. J. verdict, I was thinking about the night of my accident. I was thinking about close calls and second chances. I was also thinking about the Million Man March, which was just two weeks away.

"Black, I need you to pick us up from the airport."

I was calling my friend Sean Glover, known affectionately as Black, for him to come pick up a group of us and take us into DC. It was Thursday afternoon, October 12, 1995, and the Million Man March was scheduled for the following Monday the sixteenth, with events taking place all weekend.

"Which airport?"

"Duels."

"Duels? You mean *Dulles*?"

"Yeah, whatever."

Black pulled up in his Nissan Altima, and five of us piled in, bags and all. Needless to say, it was a tight fit. I don't think we noticed, though, because we were all so excited. This was such a historic moment. Racial tensions were high after the O. J. acquittal, but we were focused on the positive. Our generation hadn't had its civil rights moment, its March on Washington with Dr. Martin Luther King Jr. This was going to be it.

Standing on the National Mall, surrounded in solidarity by brothers of all ages and colors, that was the first glimpse of heaven for me. I had never felt that much love among black men in my life. The way we grew up, it was about competition, this dude getting ahead of you. You're cool with your tribe, but the rest you're pretty much trying to fight against for something at any given time. It was a humility I had never felt among black men. Every person was so happy to be there.

A million black men walking towards one direction
The cream of the planet, resurrection.
—"RESURRECTION '95"

The thing I remember most about the day of the march is looking around and seeing all the people behind me, around me, and all of them were black men. Multitudes of black men. It made me think, "They're going to write about this in the new scriptures."

I was a black man saying I was proud to be a black man. I was there with other brothers on this day of atonement. And even though I hadn't stopped fucking around at that time, even though just a year before, I had almost hurt myself and someone else because of my poor judgment, I still felt like I had the capacity to start making those steps toward doing the right things. It made me recognize the importance of making conscious choices in all aspects of my life. In my heart and in my spirit, I knew I really wanted to do the right things.

The first thing I remember from that day was the little brother from Chicago, just fourteen at the time, who spoke, Ayinde Jean-Baptiste. He spoke about our tradition of struggle and our need for self-determination. That inspired me. He kind of kicked it off. I remember that for sure. I remember Rosa Parks, too. Everyone started chanting, "Rosa! Rosa! Rosa!" Her name echoed across the mall. We were there for a purpose greater than ourselves, greater than the individual. I'm glad to say that I was a part of it. I wanted to be able to tell my children I was there. Our generation doesn't have too many moments like that. Now's the time to live your truth.

It was a challenge to be a man—a black man—and to express love for a woman in public. When I did "I Used to Love H.E.R.," I didn't have the heart to write a love song. But after the Million Man March, it was like a seed was planted. "This is how you feel any-way, *and* this is the right thing to do." I was growing up—and hip-hop was too.

7 "RETROSPECT FOR LIFE"

To My Unborn:

I have a lot to say to you if I can find the words to give it shape. Though I never knew you, I can't forget you. Let me begin by saying I'm sorry—sorry for my selfishness and my irresponsibility. I'm sorry for not allowing you to come into this world. I know your soul is precious.

I truly believe that every child that's conceived chooses his parents for a reason. I know you chose me. I know I failed you.

Your mothers and I made the choice together. We agreed that it was the best decision for us at the time. We were too young. We weren't ready. She was working or going to school or launching her career. I was on the road or in the studio or just not ready to be a father. We thought we were doing the right thing, and perhaps we were. But right doesn't always feel right.

After the first time, I told myself I wouldn't do it again. But I did. I wonder: Would you have been boys or girls? Would you have grown up to love music or dance or sports or science? Would you have been protective of your baby sister? Would you have whispered secrets together in the dark at night between two single beds?

By now you would be a young woman or a young man. Maybe you'd be in college. Would you have followed your father into music or acting? How would your life have changed mine? Would I have become an actor at all? Would I have just given up rapping? Would I still have been able to pursue my dreams, even past the hard times, if I had the responsibility to provide for you?

I know these are selfish questions. I know that for you, the matter is simple. Life or not life? I denied you your say. So I ask your forgiveness. I ask your forgiveness, and I ask your mothers' forgiveness, too.

At many points in my life, I've been spoiled and selfish, not living up to the man I'm supposed to be. I know I am capable of being a better child of God, a better human being, a better man. I will continue to break down the walls I have up and I will strive to live by my convictions. I will become who I was created to be. I hope and pray that you recognize that I value your spirit, your soul, and who you might have been on this earth.

I am a father now to a brilliant and beautiful young woman, your sister. Perhaps I don't deserve that blessing, but I strive each day to be the best daddy I can be. Even now, I'm still learning what it really takes to be a father. I haven't always been as responsible as I know I could have been. I have lived through selfish times. But

I know that the proudest title I bear is "father" and I will continue to follow that into the light.

Years ago, I wrote you a song. I apologized for taking your first breath, first step, and first cry. I'm not just sorry for you, though; I'm sorry for myself that I missed that. I want you to know that I love you and that you remain a part of me. From this point on until forever, your soul and my soul will remain one, even at a distance.

Love,

Rashid

ABORTIONS NEVER LET YOU FORGET.

I had been here before: driving my lady in silence on a Chicago winter day, crossing the street with her leaning hard against me, braced against the cold. The waiting room where we sat for her name to be called was all sharp lines and antiseptic white. I remember the time and the tick of the clock in the silence as I waited for her to return, and when she did, her face . . . told so much—not for what it showed, but for what I couldn't see.

We told ourselves it was timing. I was on the road touring. She was getting her career going. It was not an easy decision. Can it ever be an easy decision to take a life? And make no mistake about it, we did feel like we were taking a life even if what had just begun to grow within her hadn't yet become a child. For me it remains a moment of ambivalence and contradiction. I regret our decision, but at the same time, I don't know if given the same time and circumstances, I would have wanted us to do something different. That's tough emotional space to inhabit, living with deep re-gret that you wouldn't undo if given the chance.

Even in the face of those losses, I knew that one day I would be a father. I knew that one day I'd meet the mother of my child. What I didn't know was that we would meet in 1996 at a Goodie Mobb show that Biz Markie was DJ-ing. February 13 was the date, I think. I was there with Sean Lett and Rasaan. We were about to leave when I saw this girl at the bar talking with my boy Luther. Luther was one of the big-time Fours in our neighborhood, a straight enforcer. As it turned out, Luther was messing with my mystery girl's sister. I walked over and introduced myself to Kim. One of the first things I asked her was "What's your sign?" I know that sounds corny, but I was genuinely interested. She could tell, and that intrigued her. In fact, at the time, she said she wanted to write a book on astrology. We had a cool conversation. It was quick, but it was good.

The experience wasn't love at first sight with Kim, but I felt an undeniable connection, a sense of belonging. During my visits to her house, she would introduce me to new things: music, food, art, whatever. We enriched each other's lives. Some of our first dates were about discovery. We went to see the film *Basquiat* together. She'd teach me about astrology. Of course, she was beautiful.

The other thing I loved about Kim was that she had that street sense about her. She grew up poor, point-blank. She was not in the projects but one step above. She grew up in the 'hood, but was on the North Side, so she went to a very good public school. Kim was like, "I understand you a South Side nigga. You crazy." She was savvy in that way; she understood people. She knew how to hustle, just like my mother. She was honest, too: "I'm not going to have a baby with just anybody. You're a nigga with a future." I felt something around her—I'd get that tingle in my stomach. Maybe our unborn daughter, Omoye, was tapping us through the esoteric rain. I felt certain that I would have a child with this woman.

When Kim got pregnant, all the old questions came back into my mind. Was I ready to be a father? Did being a father mean that I had to be a husband too? Kim and I were in a relationship with each other, living together, but in a kind of uneasy commitment. Was this a stable enough home life in which to have a child? Could we raise a child together with love before we had made a true commitment before God and family to love and support each other? We couldn't answer these questions with certainty. I didn't know if I even wanted to bring a child into this world. This world seemed so tough to me. But God had bigger plans. My next thought was, "Man, how am I going to tell my mother?"

Kim and I were sitting at my mother's kitchen table on the evening I told my mother we were having a baby. She was cooking catfish, standing at the stove with that rich, fried aroma filling the air. I said, "Ma, I got to talk to you about some stuff." She gave me that stare. She had that look like, "Don't talk to me about no BS, 'cause I don't want to hear it right now." So I just blurted it out. "Kim is pregnant." She didn't look surprised. She just flipped the catfish over and said, "When are you all getting married?"

I almost died when Rashid told me that Kim was pregnant. I was right here in this kitchen. I remember saying they ought to get mar-

ried. 'Cause that's all I knew. And I remember him saying, "Well, I don't know if I want to get married." He was young. I thought he should. But I told them that ultimately that was their decision. I think he probably knew at the time that he and Kim wouldn't work out. Maybe that's why he made the decision he did.

EIGHT MONTHS LATER, my daughter was born. We named her Omoye Assata Lynn. Omoye means "blessed baby" because that's what she was to us. Assata was for Assata Shakur because our daughter was destined to become a fighter, even a revolutionary.

That same year, 1997, I wrote and recorded "Retrospect for Life" with Lauryn Hill as a testament to so many young people like us faced with the decision of life. I dedicated the song to my baby daughter, Omoye Assata Lynn, born on August 13, 1997.

I wasn't in town the day my granddaughter, Omoye, was born, but I remember the day or two after. She was such a happy baby. Her spirit, even as a newborn, just filled you with joy. For the first few years we babysat her while her mother worked and while Rashid was on the road or in the studio. That first year, my mother took care of her almost every day. They would drop her off and Kim would go to work. So Omoye was always in our life. Thankfully, she still is today. Other than two, she has spent every single Christmas of her life with us. And every birthday except one. She brings us so much joy.

IT SOON BECAME CLEAR that my relationship with Omoye's mom wasn't going to work out, but we had to work out how the two of us could be the best parents we could be for this little girl. I felt no pressure to stay with Kim. Maybe that's where the selfish me came out. "Look, I'm not responsible. This is responsibility? I don't want all of this."

Raising a child with someone when you're not a couple is hard work. Being around someone you don't want to live with, that's the hardest part. You have to choose the energy you keep around you. Kim must have felt the same way at some point because she moved from Chicago to Washington, DC, without leaving an address. I would get calls a little bit, but she was more or less making her break. She was taking her time to heal and maybe getting back at me a little bit, too. She was in touch with my mother, but told her not to tell me where she was. That was one of my hardest times, because circumstances didn't allow me to really be a father at all. Kim and I were able to agree that our daughter deserved two loving parents in her life.

Having a daughter has made me understand people better—particularly women. I began to consider and question how any woman I was dealing with might have been raised. Did she have her father in her life? What was she missing? What helped her move forward? Thinking about all of that makes me want to make sure that I give all I can to my daughter.

It's a challenge, though, to be there even when I'm not. For most of Omoye's life, I've been on the road, whether touring or, more recently, making movies. No matter how far apart we are, she's still the first thing on my mind in the morning and the last thing at night. We have a bond that doesn't care about distance.

I taught my daughter how to ride a bike when she was around six. I was guiding her with my hands, then just my fingertips on her back as I jogged alongside. She kept pedaling, kept pedaling, and then I just let go. She was still going, she was still going. I wasn't holding on, but she knew I was there. That's how I want her to go through life. I might not be holding on to her, but I'm there. Daddy is there.

It's a persistent process—fatherhood, manhood. It's a path you take. You're constantly looking in the mirror and saying "I am a man," and then sometimes you walk away and you forget. You're not supposed to, but you do. You have to be reminded at times about who you are as a man and what you stand for.

A man knows who he is and has a sense of responsibility for himself, his family, and his community. A man believes in something and stands for it. He does his best to practice what he believes. A man can be honest and strong. He can be emotional without fear. A man loves himself, knows himself, and will be himself in every situation. And he's not afraid—I don't even like saying the negative "not afraid." He's open. He's open to growing. A man can acknowledge his truths.

I was having a conversation recently with Sway and one of his guys about raising daughters. Omoye and Sway's daughter are close to the same age, so we were talking about the kinds of conversations we were having with them. "Yeah, Omoye doesn't tell me certain things," I was saying. Then his buddy was telling me how he was raising his daughter. I learned a lot from listening to them. It made me realize that as a young black man, I really didn't have a guide to say, "This is how you be a man. This is how you be a father." When you have an example of how to conduct yourself as a man, as a head of a family, it prepares you for the future. When that isn't there, it puts you in a position of lack. That conversation made me realize that for all my mother gave me, there were certain things she just couldn't provide. I was learning at the ripe age of thirty-eight lessons that I probably should have learned at a much earlier age.

Of course, I had male role models throughout my life. I had my father, who was a major influence on me, even though I saw him in the flesh only once in a while. And I have to give credit to Ralph. There are certain things that he instilled within me. How to conduct yourself with a woman—opening doors, pulling out chairs, standing when they leave the table—how to handle different situations. Sometimes it was simple things: "You'd better be sure you have your own house. You need a place to go if your woman decides to kick you out." That's a small example.

Back in 1997, when I was a new father, I still had so much to learn. I didn't even know what I didn't know. I was rash at times, reckless with my affection, heedless of my relationship. I believed I was a giving person—and certainly I was generous with my family and friends—but I was also deeply self-centered. I suppose on one level I knew all of this and knew what I had to do to change, but knowing and doing are very different. I had to hear about myself. Who better to tell me those hard truths than my mother?

A Letter to My Son

October 26, 1997

Dear Rashid,

I haven't written you a letter since you were in college, but I think it's time to write you now. As I told you the other day, I'm so proud of you as a son. I love you and I thank God for you. But I'm concerned about your behavior as a man.

A man makes decisions and sticks to them. Be a chess player, not a chess piece. You can't keep calling all your boyhood "friends" for advice, especially when their lives are a mess. Make your own decisions and stick to them! You can't keep vacillating or you'll lose yourself. It's okay to be wrong sometimes, to make a mistake; the problem comes when you keep making the same mistake over and over again. That's called stupid. I don't want you stuck on stupid.

A man respects himself, his body, and others. He doesn't drink beyond his ability to control himself, his mouth, or his temper. A man respects his home and anyone living in it because he chose to let them stay, whether man or woman. You don't stay out all night when you are living with a woman, nor do you bring a woman home to spend the night when a man is staying with you. I'm not judging who you choose to live your life with, but rather how you live it. These are dangerous times to be sleeping around. People are dying of AIDS. You may be fooled into thinking it's you the girls want to be with, not Common Sense. It's called respect for yourself and for others.

A man thinks about his decisions and how they will affect him and the people involved before he makes them. He realizes what he can and can't do. He doesn't say yes to more things than he can possibly han-

dle and become angry with himself and others because he's said yes to more than he can or wants to do. A man knows when to say no—even to family. He knows that he can't help anyone until he first helps himself.

A man stands for something. He has morals and values and he doesn't compromise them on a whim. A man who respects his mother respects other women and doesn't call them out of their name to prove a point or for the sake of a dollar. A man knows when it's time to grow up. He knows when, as the Bible says, to put away childish things. That goes sometimes for boyhood friends and boyish ways. He doesn't forsake his friends; he just no longer does boyish things and he recognizes his friends for who and what they are.

A man takes care of his responsibilities. He does not spend money he doesn't have. He doesn't blame others for how his money is handled. A son should know that he can count on help from his family, but should not abuse their help. You don't seem to care about money, yours or mine.

I know that you know these things about yourself, but knowing is not enough. It's time to change. I know you can. You are Lonnie's child, but only by birth. It's how you were raised that determines who and what you are. You are God's child and you need to start acting that way. You were raised by a strong, black Christian woman and man. You've seen Ralph and me work hard all of your life and take care of ourselves and others. You have a model. Even Lonnie is a model for you—he's made the mistakes that you don't need to make unless you want to be as unhappy as he has been. Believe me, he has not been happy since he was about fifteen years old.

Rashid, it's time for you to stand up and be a man. This means not saying you're a man, but acting like you're a man. Behavior is a mirror in which everyone shows his image.

I think you have a hit on your hands with **One Day It'll All Make Sense** *and that your career is on an upward slant. But there are some things you're going to have to change if you're going to be truly happy. I hope and pray that you understand all you can be and start to become it.*

Love,
Mama

UNDERSTANDING WHO I CAN BE. Becoming that person. I accepted the challenges, but change didn't happen overnight. It seems like a contradiction, but the very moment when my own life seemed to be in chaos was the very moment I started to find clarity as an artist. People sometimes think that I've always been a "conscious artist," but that reputation really began with my third album, *One Day It'll All Make Sense.* Here I was, a twenty-five-year-old man about to have his first child. I was growing into myself as a man, but I was also slipping back into old behaviors.

Here's an example. We were touring to promote the album and had a date in Boulder, Colorado, a college town. It was a great show, and we decided to keep the party going at the hotel. I say *hotel*, but it was really more of a motel: two levels and all the access from the outside. We had our little after-party on the second floor; strictly women were invited. It was me, Derek, the road manager, and a couple of the tech guys. While I was performing, they'd been recruiting. They'd say to a couple dozen girls, "Come to this hotel," knowing that maybe a third of them would actually show up.

We already have a nice little party going when there's a

knock on the door. It's two girls the sound man had invited. We invite them in, and as they're coming through the door, this dread-locked dude tries to walk in with them.

"Wait, hold up, partner," Sound Man says.

"But I'm with them."

"Sorry, man. We got enough guys at this party."

At this point, I'm sitting on the sofa across the room, politick-ing hard with this girl.

"Dude," Derek pipes in, "we don't mean no disrespect, but only ladies are invited."

That's when the two girls start in. "Oh, he's our friend."

Sound Man talks to the girls, and they seem to get the picture. They tell Dread that they'll meet up with him later.

Meanwhile, Dread is not pleased at all. Walking out the door, he starts talking all types of shit.

"I don't fuck with y'all niggas anyway," he says. "Fuck Com-mon. Common is wack."

That's when I jump up. Now, mind you, I wasn't even paying attention to him. But I heard my name and, more than that, I heard the tone in which he used it. You're going to walk into a room with four guys and start popping off like that? That's not a recipe for peace and tranquility. He should have walked in quiet and left—quieter.

I'm most of the way toward Dread when Derek jumps in to stop me. "Nah, you ain't going to jail over this dude. You're not gonna catch a lawsuit over some bullshit."

Derek's holding me back, but it's not one of those scenes where you're making lots of noise knowing that your man's not going to let you through. I'm really trying to break Derek's grip. I'm really trying to knock this nigga out. We're almost fighting so I can get to this dude. Sound Man and Stage Hand have stood up now and are circling near the door.

Now Dread is really talking shit. That's when Derek tries to appeal to his rationality.

"Dude, you are really not in a good situation here. You best just move on."

I can hear a tone shift in Derek's voice. He's just gone from manager to South Side roughneck. That's when I calm down and stop trying to break through. I know what Dread seems not to know: that this is really his last chance to diffuse the situation before it gets really bad for him.

Inexplicably, Dread says something else. He doesn't even have a full sentence out of his mouth before Derek just turns around and clocks him in the eye. By the time he hits the ground, Sound Man and Stage Hand are stomping the shit out of him. Dread catches a major beatdown; it's all he can muster to stumble down the stairs. He leaves us with souvenirs: two bloody dreadlocks that had been pulled out by the roots.

The next year, we came back through town, and that beatdown was all the buzz. "Yo, you beat up so-and-so!" I'm not exactly proud of what happened, but, then again, dude was asking for it.

People are mistaken if they assume that my conscious perspective was simply a natural expression of who I am. That's only partly true. Yes, I've always been conscious—maybe a better way of saying it is that I've always been *curious*. But the content of my lyrics was also the product of a decision I made. I made the decision during a dark time in hip-hop culture, in 1996 and 1997—when Tupac and Biggie were killed, dealing with the loss of my relationship with Kim, and the loss of my close friend Yusef. I was dealing, too, with the birth of my daughter and the meaning of fatherhood.

Surrounded by all that death and all that life, I chose to breathe new energy into my music. I wanted to shed light into the darkness. That mission came from my relationship with God and from seeing the compassionate way that my mother treated those around her. It also came from finally understanding Sef's words, the challenge he left me even after his death: be a leader. If I was going to lead, I was going to lead us toward the light.

The light I hoped to generate began with the music. I wanted to do something different musically on this new album. The new sound I wanted called for working with live musicians. I loved what Outkast was doing musically and wanted to stretch myself artistically. The new style was an expression of my spiritual awakening as well, which stemmed from being a Christian and seeking out wisdom in other faiths as well.

My bloodline is one with the divine
In time, brotha, you will discover the light
Some say that God is black and the Devil's white
Well, the Devil is wrong and God is what's right
I fight with myself in the ring of doubt and fear
The rain ain't gone, but I can still see clear
As a child, given religion with no answer to why
Just told believe in Jesus cuz for me he did die
Curiosity killed the catechism

Understanding and wisdom became the rhythm that I
*   played to*
And became a slave to master self
A rich man is one with knowledge, happiness, and his health
My mind had dealt with the books of Zen, Tao, the lessons
Koran and the Bible, to me they all vital
—"G.O.D. (GAINING ONE'S DEFINITION)"

I was now understanding that with my role as a rapper came a serious responsibility. Rap is my gift, but it is also my calling. This didn't mean that I had to be perfect or that I had to have it all figured out. Far from it. I only had to be open and determined. In recording *One Day It'll All Make Sense*, I came to believe—I still believe—that even in my own journey of discovery, even in my own imperfect course toward and away from my destiny, I can say things that will affect people for the better.

Maybe I had forgotten before just how strongly KRS-One and Public Enemy and other rap artists had affected me growing up. They said things in their raps that redirected the course of my life. Their words reshaped my sense of who I was and who I could become. Maybe now I could do the same for others.

I had always been a seeker. I had always sought out knowledge from books, people, and experiences. I was reading the Bible, the Tao, the I Ching. I was going to the mosque. I was on a spiritual quest of my own design. I was reading books of Buddhism, reading the Koran. I was reading *Behold a Pale Horse*, *The Illuminati*, and *Message to the Black Man in America*. I was feeding my mind well. Why not communicate some of that in my lyrics?

Don't get me wrong, I was still a party guy. I was that guy who would get drunk on Saturday night but make sure to be in church on Sunday morning—and bring my guys with me. Saturday sinner, Sunday saint is what the old folks would call it. I saw myself as a young man with good intentions and high aspirations to go along with an unfettered sense of fun and adventure. I didn't see a contradiction. I still don't.

I made a conscious choice at a certain point to talk about my growth in my music. I decided to talk about the light at the end of the tunnel, not just the tunnel. If I don't talk about us getting to the light, then some people are never going to envision the possibility. The image reminds me of the reality. When I see certain truths and choose to make music with positive vibrations, it's because of what I want for my life and for the lives of others. I could talk about the bad always, but it wouldn't benefit me or anyone else.

The change in my subject matter corresponded with a change in my sound, too. I got connected with a lot of jazz cats. I'd go to the Jazz Showcase in Chicago by myself. I became a true jazz head. I checked out Pharoah Sanders, Ahmed Jamal—great musicians. I went to see Roy Hargrove in 1996 before I was familiar with his music. He'd been just a name to me. I walked in and was surprised by who was playing. "Damn, these dudes are my age!" I realized. And their sound and musicianship were immaculate. A drummer, Karriem Riggins, invited me to come talk. Roy said he knew "I Used to Love H.E.R." and a couple other of my songs. Karriem hooked me up with the musicians who formed my first band.

Once I started receiving positive feedback for the new work from friends and fans, I decided to focus on more progressive rap.

Conscious girls started kicking it to me. I started embracing that and taking on that responsibility and wearing that belt. I didn't want people to see the other side as much anymore. And even though that other side existed, I knew that the new was what I wanted for myself. I want to be a conscious artist, and I want to be a balanced person.

> At times my going forward seems like retreat
> As I rewrite rhyme after rhyme and throw away beats
> Growing into my britches, outgrowing the streets
> —"INVOCATION"

I said I'm "outgrowing the streets" because some aspects of the street mentality can keep you standing in one place. I gotta make some moves. I'm not going to be stuck on the same level mentally, spiritually, and financially. I can't have eight niggas knocking at my door talking about their demos or be worrying about how my rent's going to be paid with everyone else thinking I've got it made.

One Day It'll All Make Sense is expressed visually by that picture of me and my mother on the CD cover. Parenting. Love. Life. Responsibility. My soul was saying, "I got to grow. I have to contribute something." I can utilize my music to say something to help somebody's life. I can talk about God, about love, about my experiences. If you listen to my music before then, you don't hear a lot of substance to it. "Book of Life" gave a glimpse of that new self, but now I wanted to make songs to move people, to move mountains.

The pinnacle of this new artistic vision was embodied in a single song from the album: "Retrospect for Life." That was a very personal song for me. It was also a public song in that I wanted to reach out to women by talking about something that matters deeply to them. So much of hip-hop in that period is about masculinity and swagger. Believe me, I have my share of bravado, but I also wanted to write a song that would speak to—and even speak for—women like my mother, women like Kim, women like my daughter one day would become.

When I think about "Retrospect for Life," I think of another great woman: Ms. Lauryn Hill, one of the true geniuses of our time. I've had the privilege of calling her a friend for well over a decade now. The one and only time we recorded together, though, was on "Retrospect for Life." I had already chosen the track and written the lyrics, but I felt like the song needed something more. It needed a woman's voice. It needed Lauryn. So I called her up, explained the concept of the song to her, and asked if she'd be willing to collaborate. She was so enthusiastic about it that not only did she agree to sing the hook on the track but she also agreed to direct the music video.

Working with Lauryn, I got to see her genius up close. I also got to know a truly beautiful human being, inside and out. We'd spend hours in the studio laughing and listening to Stevie Wonder songs. (She eventually chose to interpolate "Never Dreamed You'd Leave in Summer" as the hook.) The song became so much more powerful once her voice was added into the mix. It's still one of my favorite songs that I've ever recorded.

The video was another experience entirely. It was my first attempt at acting, and, needless to say, I was a work in progress. But even though I was obviously uncomfortable in front of the camera—worried I might forget my lines, glancing down at the ground to make sure I hit my spots—Lauryn never lost patience with me. I remember after one particularly poor line reading, she drew me aside.

"Rashid, where are you from?"

"I'm from Chicago."

"And what's your mother's name?"

"Her name is Mahalia Ann Hines."

"You hear how you answered those questions? How natural you sounded, how comfortable?" she said. "That's exactly how I want you to sound when you deliver your lines. I want you to be you."

Those words really reached me. And although there was only so much I could improve upon in my performance—my guys still clown me for it to this day—I would take that lesson with me into my first professional acting jobs. I still carry it with me today. That's the kind of wisdom that Ms. Hill has to offer.

In the years that followed, I'd keep up with her from time to time. Like the general public, I'd read about her hard times and longed for her return to music. What I saw, though, wasn't a person in crisis but a person in pain. Every so often I'd call her up just to let her know that I was here for her if she needed me. I didn't ask her any questions; I didn't need for her to explain anything to me. I just needed her to know that I was here if she needed to talk to someone. That's how I understand friendship.

AS 1997 CAME TO A CLOSE, contradictions became clear to me. The year had been one of birth and death, of sadness and self-discovery. It was marked not only by the pride I took in recording a new kind of album but also the disappointment in yet again seeing it fail to gain the attention I thought it deserved. I lost hope when I was on Relativity, and I felt like I was trapped on the label—like I was in an unhappy marriage. The execs at the label probably felt the same about me. But they wouldn't let me out of my contract. There was nothing I could really do. I was in a holding pattern, and I'm a person who always wants to keep moving. I could work on my art, but I wanted it to reach an audience. The stalemate was starting to affect my psyche. In this moment of need, I reached out to my father.

I don't know what made me think that my father could help me get off the label. He wasn't a lawyer. He wasn't a businessman. But he was—he is—a powerful communicator. When I asked him to help me, he got on the next flight from Denver to New York City. Without an appointment, he headed directly to the Relativity offices and asked to see the boss man.

"My name is Lonnie Lynn, and my son is Common. He's on your label. I'm here to speak to the general manager."

The receptionist was polite but suspicious. In the music industry, particularly in the hip-hop industry, a stranger showing up could sometimes be a threat.

"He isn't available right now. Perhaps if you make an appointment—"

"Thank you, ma'am, but I'll wait."

He sat down in that lobby at ten in the morning and stayed there through lunch. He didn't complain. He just waited patiently until finally the general manager agreed to see him.

"I had on my five-hundred-dollar suit, my one-hundred-dollar tie," he told me later. "I sat there like I meant business. And I did. After an hour passed, I could tell the momentum had shifted. In total, I sat there for two hours and fifty minutes. The guy came out with his security guard."

"What can I do for you, Mr. Lynn?" he asked.

He stood there in the lobby, security guard by his side, as if he expected my father to swing on him.

"Sir, I'd like to speak to you about my son," my father said in an even voice. "If you don't mind, I'd like to go somewhere that we can sit down."

He looked at my dad like he was taking his measure, then he ushered him into the office.

"Now," he said, "tell me what I can do for you."

"Let me ask you a question: if your son wanted to get free, and he couldn't, how would you feel? I know for a fact that you wouldn't let me suffocate your son. Well, I won't let you suffocate mine."

"Mr. Lynn, this is business—"

"Don't hurt my son. Don't hurt my son. Don't hurt my son."

He said it three times. Each time, he looked him dead in the eye. He wasn't threatening him. He knew that guys like him understand when they're being threatened. Dad was respecting him and demanding that same respect in return. His eyes were saying, "Look, I got as much juice as you. I've got partners up in Harlem on 145th and St. Nicholas who have my back. But I'm coming to you as a man. I'm asking you as a man to do the right thing."

A few weeks later, the label granted my release.

8 "DOOINIT"

Dear Jay Dee:

What's up, Chief? Man, I gotta say that I miss you much. I still call the place we shared in LA my home. Some days I drive up and be like, "Jay Dee used to drive through this driveway. Jay used to be up in our front room right here on the couch." Some days I might see a lighter or some other small thing that was yours—traces that bring me back to your presence.

Sometimes I'll turn the corner down the hall and expect to see you there. I see you after I invited you to move out with me to Los Angeles from Detroit, before the illness had taken its toll. You'd be jumping from one place to another, making a beat in the living room, body bent low, headphones cupped to your ears. "What you cooking up?" I'd ask. Sometimes you'd play me a taste of the groove, what we used to call that hump. Sometimes you'd just give me a look that said, "Man, don't bother me when I'm in a zone."

Now and then, I'll see visions of you after the disease had stripped away your strength. I see your narrowed shoulders and withered arms, your wheelchair sliding across the hardwood floor. I see you after your mother arrived to stay with us, caring for you around the clock. Sometimes I'd come in from a late night out, buzzed off the bright lights and the liquor, to find you on the couch with your head in her lap, a child once more in his mother's arms.

There are still parts of the house I have a hard time visiting. I almost never open that closest where all your records are because when I do I get sad and down. I try not to let it get to me, but all I'm doing is hiding from my feelings. Man, I do feel your loss sometimes more than others. To me those records are something sacred. I don't know if it's right to touch them. So I keep them there as a kind of makeshift monument to your memory.

You were my brother. Beyond music. I felt like my soul knew your soul from sometime before and the music was just one way we expressed that connection. From the first time you flew to Chicago on your own dollar and laid down those beats for me, I was like, "This is my guy." I think about being in your basement and going to Korean BBQ or going to see The Matrix and creating music. I really began to appreciate Detroit, too. Some of them thick girls y'all had out there . . . Man! Those were some of the most fun days of my life. It was just a beautiful time.

I think about your family. Your mother and your daughter. One of the hardest things in my life was seeing you sick and watching you go through the pain you did. It was really, really hard for me, so I can't even fathom how hard it was for you. I kept telling myself, truly believing, that you were going to get better. It hurt me to see you suffering, seeing your body deteriorate. It brought the fear out of me.

Part of my fear, I have to admit, was in doubting my own invincibility. Seeing someone so close to me dying, it forced me to confront my own human frailty. It's funny how James and Ahmir and them would call you "The God." Because we all looked at you and knew you were this special human being, this Divine Gift. You were a divine gift of creativity and genius, and now that you're not here in the flesh, the world is missing a true spirit. I feel like music would be different if you were still alive; after all, you've affected so much of it even after death. You influenced so many. You kept growing so much—there was something new and soulful about every "batch" you cooked up.

I heard Rob Glasper and Derrick Hodge playing your music with a jazz combo, and I thought to myself, "Dilla was our Coltrane. He was our Miles. This dude was a classic in the truest sense." When I hear orchestras playing your stuff, I know that the music you made was timeless.

It hurts to think we can't get any more music from you. It's really painful. Some of my most joyful times were knowing I was getting a Jay Dee beat CD. When your mom would call and say, "It's on the way," or she would say, "Hey, you can come work on Tuesday and Wednesday," it felt like Christmas morning. When I think of you, I think of how much I love music. I love music. I love you, brother.

I hope and pray that your soul is at peace. I have dreamed

of you many times, and sometimes I feel like you are all right, and sometimes I feel like you feel cheated, left behind. I know that as a fan, a comrade, a creative partner with you, I sometimes feel cheated. But there are also parts of me that know I must appreciate all that you gave us in your thirty-two years on this earth. You left your mark. You left an incredible imprint on our souls and on the music. I just want your soul to be at peace.

I used to have a hard time coming home and seeing you sick. The way you were, I felt guilty that I could walk in the door on my own, that I was healthy, and that I was embarking upon new dreams. I know you were happy for me and proud of me, but sometimes I could see a little bit of sadness in your eyes—like you realized just what was slipping from your grasp. I watched you fading away, but my heart is always on your side. My soul will always show love to yours and recognize your spirit as my brother. You are the greatest. You are timeless.

Love,

Rashid

I MOVED TO NEW YORK IN 1998 WITH FOUR CHANGES OF CLOTHES. I told myself I'd be staying only for a couple weeks. I just had to make a few connections in the industry, let them see my face. Then I would head back to the Chi, where I belonged. I ended up living in New York for three years.

New York in the late 1990s was a cultural mecca for the hip-hop generation. Walking along Park Slope in Brooklyn, or up on 125th Street in Harlem, or down in Soho, you were bound to run into someone making something beautiful. Maybe it was a street mural. Maybe it was a saxophone solo. Maybe it was a beaded necklace. The point is, beauty and creativity were all around.

For an imaginative kid from the South Side of Chicago, New York City was something like paradise. It was riding the train. It was hailing ghetto cabs. It was life on my own. I'd take the train into Manhattan from where I was staying in Brooklyn and go to the Metropolitan Museum of Art, to the Museum of Modern Art, and then farther north to the Studio Museum in Harlem. I got to see the work of Basquiat and Romare Bearden. I studied how they'd bring a human figure to life in a single line. I'd go to off-Broadway plays, studying how the actors projected their voices into the echoing space. I'd go to out-of-the-way jazz clubs to hear young musicians about my age playing the tradition in their own key. For someone with an artistic temperament, New York was—and remains—perhaps the best place in the world to find inspiration.

> *Envisioning the hereafter, listening to Steve Wonder*
> *On a ?uest for Love like the "Proceed" drummer*
> *I strike like lightning and don't need thunder*
> *Inhale imagination and breathe wonder*
> —"INVOCATION"

Living in the city, you end up creating a kind of artistic community. Mine radiated out of Electric Lady Studios, the famous recording studio, built by Jimi Hendrix, where Curtis Mayfield laid down "Superfly," where Al Green and Stevie Wonder and many others recorded. They had three studios, and on any given day, you could find the Roots in studio A, D'Angelo in studio B, and me in studio C. We'd hop from door to door, sitting in on one another's sessions, guesting on one another's records, and building an informal collective that we would eventually dub the Soulquarians. The name was devised by the Roots' drummer and musical director, Ahmir "?uestlove" Thompson, because so many of us—though not me—had the astrological sign of Aquarius, and all of us were soulful. We produced some great music in that time: D'Angelo's *Voodoo*, the Roots' *Things Fall Apart*, Erykah Badu's *Mama's Gun*, my *Like Water for Chocolate*. All of these albums, as different as they were, shared the same spirit of soul.

One of the Soulquarians I started working with a lot was the soul singer Bilal. He and I would work on lyrics together. I had never written lyrics for an R&B song, and I had never really written with someone in the studio, either. We were in Jive Records' studios working on a song called "All That I Am (Something for the People)," coming up with the story. We worked on a song called "Sometimes," too. For that one, he called up a bunch of different people and asked them a question, not revealing that their answer would end up in the song. He called me up and said, "What do you sometimes wish you were?" He used what I said, too.

Bilal worked a lot on my stuff as well. He ended up being kind of like the unofficial house vocalist for *Like Water for Chocolate*. You'll hear him on several tracks that he wasn't scheduled to be on. Sometimes I'd just bring him into the studio when I was working and if the spirit moved him, he'd put something down. When I was working with DJ Premier on "The 6th Sense," one of Primo's guys called him in and said, "Man, Rash got some dude in here singing." Premier burst into the studio ready to be mad, but when he heard what Bilal was doing, he was blown away. It was right before Thanksgiving, and we laid down the vocals for "The 6th Sense" in D&D Studios on West Thirty-seventh Street. His melody added another dimension to the song.

> In front of two-inch glass and Arabs I order fries
> Inspiration when I write, I see my daughter's eyes
> I'm the truth, across the table from corporate lies
> Immortalized by the realness I bring to it
> If revolution had a movie, I'd be theme music
> My music, you either fuck, fight, or dream to it
> —"THE 6TH SENSE"

The change I was undergoing inside manifested itself on the outside as well. I took a lot of fashion risks when I moved to New York. It gave me a sense of strength knowing my individuality was there, wearing my patchwork vests or whatever. I've never had a problem with people laughing at me. I can laugh at myself. That's cool. I'm still a real cat. I feel good about it. You laughing 'cause it's different. I think it's fresh. My dudes at home were getting on me hard, though. "Why don't you got on something regular?"

Rashid really never fit into Chicago, as far as his style goes. That's why he was so happy when he moved to New York: he could be freer. He'd go to thrift shops, find hats and vests and shoes that he just couldn't find back home. Then again, I guess he was always sort of Bohemian. But with me—no! We were straight middle-class. I guess you would say that growing up his style was preppy. But then again, that was really my style. I wanted my son to look clean cut and put together. That's pretty much how he operated.

New York meant more to Rashid than clothes, though. I think it meant liberation, too. Chicago was getting a little bit claustrophobic for him, hanging with the same old friends in the same old places. I'd tell him, if you hang around with nine fools, then you're sure to be the tenth. Don't get me wrong: I love a lot of his friends. But I think Rashid had to leave Chicago for him to grow—as an artist and as a man.

It's hard to turn on the 'hood that made you
To leave, we afraid to. The same streets that raise you
Can age you, with other black birds that's caged, too
The rage up in Harlem and the South Side
Brothers is starvin' with their mouth wide
Open . . .
—"U, BLACK MAYBE"

THAT MOVE TO NEW YORK really was a life changer for me. The world just expanded in my eyes. There was so much to explore, so many creative people to meet. In a strange way, I was also meeting myself. My individuality was coming out. The new music—Fela Kuti, underground jazz—and being around MCs like Mos Def and Black Thought, that all influenced my style. I was gaining knowledge, too. Mos and his collaborator Kweli had a bookstore where they would have readings and performances. I'd go a lot. I'd go to Gordon Parks photography exhibits. I'd talk to people who were into astrology or different spiritual practices, and that would open me up to a new metaphysical reality. It was a journey I had begun in 1995 through books that I was now continuing through life itself.

More than any one influence, though, it was the spectrum of culture in New York that affected me the most. It made me open up and think, "Man, an artist is an artist." I might be able to pick up a paintbrush and be cold-blooded. I might be able to go into the kitchen and whip up a culinary masterpiece. Well, maybe not. But I could eat. And the food in New York was otherworldly. It's rare that you're going to find health food on the South Side of Chicago.

Chicago made me an MC, but New York made me an artist. I'd go to Black Lily, the weekly gathering of hip-hop and soul musicians, and make music with whoever happened to be there: Bilal, Black Thought, Ahmir, whoever. I would go to the New School and meet all these jazz cats through my friend, the pianist Robert Glasper. These young guys were pursuing their art as a discipline. That energy of wanting to get up early and go get it, particularly if you can go get it in your field of dreams, is an inspiring thing.

The greatest single influence upon my artistic development was one person: Jay Dee. I first met Dilla at Q-Tip's house in 1995. There had been a *Vibe* magazine party hosted by Quincy Jones, and I ran into Q-Tip there. We got to talking, and he invited me over to his crib for an impromptu jam session. I got over there, and there was a bunch of musicians doing their thing. I saw this dude in the corner going through some records. He was sitting there on this carpet, Indian style, just looking through Tip's collection. That was Jay Dee, making beats at Q-Tip's house. We struck up a conversation, and it felt like discovering a long-lost brother.

Jay Dee was a genius, a powerful spirit. There are only certain people I've come across in my life who I believe are that gifted—who you already know are a living monument to human capability. When I looked at Dilla creating, I felt like I was watching history. The history Jay Dee was making wasn't the same as Tupac history. It was more like a shadow history, just this side of the spotlight. Dilla would never have been as big a celebrity as Tupac. That wasn't him. He was an influence, a musician's musician. He was the guy who influences the guy who influences the world. You can have an artist like the late Gil Scott-Heron, for instance, who influences Stevie Wonder, who influences the world. The French painter Henri Matisse influenced Pablo Picasso, and Picasso influenced the world. Dilla was like that: a quiet mover of cultural mountains.

The thing that cemented my friendship with Jay Dee was this: after we met at Q-Tip's house and struck up that conversation, he flew himself from Detroit to Chicago just to leave me some beats at the studio. That's the kind of generosity he'd show—not just to me but also to everyone he worked with. Before long, I was heading up to Detroit to work with him and the Roots.

The Soulquarians were a movement, and Dilla was one of its governing spirits. For as diverse and divergent as our talents may have been, we shared a common cause. Sometimes we even sought after the same music. I remember one afternoon, I came into Electric Lady to find Ahmir, D'Angelo, and musician-producer James Poyser in studio B working on a track for me. They were playing this groove with a funky guitar riff on top and a loping bass line on the bottom. Ahmir punctuated it all with his kick and snare.

"How you like this, Rash?" Ahmir asked.

"It's real nice. Real nice."

And it was, though I wasn't feeling it quite as much as they seemed to be.

"I'm glad you dig it," Ahmir said, "because it's all you."

I left to hit the restroom and came back five minutes later to see D'Angelo and Ahmir conspiring about something. Ahmir glanced over at me with a look I couldn't quite decipher, then back at D. I just went on into studio A and recorded my vocals for another song. I was heading to Brazil the next day and wanted to be sure that I got the track done before the trip.

Well, two days later, I got a call from Ahmir while I was in Rio.

"You remember that song we were composing for you?"

"Yeah, of course."

"D wants it."

Even though I wasn't crazy about the song, it was still hard to hear that they were taking it away. I guess it's natural human psychology to long for the thing that's denied to you. I've felt the same way about women. The moment she decides that she's going elsewhere is the moment you decide you're interested again.

"Tell him he can have it."

"Thanks, Rash. And don't worry. We're cooking something else up for you right now. It's going to be classic. You'll see."

D'Angelo ended up recording the song—and killing it. He called it "Chicken Grease," and it became one of the funkiest songs on *Voodoo*. And me? Well, the song they ended up putting together for me was "Geto Heaven Part Two." I think it worked out for both of us.

To this day, I keep *Voodoo* in constant rotation. It's one of three discs that haven't budged from my six-CD changer for the last two years. The others? Lauryn Hill's *The Miseducation of Lauryn Hill* and Radiohead's *Kid A*. Those three albums can just about cover any mood I happen to be in. Those are artists who turn you into an evangelist: you hear them once, and you want to convert every-one you know to their music. When I first heard D'Angelo's songs before his first album was released, I would drive around calling people and putting the phone up to the speaker so they could hear it too.

The first time I met D'Angelo was when the producer and label exec Kedar Massenburg invited me to the set of D's "Cruisin'" video. They were shooting on Harlem River Drive, near these boats. I got to the set to find the director, the crew, and the label execs, but no D'Angelo. He finally showed up, and his knuckles were bleeding, and his jacket was hanging kind of loose. He told us some guy had spit on him—whether accidentally or otherwise—and he had just mopped him. Believe me, D is a real cat. He ain't no punk. That's what I love about him as a soul singer. He has that smoothed-out lover-man side to him, but he's got the grit to match.

D is also one of the most generous artists I've come across. Back when I was recording *Like Water for Chocolate*, he would sometimes just drop into the studio to see if he could get on something. For instance, "Time Traveling." That song was born when Jay Dee started playing this little riff on the keys. Then James and Ahmir and bassist Pino Palladino started adding on. It had that Fela vibe to it, an easy groove you can imagine going on for forty minutes and you'd still want more. D'Angelo came by when we were mixing in studio B. He ducked in and added this crazy part, then got up and left. At first I was thinking, "Do I like that better or not?" It would be the part that I'd rhyme to. It wasn't long before I said, "Yeah. Yeah, I do. This sounds epic." Damn, D knocked that out in like three minutes. Now it's one of my favorite pieces of work that I've done.

I really grew close with Jay Dee working on *Like Water for Chocolate*. I'd travel to Detroit and get down to work. Dilla would come get me at the Atheneum Suite Hotel, and we would go down to his basement studio to create. He would sit at the mixer with his headphones on, come up for air an hour later, play you something, and you'd be like, "Where did you get *that* from?!?" Sometimes he would let you hear while he was composing. We'd work into the night, then out of nowhere he'd say, "Man, you want to come with me?" And we'd hit the strip club. Eating chicken wings, drinking. I'm not really a strip club dude. I guess I'm just a little too egotistical for a woman to kick it to me just because I'm putting out a dollar or two. And the next man gets the same treatment? I like a woman who comes to me because I'm me. But I would go with Jay Dee just for the company. "This Negro is crazy," I thought, but he is one of the most gifted people I've ever met.

Like Water for Chocolate, next to *Be*, is my proudest accomplishment as an artist. It marked a turning point in my evolution. It was the realization of a musical dream. One of my favorite songs on the album is "A Song for Assata," not just for the music but also for what it represented. When I met Assata Shakur in 1999, I realized that no matter how conscious you are, you're a human being whose gifts and flaws equally define you. That humanity came through when I sat down to speak with her. I even recorded our conversation, which you can hear on "A Song for Assata." When I met her I thought, "This revolutionary woman has fought so much for us." I was in awe. But when we got to speaking, I could feel her humanity.

She discovered freedom is an unspoken sound
And a wall is a wall and can be broken down
—"A SONG FOR ASSATA"

I think I realized Assata's true complexity when I met her down in Cuba. I had read her autobiography years before, and it changed my life. Here was a woman, a freedom fighter, who was falsely accused of multiple crimes and hunted across numerous states. The story goes like this: In May of 1973, Assata and several other members of the Black Liberation Army were stopped by state troopers on the New Jersey Turnpike. A shootout ensued, and State Trooper Werner Foerster and BLA member Zayd Malik Shakur were killed. Assata and another trooper, James Harper, were wounded.

Over the next several years, Assata faced indictments in six other crimes: murder, attempted murder, armed robbery, bank robbery, and kidnapping. In each instance, she was exonerated— three acquittals and three dismissals. But they wouldn't stop hunting her. Finally, in 1977 she was convicted of the first-degree murder of Foerster and of seven other felonies related to the shoot-out. Two years later, she escaped from Clinton Correctional Facility in upstate New York and found her way to Cuba, where she's been living under political asylum ever since. She's still a fugitive. As recently as 2005, the FBI classified her as a "domestic terrorist" and offered a million dollars for information leading to her apprehension.

So here is this larger-than-life figure, the stuff of modern-day folk legend. Here is this woman I'd write a song about and name my child after. Here is this revolutionary woman who has fought so much for us, but when we sat down and started talking, she was just an ordinary person. I guess I had built her up so much in my mind that I had lost sight of her humanity. But here she was, in the words of my friend Cee Lo, "perfectly imperfect."

All great leaders are like this. Martin Luther King was a real human being. He was a great man who did God's work, but he also did his share of dirt. All of us have dirt under our fingernails from time to time. The dirt, along with your great acts, is what makes you a beautiful human being. There's not one person on this earth who's all positive. Life exists as we know it with sin. A man and a woman are strengthened by the work they do to overcome that sin and the process they go through to defeat it, to live above it. So when people call me a conscious artist, I'm flattered, but I'm also a bit confused. "Man, you all don't hear me saying 'bitch' still sometimes?"

When I look back over my life and see my flaws, a few seem to crop up consistently. When I was younger, I was a hothead, quick to throw down, quick to take offense. I cooled out a bit by the time I reached my mid-twenties, though. My other flaw? Well, I think Q-Tip said it best: "Shorty, let me tell you 'bout my only vice / It's gotta do with lots of lovin' and it ain't nothin' nice." I always loved being around women, not just for the physical pleasure their companionship could bring but for their energy too.

As my art evolved, so did the women who approached me after shows. You'd think that conscious girls would be harder to seduce, but you'd be wrong. These conscious girls, they're coming up with a different approach, but they still want to fuck. They just want to fuck with the mind first, and I like that. We're all human, and we all have sexual desires.

> Yo, *if I'm an intellectual-al, I can't be sexual?*
> *If I want to uhh-tah-uhh does that mean I lack respect for you?*
> —"THE QUESTIONS"

Because I had a reputation as a thoughtful artist, I'd get girls approaching me on a conscious tip. "Brother, what do you think about this?" That was their hustle. Women can be just as raw as men. They'll go for theirs. They'd want to talk about spirituality and politics and literature. We'd talk, but they'd still end up with their legs over their head.

By the time I got a little fame, the opportunities for sex expanded, but the chance for love contracted. I think that's why a lot of celebrities fall into sexual addictions. Sex is so readily available that you gorge on it. I certainly had my share of fun. After all, I come from a city where popularity is pussy. Of course, I was getting girls—more than I could handle—so I'd put my boys on. "Hooking up my homies on deuces" is what we called it. I was like the Noah of the deuce move—two by two.

On tour, I'm always most interested in talking to the girls who don't seek out attention. My people know this. If a crew of girls comes backstage, my guys will pick out the one who's most likely to get overlooked—the one who's too this or too that. Maybe it's the sister who's been waiting forever to meet me, who may not be considered conventionally beautiful. That's the one I want to see. I see the inner beauty in all women. When women come backstage, I treat them with respect. Most of them only want to talk; they might think they want something more, but in the end, the best thing that can come of it is a human connection.

When it comes to the women I've been with in my life, I always wanted them to enrich me in some way. If we had sex and you weren't bringing anything to my life, then that would be the end of things. But if you were bringing new experiences to me—play new music, art, whatever—then I was turned on, especially in the mid-1990s, when I was breaking out on my own away from home. I can tell the difference between game and the truth. Some of these women will try to run games. But they don't know that I might spit conscious rap, but I'm from the streets of Chicago. I'm peeping you. If you're coming with genuine energy, then I'll feel your pure intentions.

Likewise, I always want to leave the women I see with a little bit of knowledge. "I don't spit game, I spit reality." That was my motto. I always wanted the same from them. If you're a ballplayer, you don't want people coming up to you every day just to talk about basketball. If you're a musician, you don't always want to talk about beats and rhymes. Why not talk about something real? What's on your mind? How can you relate to a person on a human level? That's been my way. Say what you're really thinking. Be authentic. I think that's the Chicago in me. I don't spit game, I spit reality. If reality is my game, so be it.

I like sex, but I love romance. I enjoy the journey even more than the destination sometimes. I like the touch of a woman. I like her scent. I like the passion of shared emotions. You can feel it in your stomach. It goes beyond the body, even. That's the type of intimacy I crave. The best sex I've ever had has come when the woman and I have been aligned in our bodies and our spirits. Don't get me wrong, I've had some good fucks—just trying shit, experimenting, having sex for sport. But when you get sex and love intertwined, you feel it all over your body. You feel it in parts of your body you didn't even know you had.

I always look for a woman who has been through something, who has struggled. I wanted a woman who has known pain, because I felt like that was the thing that built true character. They know what it is to carry pain, so they're prepared for challenging situations. They can support you. Maybe it was subconscious, too, because I had seen my mother go through pain. I always thought of women like that as strong women. I couldn't deal with a woman who had been sheltered all her life. I wanted a strong woman with intelligence, but a street thing too. I wanted—I still want—a woman who is spiritually wise, culturally smart, academically adept, and naturally streetwise.

Put down your bags, love

I know in the past love

Has been sort of hard on you

But I see the God in you

—"COME CLOSE"

The way you are in your romantic relationships is a good barometer for how you'll be in your life as a whole. That's why I seek balance, in love and in life. There was a period shortly after *Like Water for Chocolate* when I was striving hard to become more peaceful. I sought that inner peace so I wouldn't just lash out and fight. "Nigga, what the fuck? I'll beat your ass." I didn't have that calmness about me to make good decisions. But when I sought peace, I went so far to the left in my Buddhist state that I was losing myself.

That's when I started moving back to the center. "Yeah, I'll drink a little wine or whatever, but I won't get silly drunk. If there's a time I need to cuss somebody out, I may. If it takes me to warrior some shit out, I will. But I know how to make wise enough choices where it's usually not necessary. I have that self-mastery. I got enough vision to think two or three moves ahead."

People who know Rashid know more about me than people who just know Common. There are other things that I don't say, that I don't express in music. But there are things that I can express through acting. There are things that I can talk about in this book. I need to talk about them. I need to let it out.

Our purpose should be to become one with ourselves, to achieve a completion of personality. That doesn't mean perfection or sainthood. It means making a genuine effort to see that our actions match our good intentions. It means trying to walk the righteous path. God will guide those righteous steps. I truly believe that. God will help you keep the path if you do your part to follow it.

9 "LOVE OF MY LIFE"

Dear Erykah:

Peace. What's up with you? How are you? I haven't talked to you in a while. Your birthday just passed, and you crossed my mind, so I'm sending you this message.

Truthfully, I felt I should have called, but you know I've kept a distance between us. I keep this distance not because I don't like you or even hate you; I guess I just decided it was time to close that chapter of my life. There was a lot of hurt there, a lot of pain. At the same time, it was one of the biggest growth spurts of my life. I look back and think that I wouldn't be who I am today if I hadn't been through that love—and that breakup—with you.

What was so revealing about you and me together was that I only knew how to love freely, to love and to give my all to love in a pure way. I don't know if it was always the right way, but it was the only way I knew. It was love. True love.

You were the first woman I had ever been in love with as an adult. I had never loved a woman like I loved you. I think we both knew it came from a deep place and maybe from a lifetime before. Wherever it came from, it was very strong. I know I gave my all, my whole being, to our relationship. I know that when I met you, there was something about you that would make me fall in love like never before. I knew when we first talked on the phone as friends that you and I had a profound connection. I knew we had a purpose in each other's life.

When we first met, I remember being mesmerized and over-taken by your presence. We went over to your apartment in Brooklyn, and I was happily overwhelmed just being your friend. You appeared on my album, and I was geeked that you wanted to do something different, geeked to have you care enough to create in the way you did.

Do you remember that night in the studio back in early March of 1997? You came through in the late afternoon, and we chilled for a minute. The vibe was so right. Then someone came in and told us that Biggie had been shot. All of a sudden, the night turned sad and solemn. The whole mood, the energy, was low knowing that part of hip-hop had died.

I think we needed each other's support that night. You came with Bless, and you dedicated your time and energy even when we weren't in the best of spirits. We ended up creating something special, recording "All Night Long" for One Day It'll All Make Sense. I still love that song. I've watched you create numerous times, and it's *always something to see. You are a blessing—one of the legends of our generation—and I want you to know you blessed my life.*

E, I call what we had X-ray love because it showed the very shape of who we were as people. You could see I love deep and strong and dreamy. You could see my heart was free. But I know that I didn't stand up for certain aspects of me. I didn't set boundaries for myself, wasn't true to the totality of my being. I don't put that on you. Most of that was just me being in the process of learning who I was and deciding who and what I wanted to be, what I wanted for me. I was so used to pleasing others, trying not to offend. That's no way to build a relationship.

Looking back, I think I learned as much from our breaking up as from our being together. I learned that I had been willing to play the back, willing to dim my light in the face of someone else's shine. I know that's something you never asked me to do. At the same time, you didn't seem to mind that I did it, either.

Why did I hold myself back? I guess in part it was out of fear of being left alone. I feared losing our love. The funny thing is, though, that once I lost you, I gained so much of me. It wasn't your fault. I know now as a man that I have to lead when it's time to lead and know when it's time to listen and follow.

I know we don't talk as much as we used to. I know we are not as close, but you will always have my love and respect. I thank you for being the friend you have been. I thank you for your wisdom and your light. I thank you, too, for your art. You a cold girl!

Remember, if you need me for anything, I'm here.

Love,

Rashid

. . .

ERYKAH GOT MY HEART. LOVING HER WAS THE FIRST TIME I TRULY understood what it meant when people say they "fell in love." I fell for her. I fell for her in a way that I couldn't even explain back then. It's only a little bit clearer now. Have you ever met somebody that you thought you knew, even before you said hello? That's how it was between us. When we first met, it wasn't like we were strangers. It was more like we were already lovers, and one of us had gone away on a very long trip and was just now coming back home. I guess that's how I'll put it: being with Erykah felt like home.

I'm sure that our two souls were supposed to meet, like ours was one of those connections that transcend a lifetime. We were both Pisces. She would get into the astrology of it: "Our emotional connection is so intense. We're both sun signs, so when we come together it's a super nova," she said. I was mesmerized by her presence, her spirit, her intelligence, her confidence. She set-designed her environment and announced without shame, "Look at me. I am a queen."

> *It was more than bodies we shared with each other*
> *We laid under the cover of friends*
> *A place where many lovers begin*
> —"BETWEEN ME, YOU AND LIBERATION"

We were friends only, for a long time. I was with Kim, and Erykah was with Andre 3000. In fact, Erykah and Kim were pregnant at the same time. They even had the same due dates. All of that created the space for our friendship to grow without being overwhelmed by passion. We built one of the strongest friendships I have ever experienced. We supported each other. We shared things with each other: music and books and spirituality. My heart felt good when we were together. But from the look of things, we were headed to becoming one of those love affairs that never happened. We looked destined to walk parallel paths.

When she was going through her breakup with Dre, I was there for her. Maybe part of me imagined the two of us together, but I honestly wanted to be there to help her through the tough times. "When your man messes up and leaves you, I'm going to be the one to take care of you." That's what I thought. In some ways, it was similar to what I felt as a child toward my mother. "Mom, I'm going to take care of you." Even as a child, I wanted to help fill the void that my father left. Talking with Erykah is when I started working up the mentality that I'm going to do the right thing and be a man because these women have been getting hurt. I knew I had a lot of love in me and that I could be a loving person to her.

I knew it wasn't the right moment for either of us to start a new relationship. But I still wanted to be there. I think both of us were learning a lot from our conversations because our lives were mirroring each other's. We both had children. We were both in the process of difficult breakups. I would tell her how a man feels and give her insight into some of the things that he might be going through, and she would do the same for me as a woman.

Then something changed. I was at the House of Blues in Chicago doing a concert for *Like Water for Chocolate*. I was in my hometown, so this was a special show. I got dressed to the nines.

My stylist, Ashaka Givens, had put together an outfit that was cool and cutting-edge. I was wearing a blue-brimmed hat and a tailored vest. I guess you could say that I was sharp. Before the show, Erykah found me backstage. It was one of those moments that you see in movies, where things just slow down and the two lovers catch each other's eyes from across the room. She walked straight over to me and kissed me. The kiss was somehow hard but soft, deep but still teasing. Then she turned around and walked away. I didn't see her again for several weeks, but when I did, let's just say that all the promise of that first kiss was fulfilled beyond expectation.

We didn't start dating then and there, though. We continued as friends. She was doing her thing. I was doing mine. In fact, I didn't know that Erykah and I were dating until she *told* me we were. At the time, I was talking with the actress Cree Summer. I was in Hawaii, and Erykah came over to visit me. We were driving around the island one day, and I happened to mention something about Cree. Erykah looked me dead in the eye and said, "You're my nigga." I liked that. Maybe I should have been telling her, "You're my lady." Maybe that was a sign of the relationship to follow. She had a need to be needed. But she also had a need to possess.

We loved hard and fast. We weren't together but maybe four months before I proposed and she accepted on New Year's Day 2001. I did it spontaneously; I didn't have a ring yet, but it felt right. We didn't go public with the news at first. We just told our families and closest friends. I thought about what it meant to be with her—not just the intoxicating love of it but also the sobering realities. Here we were both trying to build our careers. Here I was with a daughter; here she was with a son. What would it mean for me to help raise another man's child?

Sometimes I would look around the house, and all I would see were pictures of Dre. Dre. Dre. Dre. Everywhere. I'd turn on the radio, and what would I hear? "Ms. Jackson"! The brother was everywhere. I couldn't escape him. But I knew how important it was for Erykah to have those pictures around; Seven had to know who his daddy was. And I loved that little boy, too. Imagining being a stepfather to him made me reflect upon what Ralph must have felt when he married my mother. I wanted to do what he did well, but I also wanted to do more. I didn't want to be just a disciplinarian. I was ready for the challenge.

Erykah was my first grown-up love. Loving her was the first time I had been so caught up in a relationship that everything else seemed muffled and dimmed. "I don't care what anybody says. This feels so good to my heart and my spirit that nothing can take it away." We loved like hippies, walking around her house with Jimi Hendrix, Otis Redding, and Marvin Gaye playing on the stereo. We lived to love.

I had never loved anybody as much as I loved her. The way I love is so deep and so uninhibited that I have a tendency to lose perspective. I was living in Dallas with Erykah, eating the same food, even dressing alike. My boys back in Chicago would see pictures of me in magazines and call me up to clown.

"Yo, nigga, why you wearing a muumuu? Nigga got on a dress and shit."

"Whatever, man."

"Nah, for real. If I didn't know you, nigga, I'd knock you the fuck out if I saw you on the streets."

Erykah and I were free spirits. I dressed the way I wanted to dress with her. That's why I wrote those lines on the "Come Close" remix:

I don't stress it, baby

They say you got me dressin' crazy

Eatin' veggies, wearin' shirts extra medium

And if we break up, I'ma eat meat again?

I feel complete with you

Shit, I held up signs in the streets for you

In the streets people ask about me and you

I tell them "We go through what most people do."

Let's let go of fear, love

We can grow as long as my beard does

You push me in the way you supposed to

Queen, you're the one I come close to

Erykah and I were a power couple. And I don't mean that as far as what kind of pull we had in the industry. I mean that, at our best, we were stronger together than we could ever be apart. The kind of energy that we generated together drew other energies to us. We found ourselves in some amazing situations.

Perhaps most amazing of all was our trip to visit Nelson Mandela in South Africa. Erykah and I went over to perform, but that was just an excuse, as far as I was concerned. I really just wanted to meet President Mandela and shake his hand. His great-grandson knew who I was, though I'm sure Nelson Mandela didn't. We didn't talk for long, but it was an honor just to be in his presence.

Another person we got to know together was Prince, who invited us to perform at his birthday party. Erykah, the Time, and a young girl I had never heard of at the time—by the name of Alicia Keys—all performed. Prince had invited us all a day before the show to come chill out at Paisley Park. I remember that afternoon that Erykah and I were in the back talking to Prince about the Bible. It was getting pretty heated, and I think I might have said the word *damn*. Prince pointed toward a bucket. That was where you had to put your money if you cursed. I read the Bible but also the Koran. I listened a lot, but I still had some things that I had to say.

We were chilling in one of his rooms, like a den area. We had walked through the whole mansion, and they had all these Prince outfits from different years hanging on the walls. They could shoot videos, even movies, there. We talked all night. The next morning I awoke to the sound of cooing doves. You could hear them in the hallway. Now I understood what made him write that song.

Prince showed so much love that he invited me back to his studio to record. Ahmir, James Poyser, and Pino all came along. Prince wasn't there, but when we walked in, Prince's father was playing on this big white piano. A couple months later, his father died.

Prince was part of another major moment in Erykah's and my relationship. For Erykah's thirtieth birthday in 2001, I planned a surprise party like no other. I flew in her favorite musicians—all of these people she had known at various stages of her life—and put on an all-star concert. I rented out a performance space right next to her grandmother's house. The night of her birthday, I had a car pick us up and drive us to the venue. She knew we were going to a party, but she had no idea what to expect. The first thing she saw when she walked in was a crowd of faces: people from high school and college, from the music industry, from every walk of life.

Then the music started. It was our favorite singer, the British artist Omar, singing his song "Golden Brown" with ?uestlove on the drums, Pino on the bass, and James Poyser on the keys. Then Roy Ayers took the stage. Then Chaka Khan. Finally, I took the stage with Prince and performed "The Light." Later that night, exhausted from all the celebration, she said that when she walked in, it was almost like she had died and was watching her life flash before her eyes. Like, "This is your life."

For all that was good about our relationship, there was much that was difficult. Maybe I should have seen the signs. I loved Erykah so hard that I didn't have any love left for myself. Erykah is a strong woman who is set in her ways. I felt immense pressure to do right by her and by the relationship. I started feeling that sacrifice was what I needed to do to be a good man. So when I needed to go to the studio to write rhymes and she wanted me to do something around the house, I'd stay at the house. Both of these things were important, but there's got to be a balance. The emotional pull she had on me was so intense.

It all came to an end with a single phone call. It was April 3,

2003, and I was back at the House of Blues Hotel in Chicago. *Electric Circus* was out, and I was in the middle of my first headlining tour with Gang Starr, Kanye, and Talib Kweli. I remember picking up the hotel phone, knowing somehow that she was calling.

"I don't want to be with you anymore. I like somebody else."

She articulated each word with precision. As she spoke, I heard another man's voice in the background.

I should have seen the signs earlier on. I should have listened to my closest friends and family, who kept saying, "Rash, this relationship is changing you. You're losing yourself." But I was so far in love that I couldn't see that the relationship was asking me to give up more than anyone should. Maybe it was those nights when I would smoke weed just because Erykah did, even though it made my lungs hurt. Maybe it was when I no longer felt that I could pray the way I wanted to pray. Whatever it was, it never really hit me until after that phone call.

"I'm in love with someone else," she said.

"Who?"

I don't know why I asked, because I already knew. She had been talking a lot with the West Coast rapper the D.O.C., but it was strictly platonic, she told me. Now I could hear his voice in the background. I felt eight different emotions at once. Anger. Despair. I wanted to hang up, but also to beg her to reconsider.

The funny thing was that about a month before, I had been scheming on ways that I could get out of the relationship. She had called me up talking about, "Man, you better start talking with me or I'll have to start talking with somebody else." Maybe she saw me breaking out on my own too much. Maybe she feared that if I had something going on of my own, what we had wouldn't matter as much. I don't think any of that is true, but who's to know. All I know is that I was feeling the pressure of being asked to be someone I was not. I didn't feel I could be the man that I wanted to be and the man that she wanted me to be at the same time. But I had stuck it out, hoping that things would get better and relying upon love to fix whatever was wrong. Maybe I withdrew from the relationship too in order to protect myself. Maybe I thought that would make her realize how much she needed me. I should have known better.

There's a difference between thinking something might happen and having it really go down. I wasn't preparing myself for the breakup; I was still thinking about the ways that we could make things work. But I guess God had a plan. What happens when the person you love tells you they no longer love you? What happens to the love you have that you can no longer express? You send that love to the skies. You keep your thoughts in a good place. You do your best.

Losing Erykah definitely opened up some doors that I had kept locked in my psyche. You know that room you haven't visited in a long time, that you sealed up to protect yourself from the truths inside? I opened up those rooms, and what I found was pain— but also a new beginning. It felt at times that I was taking on her pain, too. I had loved so purely that for someone to reject that love caused a pain that I could not have imagined. I was a child asking, "Why would somebody want to hurt me?"

Erykah was a chapter in my life. When she broke up with me, my whole heart dropped. It felt like a death, but worse because she left me by choice. That year, it seemed like everything fell apart. My heart was broken. I lost the love that I thought was supposed to be for life. My latest album, *Electric Circus*, had sold poorly and been panned by critics and fans. I was wondering if my career was over. I didn't know how I was going to make it as an artist if people weren't in tune with my creativity. Am I going to be able to keep making records? Is this the end of my career? I had hit the lowest point of my life, personally and professionally. This was a turning point. The only options were to give up or to get up.

So I got up. I stepped into manhood and started believing in myself—as an artist, as a man. It was a spiritual transformation. "No longer am I going to dim my light for anyone or anything. I'm going to let it shine. This is what God gave me, so I'm going to wear this. I'm going to wear my greatness."

I had to trust that God knows best. God has the greatest things in store for you if you just allow them to happen. You may feel pain, but those pains are really the labor pains for the birth of the best things in your life. Emerging from my relationship with Erykah was like one of those butterfly-from-the-caterpillar moments. It was like the light was beaming down upon me. I had won the battle for myself, and because of the battle, I became myself.

It took me months to grieve the loss of the relationship. I'd spend hours on the phone with close friends and family. After all of it, though, I came to the realization that I was better for having been in the relationship—and for being out of it. Loving Erykah taught me how to love a woman right, but it also taught me certain things about being a man. Part of what I came to understand about manhood—really, about life—is that there are certain things one should never compromise for a relationship. The most important of these is your relationship with God. I was distanced from my faith when I was with Erykah, even though I was also exploring a host of other forms of spirituality. It took losing her to realize what I had to regain.

Breaking up with Erykah marked the beginning of a new phase of my life. It was one of independence, but also one of understanding. I'm a better man for having been with her—a better lover, a better person. We still talk from time to time to this day. I think we always will. We just have that soul connection; whatever bound us together can reach beyond the limits of place and time.

When I travel around the world, people still ask me about Erykah. "Why did you all break up?" "You were such a wonderful couple." I hear that, and I feel at once wistful and warm, knowing that everything in life happens for a reason.

That time with Erykah was interesting. I think that was truly his first love. She invited us all out to Dallas once. She wanted our family to come and meet her family. I really liked Erykah. And even though his little heart got broken, she was sort of responsible for teaching him—particularly about his health. They were strictly vegans. I said, Lord! He was walking in them sandals, wearing smocks . . .

When they broke up, I tried to be supportive of him. I tried to be good in hearing him talk about Erykah. But after the third or fourth late-night call, I told him, "Boy, you better get up. I'm tired of talking about all this." Erykah took away some of his manhood because everything was to please her. But he walked away a better man.

I still stay in touch with Erykah. One day she called me and told me how good he looked and all that. Rashid probably would have been a good person for her, but she was so lost herself at the time. That was part of the problem with that. I'm never shocked by what Erykah does. She's a person who's brave, and bravery sometimes can look like foolhardiness.

SURPRISINGLY, I DIDN'T TALK TO MY MOTHER a lot about my relationship. Maybe part of me wanted her to feel that she was more important. I wanted her to know that she was the most important woman in my life. I had a lot of talks with my aunt Mattie, though, calling her at three in the morning, then calling her again at five thirty in the morning. I had a lot of conversations with different people who knew Erykah, like a spiritual advisor who worked with her. I was just gathering information. I would ask God, "Why? I gave all my heart to this and felt like I was doing the right thing. Why is this hurting like this?" There are some lessons to be learned. There are some things you've been doing in your life that you must recognize are not good qualities in order to become a stronger person.

When I was with Erykah, I held myself back. Something magical happened after we broke up. Out of my grief at losing the relationship, I found a way to reshape myself as a man. I started owning my excellence and the recognition that came with it. It helped that Kanye was around at that time, too, because his confidence bolstered mine. Seeing somebody so uninhibited about his art was an inspiration. "Listen to this!" he'd always be saying to me and anyone else who would listen. "This is good. Check it out." It made me ask myself, "I feel the same way about my music, but why don't I say that?" I started realizing that the more that I speak the things I want, the more they come to me. If you're doing things out of love, why shouldn't you be letting people know about them?

You can feel me all over, I'm live, I help culture survive
I opened the eyes of many
Styles y'all wrote in the skies with your lows and highs
Open your mind to hear me
—"I AM MUSIC"

Success didn't come to me overnight. It's arrived in stages over a period of years. You look at some artists, and it seems like they're propelled into the stratosphere. One day their feet are planted squarely on the ground, and the next, they're thirty-five thousand feet in the air. It's been different for me. I've soared and dived over the years, but I'm fortunate enough to say that the trend has always been upward.

Finding success in stages, as frustrating as it's been sometimes, has helped me keep perspective. Sometimes I feel bad for kids who get famous at age twelve or thirteen. If you've reached the pinnacle of success as a teenager, where do you go from there? That's never been a problem for me. Part of it may be because of where I'm from. Just try copping a superstar attitude in Chicago.

Folks won't go for that. Part of it, too, is that I've kept the same people close to me since I was young. I have the same friends. Derek, my friend since high school, has also been my manager from the beginning of my career up to now. They help remind me who I am—and who I'm not. My friends are quick to tell me when something I'm doing ain't fly. They'll speak their minds.

Thank God that there are certain things I didn't get too soon as far as success and recognition and popularity and money. It made me develop my character. I had to work for these things. It made me appreciate each level of achievement. I appreciate it and respect it. I may see my face on certain magazines or on a billboard, but I never think, "Celebrate me! I made it." There's more to do: higher levels to get to, more rhymes to write, more souls to affect, more scenes to shoot, some Oscars to get.

> *I break bread with thieves and pastors, OGs and masters*
> *Emcees and actors that seize and capture*
> *Moments like the camcorder*
> *You ain't killin' it, yo, that's manslaughter*
> *Though paper can't change a man's aura*
> *It can feed a man's daughter*
> *I stand for the blue collar, on the side makin' a few dollars*
> *Like Sam Jack they maneuver through drama*
> —"THE FOOD"

I used to feel self-conscious when people called me a celebrity. I wanted to prove to my mother and my friends that I hadn't changed, that I didn't think I was somehow better because I had a little fame. So I'd go out of my way sometimes to show them that I was just Rashid. That's why I squeezed myself into the small seat in the hatchback after signing my first record deal. That's why I turned down certain gifts or special treatment. The problem, though, came when I started holding myself back in the name of staying humble.

The people I look up to the most—Nelson Mandela, Muhammad Ali, Barack Obama, Harry Belafonte—they are all what I call humble kings. They wear their greatness like Jesus wore it. Jesus knew that he was the Son of God, the Messiah, but he still kept his humility. So many of the greats carry themselves as humble kings and queens.

10 "IT'S YOUR WORLD"

Kanye:

You've always been my brother. We're both from the Chi. We're both mama's boys. We both love this music. We've known each other for years, but we really became close at a critical time in my life.

I was coming off of a broken relationship, a disappointing album—a series of setbacks, both public and private. We started working together, and your confidence was contagious. Your belief in yourself—and in me—brought me back in tune with my potential.

I was stepping into manhood. I was beginning to see things clearly and beginning to feel who I was as an artist and as a man. At the same time, you were just beginning to flourish as an artist on your own terms. This was a wonderful time of development and discovery for both of us.

We spent hours in the studio. I was putting rhymes to your beats; the musical synergy was off the charts. But what I recall most were the conversations, bonding and beefing and airing our thoughts. That was golden. I really appreciated that time in my life, and you were there for me as a friend, as a buddy. We created some special music for the world to hear.

Back in the Chi, you used to come by Dion's basement when we were making tracks—a little dude talking crazy shit. "This nigga's wild," I thought. "Does he ever stop talking?" But I could tell that there was something special about you even then, a power you had and still have today.

I know I'm your older brother, but a lot of times, you've been my teacher. You never tried to tell me what I should do; you taught by example. What I appreciate most about you is your honesty. That honesty, that truth, is raw—straight, no chaser. You always speak the first thought on your mind, which can get you into trouble sometimes. But it's always coming from a pure place.

People sometimes ask me, "What's up with your boy?" They point to a telethon or an interview or an awards show. They look to me to explain or excuse what you do. I always tell them, "Look, I support him unconditionally. He's my brother." Those who don't know you find it hard to believe that you're as genuine as you are. They see calculation in your actions. I think that says more about them than it does about you. You know, I might not always agree with everything you say or do, but I know that whatever it is comes from a genuine place. That's one thing you should never change.

I don't know why I'm telling you this—you gonna do it your way anyway. I guess I just want to remind you that I am here. I want you to have all the happiness you can grasp in this life. You deserve it. You are a good-hearted brother. And as long as you keep your heart in a true place, guided by the right intentions and purpose, no one else's opinion should disturb your path.

I wish I had the courage and the boldness to say what I feel all the time like you do. I once had it as a child, but life has a way of taking that from you. I always admired the fact that somehow you found a way to keep that childlike honesty. I really think that's how we're supposed to be as human beings: able to express ourselves in the purest possible way.

Ye, I learned a lot from you about how to believe more in myself and apply that belief to the benefit of others. From the very moment I met you, you never ceased to amaze me with the depth of your belief in yourself. Then to see that belief made real, to see your faith brought to fruition—it's a powerful lesson that I could carry with me throughout my life.

You've gone through some tough times, and you've done it all in the face of fame. I know how hard it was to lose your mother; I can't imagine what I would do if I lost mine. You turned your pain into beauty; you let it sing through your music. I watched you do it. And I want you to know, man, God has you. He is not through with you yet, and as you experience the peaks and the valleys, God will carry you and see you through.

Your talent and your pure soul will always manifest themselves in Divine Excellence and Genius. Continue to use it to fulfill your higher purpose. Not many will be able to say they are as gifted as you are. I know you appreciate those gifts; you tell us about them all the time! I know you want to continue to spread those gifts to the world in your way, and you owe that to yourself to seek greatness.

Looking back, I had to be crazy to pass on those beats you were pushing back in Dion's basement. Then again, I wonder if they were as cold as you thought they were or if your skills have finally caught up to your mouth. I'm just playin'. But you have gotten better. And the great gift to the world is that you keep getting better with every album, every song. You truly are one of the great creators of our time. Wear your greatness as a humble king.

Love,

Rashid

I ALWAYS LOVED THAT STORY ABOUT THE PRINCE WHO TRADES places with the pauper. He exchanges his robes for rags. He leaves the palace for a shack. He lives life down on the ground. Then at the end, when he reassumes his rightful place in the kingdom, he's better and wiser for his experience and his struggle.

In 2000 I was a prince in the rap game. I had just released *Like Water for Chocolate*, an album made with a lot of love and soul. I felt like it was the best work I had done to that point, and many people seemed to agree. It was a breakthrough for me, critically and commercially. So why did I decide to take up a new art, one in which I would have to start at the very bottom? Why would a prince choose to become a pauper? Maybe so that one day he could become a humble king.

I love what it takes to achieve great things. I'm not afraid to work for it. I thrive on the slow progress born of struggle. Those are vital aspects of what motivates my life and gives me a sense of purpose. I've always thought of myself as an artist first and foremost. An artist creates beautiful things, regardless of the art form. Who's to say that I can't become a painter or a sculptor or a pianist if I haven't tried? Who's to say, then, that I couldn't make myself into an actor?

My acting career almost ended before it began. Back in fifth grade at Faulkner the teacher announced that there would be tryouts for a holiday play, *A Christmas Carol*. It became this competitive thing for Derek and me. We both wanted the lead role of Scrooge. I told Murray about it, and he said, "Man, that's some punk shit!" But I didn't care. Well, the audition came along, and Derek beat me out for Scrooge. I ended up as Tiny Tim—a good role, I guess, though it wouldn't much help disprove Murray. We did the play and they just couldn't stop talking about Derek. "Derek, you were so amazing! Derek, you stole the show." What about Tiny Tim? I decided that if I wasn't going to be the best, I might as well keep it moving and try something else.

I really didn't think about acting again until late 1999, right after we finished recording *Like Water for Chocolate*. That album awoke my spirit as an artist. I was starving for new challenges. I tried playing the keyboard, but I had a hard time getting past the scales. I'd wake up from dreams sometimes and still hear the elaborate solo I had just finished playing in my head, but when I sat down at the keyboard, it was strictly "Chopsticks." I like to say that I was a piano player in a past lifetime, but it looks like it passed me by this go-round. I was looking for something else, something that could help me take my artistry to a higher level.

Starting in 2001, I enrolled in an acting class taught by the incomparable Greta Seacat. I remember that first session, because she had us do an assignment over New Year's in preparation for it. She asked us to work with our dreams and draw the energy for our character out of our subconscious mind and emotions. It was a powerful exercise, a beautiful experience.

I remember one session in particular. I was between tour dates at the time and had decided to attend a class. I had just gotten back to New York from Australia, where it was summertime. New York was in the dead of winter. A group of us came out of class, and another three feet of snow had fallen on Manhattan while we were inside. On my way out, Greta pulled me aside. "Rashid, you have a gift. You have something special. You need a whole lot more ex-perience, a whole lot more work, but the gift is there. Embrace it." That felt like magic.

At first I doubted her. The Chicago in me came out: "Is she hus-tling me? Is she just saying that so I keep coming to the classes?" But I decided to embrace it. I would accept her words as a blessing and a challenge. So I got to work. I couldn't believe how I felt after each class. It was like discovering that you had lived your life trapped in a cardboard box, and someone has finally shown you how to punch your way out. Every class felt like I was knocking holes in that box, letting the fresh air in. The more I went to her classes, the more I knew I wanted to be—I was *destined* to be—an actor.

Being an actor has helped me to articulate my feelings with greater clarity and precision. I think that comes from the discipline of preparing a character. You're always asking questions of your character: Where does this emotion come from? Why would he do that or say this? How can he go from this place to the other? Pretty soon you start asking those same questions of yourself.

In 2005 I moved out to Los Angeles so that I could pursue acting full time. If this was going to be my job, I'd have to treat it like one. I'd have to grind the same way that I did when I was breaking into music, the same way that I did after the disappointing sales of my first album. I spent most of my days auditioning and my nights reading scripts. I wasn't seeing a lot that appealed to me. I guess it's no surprise, but there's not exactly a plethora of roles for a thirty-something black male actor in Hollywood. You're either bouncing a ball or busting a cap.

I once auditioned for the role of a basketball coach. I embraced the challenge and got into my character. I came in with a whistle around my neck and a decade's worth of coachspeak in my head. I felt like the audition went just okay. The casting director told my agent that I was "green." After all the work that I had put in, it was hard to hear that. I took it as a challenge, though. I had one thought: "I'm gonna show these motherfuckers now!"

The very next script that came in was for a movie by a young director named Joe Carnahan called *Smokin' Aces*. I read it, and it was like the sky opened up for me. It was the first time that I had made it all the way through a script. It was that compelling. It had the flavor of *Pulp Fiction* but with a style all its own. They wanted to offer me an audition, but first I had to sit down with the director. We talked for a while, but one question he asked sticks out in my memory:

"I know you can rap. I know you can do the solo thing. But do you think you can work with a team?"

That one was easy.

"Man, I played basketball. I was a point guard. I distribute. I like keeping the team happy."

They agreed to give me an audition. I would play the role of Sir Ivy, a hitman for hire. I wanted this role so bad. I didn't want a repeat of the coach debacle. So I tried something different. While I was out on tour, I started reading the sides—the audition scenes— and I started performing them for people. All along, I was building my confidence. I had Karriem Riggins film me reading my lines, too, so I got to see myself back. Then my boy Brian, who's a video-grapher, started working on it with me. I would look back at the tapes and see what was working and what wasn't. I could see with my own eyes what was really translating as pure. It was amazing to learn like that.

And I ended up going in and nailing the audition. That was my first callback. It's a wonder that I got the role, in part because I was a rapper. You see, Alicia Keys already had the gig. It was her first movie. They didn't want to stack the movie with rappers and singers. Luckily, we both could stand on our talents.

The way I approach acting, it's very difficult for me to go in and out of the role. When I'm on set, I'm locked in. Between takes on the set of *Smokin' Aces*, one of the assistant directors came up to tell me that he was doing music videos now. I told him, "Hold up. We're going to have to talk about that later. I got to go kill this motherfucker right now." That's the type of zone I've got to be in when I work. I don't take it from the perspective of "Man, I'm Com-mon. I'm a star. I should get special treatment." That's not the way I thought at all. I'm a point guard.

I'm sure that being a rapper sometimes hurts me when it comes to getting roles. But I think I'll always be a rapper and an actor—though I never want to be a rapper/actor. When I do one or the other, I'm all in. I can't imagine giving either one up, because both of them feed me in different ways and both of them help me reach different audiences. Rapping is more of a personal experience. It has its sacred element. You're composing by yourself; you're living in your head and in your voice.

Acting is a collective effort. There's a special joy that comes from working with other actors. You're creating with other people, so it's not all on you, one individual. As much as we love attention as actors—you want to be a movie star—we also love it for the artistic expression, for the communal feeling. You want to bring what you can bring, let that character be alive and breathing, but that's only one piece of the puzzle. You want to give what you have to the director, the lighting guys, the film editors. You relinquish sole control. You have to give and receive. There's something sacred as well in that selflessness of working together.

When I first started acting, I had to audition and sign my name on the audition list like everybody else. It's a humbling experience. Players in that world don't care if you're a rap star. They ask the same things of you that they do of everyone else: Say your name when we start the tape. How tall are you? Okay, you ready? Then . . . you're doing the thing. Acting—the constant cycle of auditioning, getting callbacks or not getting callbacks—has been a humbling experience for me, having to pitch myself for acceptance in a new game.

Sometimes, though, the ideal role just comes to you. Right

before the Hollywood writers' strike in 2007, I was cast to play the Green Lantern in George Miller's *Justice League*. Like so many movies around that time, the strike crippled the film even before it could get out of preproduction. That movie would have made me, for all intents and purposes, the first black superhero on film. Another actor D. J. Cotrona, who's Hispanic, was playing Superman. He and I used to talk all the time about what it would mean to young kids for them to look up on the screen and see us there. Kids need to see that. They need to see themselves doing amazing things. It helps them dream. It helps them see that they can be extraordinary.

That was a powerful thing that we set out to do. George Miller had us down in Australia doing rehearsals. He had this metaphor for what the Justice League could be about. We had this picture. We'd do our table reads. I really loved the preparation we were doing for that movie. I tried on my costume and everything. I walked into the room where all the Warner Bros. executives were, and they said it just clicked. There had been a lot of controversy on the web about casting. People were saying, "How are you picking this person? How are you picking that person?" I was one of the few casting decisions that the blogosphere seemed to like. "Okay, that's the right choice for John Stewart." Even before I knew about the Green Lantern, I used to wear the shirt. It was meant to be, and then, well, it wasn't. I take a lot from the experience, though, another step in my evolution as an actor.

Luckily I've had the opportunity to work with some amazing actors who have helped me along the way—not just with the craft of acting, but with life in general. Denzel Washington taught me what being a king means. He carries himself with humility and kindness, but also with full knowledge of his gifts and his position. He's also just good people. One time when we were on the set of *American Gangster*, I brought my boy Monard with me to watch the filming. Of course, he wanted to be introduced to Denzel, so I took him over and left them to chat. Denzel talked to Moe for damn near a half hour. After they were done, Moe walked over to me with this dazed look on his face, eyes all wide, mouth agape.

"Man, what happened?"

"Denzel Washington just gave me a pound and said 'My nigga' to me!"

I had to laugh. Denzel really taught me to trust myself and to act like I know what I know. I had only a few lines in the movie, but they were big for me. He came up to me between takes and said, "Man, you *know* how to read these lines better than whoever wrote them. You know how we would say this, so say it like that. Look, we black. We doing something that's expressing something we express as black people. So you'll know how to say it better than any screenwriter can tell you."

That meant so much to me that he took the time to break it down for me and that he had faith in me to succeed.

Now, Morgan Freeman taught me something else entirely—more subtle, but just as important. We were working on a scene together from *Wanted*, and I really wanted to nail it. I mean, this is Morgan Freeman we're talking about. He's played God! So we're doing this scene, and I know I'm pressing. You know how sometimes you can want something so bad that you forget exactly what you need to do to get it? Well, that's what happened to me.

We ran through the scene a couple times, and all the while I can see Morgan peeking at me through the eyes of his character. After one more pressed take, he pulls me to the side and says, "Rashid, I know you want to do this scene flawlessly, but you're trying too hard. Don't try. Don't try. You know the lines, you've studied your role. Now you just need to forget about it all and be."

He was right. I had learned this same lesson as an MC. When you're performing, you can't worry about your technique. You just have to be in the moment with the performance. It's the same with acting. The only way to act natural is to *be* natural. There's no trick. There's no shortcut. I learned a lot that day.

On that same set, I also got to know Angelina Jolie. She didn't know who I was before we started filming, so she called up Wyclef Jean and asked what he thought of me. "Yo, Common's one of the illest in the game. And he's conscious, too." I guess that intrigued her. She was already a tabloid staple by then for her relationship with Brad Pitt, her adopted children, and her work as a humanitarian. But I got to know her just as Angie. I'll tell you this, she's probably the realest person I've ever met in any industry. Even if she had a nine-to-five, she'd still be doing what she's doing now: giving, loving, nurturing, exploring. We shot the movie in Prague, and I'd be amazed at her schedule: she'd start the day by taking her kids to day care, then head to the set for a day of shooting, pick her kids up, put them to bed, and then sometimes go out with us. Brad was big into go-karting, so we would be getting it in on the track. Brad was getting us, too. And I'm a competitor, so I hated getting beat.

A few months later, they were in Chicago, and we met for dinner. I'd been telling them so many stories about my life in the Chi that they asked if they could meet some of my friends. So I gave my guys a call and asked them to come down and meet me at the restaurant. That's all I said. So Murray comes down, and the maitre' d brings him over to the table, where I'm sitting with Angelina and Brad.

My friends were like, "What the hell?!?" I had to tell Rasaan, "Don't be doing too much." That didn't stop him. "Let me get a picture," he said. Monard tried to sell Brad some real estate on the South Side, gave him like three or four business cards. Brad and Angelina hung out and kicked it. We went out on the patio and were listening to *Finding Forever*—my first album to debut at number one. I had made Angelina a CD of Fela and different stuff. She said, "That's some real dark warrior music." It really felt wonderful. This was just a great time. There was a lot of love and respect there.

As for *Date Night*, I played the straight man. It was a comedy, but my job wasn't to crack jokes. I think the role fit me. I could play tough, so I was bouncing off of Steve Carell and Tina Fey more than anything. Some people say I have a knack for comedy that I've yet to express. I'm not sure. I think that my strengths in acting are on the dramatic and action sides. But I can do comedy. I think I would be great in a comedy that comes off as authentic and real. I learned a lot, though, from watching Tina and Steve improvise. But off the set, we spent less time talking about acting and more time talking about Chicago deep-dish pizza.

Queen Latifah is one of the most sincere, bright spirits I've come across on this earth. She just has a smile about her, a certain warmth. It's okay to talk to her. I developed a friendship with her around 2005. We hung out. She gave me this book about the science of breath. When she did that, I thought, "This woman is on a higher level." At the same time, we would still sit and drink and get bubbed out. We became friends in LA, but we met for the first time more than a decade before. I have a videotape from the 1991 New Music Seminar with Monie Love, Latifah, and a bunch of others. She showed me love even then.

Throughout her career, Latifah has stayed true to hip-hop but has also been about personal elevation. She handpicked me for *Just Wright*. I remember she came over and picked me up one day to listen to her music, and I told her I wanted to do this movie. "They're saying the schedules won't work," she said, "but I want to do it with you." She just really supported me, and we made it work.

Just Wright was one of the best and one of the toughest times I've ever had filming a movie. It was my first leading role, and there was just so much pressure. My mother was saying, "This movie can make you." I felt the same way. My team was thinking this could be a game changer for my career. There was pressure from the director and the producers on the set. I felt like the scapegoat at times. They said I was taking too long for takes, taking too long to get into it. Don't get me wrong: it was beautiful and fun, but it was pressure. It was a stressful energy around the set. Because I had worked with these people before, I could feel what was going on more. People looked worried, too.

Throughout it all, Latifah gave me support in a way that pushed me, but was still warm and loving. I remember her saying, "Man, we just did a take with Elton Brand. He knocked it out quick. You supposed to be doing like that! That's how you supposed to be coming." She understood my competitive spirit, my athlete's mentality. At the same time, she'd pull me aside and say, "You need any help here? You straight? That come out good?" We had a great connection when we were filming because she took the time to understand me. I hope I did the same for her.

Latifah is one of those people I think I've known in another lifetime. I feel at ease and at peace with her. And I think she feels the same way about me. I just really do love her. That's one person in the industry I can say I love. I can have a conversation with her about anything. Even if I haven't talked to her in months, there's an understanding, and we reconnect right off the bat. We've had some fun, some drunken nights just kicking it. She and some of her buddies, me and my people.

Acting is one of the deepest forms of artistic expression I've ever experienced. To take pieces of yourself—some of the most vulnerable, painful pieces of yourself—and explore them is a deep form of healing. You go to some of the most painful places of your life. You open the locked rooms of your soul. You open a door to find a room that someone may have died in, and you can still feel his or her presence hanging in the air. You open another door, and you're flooded with a feeling of abandonment. You're a child again on the basketball court, wishing that your dad were there to coach the team. You're a lover stranded in a place where love doesn't live anymore. You don't visit those rooms without a reason. Acting forces you to visit those rooms, forces you to feel the pain, and then gives you a safe way of releasing it. It's a tool for life if you use it right.

I want to show all parts of me in my music as well as in my acting. Have fun, be clever, but have substance in the language that I speak when I'm with my guys and in the language of the people. I'm not afraid to express certain words that I say. I have a tendency to show only my best side, but sometimes people need to see the man in full. We need images of black men that have a positive energy and positive light, but that are real. I'm not saying I'm going to do something positive and then go out and fuck seven broads. But I will show my true self. I find a place to show that I'm a man making the best decisions for my health, my family, my community. But I'm still gonna party.

I feel like I'm a better actor when there's some drama. I'm better with some weight. Then, too, I don't like playing the good guy because I play the good guy every day in real life. There are things in me that are painful, that are shameful, that are a struggle that I get to express through these characters. I get to let these characters express what's inside of me. I don't want to play no perfect guy. I don't want to play the prince, unless he's doing some dirt too, unless he's got a dark side or got some freak in him or something. I don't want to play the prince unless he's Prince.

He needs to grow in all areas as an actor. I want him to be able to do comedy, drama, action. Gangster roles. I think he's going to become good at dramatic roles. The biggest thing with Rashid is that God has really given him some gifts. He says it, but he doesn't really believe it. Not yet. If you were in the presence of Al Pacino or Denzel, you should be humble. But if he's among his peers, he doesn't even feel comfortable to walk up and say hi.

I think he's more than what he thinks he is. And I don't think he thinks it yet. I guess that's better than the opposite. I want him to stay the way he is, but I want him to recognize that he is special. Stay humble. It's okay to be both humble and great!

People— not people who know me well, but others—sometimes ask me if Rashid buys me things. "What does he get you? Has he bought you a car? A house? You must be so proud." And I am proud, but not for any material things. The greatest gifts that Rashid has ever given me have been from the heart. He knows I don't go for fancy things. He knows I don't want other people to do for me when I can do for myself. He knows all this, and so when he gives me a gift, he gives it with these things in mind.

Ever since Rashid was little, he would write me cards. When he was six or seven years old, I bought him his own little stationery. Whenever someone would give him a gift or do something nice for him, I would sit him down and have him write them out a card. It's a simple gesture, but it meant so much—not just for the person who received the thanks but also for Rashid in learning to give thanks to others for what they bring to him.

So whenever he wanted to give me a gift—whether for my birthday, a holiday, or any old day—he usually sends me a card. Flowers and a note. The notes are what I treasure most. I still have just about every card or letter he ever wrote for me. Looking back over them is like looking at snapshots of my son in words. I see him as a second grader proud to be on the peewee baseball team. I see him as the valedictorian of his sixth-grade class. I see him as a college *freshman writing back home from Tallahassee. I see him as a young father, struggling to figure out what it means to be a parent. I see him as a young man, a young artist breaking out on his own, leaving Chicago to find himself in New York City. I see him today, a man in full, living his life by God's plan. I see all of these things in the letters that he's written me. They tell a story. They paint a picture.*

I remember a letter he sent me several years ago on Christmas morning. We almost always spend the holidays together—Rashid, Omoye, Ralph, and me, along with our extended family. It's our holiday tradition. That morning I came into the family room to find a beautiful arrangement of flowers with this note attached:

December 2004

God is Everywhere—Believe and Know—Love, your Son Rashid

To Ma,

I woke up this Christmas morning thinking about the greatest gift I had, and it had to be you. I thought about all the things you had guided and loved me through. I thought about all the strength it takes to be a mother and how you have been the truest and best. And so much do I love you. I thought about how much you have inspired me and encouraged me to do right, and how much you want me to be successful "by having another Light." I know you'd give the world for me, and for you I'd do the same. So when I picture love at its purest, our relationship is the frame. Thank you for being my Ma, my teacher, my friend, my inspiration. Thank you for being you. Just know that you exist in all that I do.

EVERYBODY HAS LIGHT and dark in them. The best thing you can do is not to express your darkness to hurt other people. You gotta take your darkness out in song, in athletics, in safe places. Let it out. To me, that's the cycle of pain we seem to generate. Our people, black people, go through a lot of pain, and we've inflicted it upon one another at some point.

The thing that acting shows me is that expression can release a lot of things. It's one of the keys to being able to move on and to grow from something. I always knew I could grow as an actor because as long as you're living life, you're growing: going through joy and happiness, love, doubt, questions about yourself, aging— all those things. You're experiencing life. Life is surreal, though, sometimes—particularly in Hollywood.

The William Morris Endeavor Entertainment offices in Beverly Hills are white-white with an occasional touch of blue. They are all reflective surfaces, enameled and polished to a shine. I remember the first time I took the elevator to the third floor and walked into the lobby to meet with my agent. It was like stepping onto a set with you as the star. The entire east wall is window. You can see all the way to the "Hollywood" sign. I know that's by design. Here you are, looking over the entire city of Los Angeles, a literal sign of stardom hovering in the distance.

My boys from back home always ask, "So is it just like *Entourage*?"

I have to say, yeah, it is kind of like that.

I've had friends ask, "How do you live in LA? I hear everyone's fake out there." When you already know who you are, being around people who are posturing doesn't make you start posturing too. You stay you. Yes, in LA there are a lot of people chasing material things. A lot of life is lived on the surface. But there's a rich culture here, too. It's a land of dreams and dreamers.

I came out here when I was thirty-two. By then, Chicago had already shaped me. I'm Chicago through and through. I try not to judge others for how they live their lives. I'm not always successful, though. Just the other day, I walked past this guy talking loud on his cell phone. "Yeah, HBO is looking at my new show . . ." Part of me wanted to say, "Shut the fuck up!" But I had to shut that emotion down.

I try to bring realness to whatever situation I'm in. I set the tone by my example. Of course, you're not going to change an entire city in one swoop, but I'm still going to be me around everyone. I'm going to say some raw, real things. That's what I know, and that's what I'll be. I also tend to look at the brighter side of things. So I look at LA, and I say, "Man, there's sunshine. There are beautiful mountains. This is a place where I can get great work done." And even if there are some people who are focused on things that are not authentic to me, I'm not going to judge them for it. I'm going to keep going about my business. If I'm in their circle, though, I'm going to show them what the real is. If they want to meet me there, they can.

I always think about Jesus when he was hanging with the Pharisees and the prostitutes. "It's the sick who need the healing." If I'm going to do my best to use Jesus as an example, to walk in His ways, then I have to be around people who I may not feel are on what I'm on. And for the greater good of both of us, we should sit down and talk to each other. I'm not one who's going to hold back if I have something good to say. If I can say it, I'll say it to pass on that energy.

I don't want to sound self-righteous or anything. Life here doesn't affect me enough to say, "What's up with LA? Why are people like that?" This is Hollywood. This is the industry. People talk about their careers, for the most part. At some point in life, a person will understand that life is about more than what you do professionally. Our lives are a complete circle, a complete cycle that's constantly evolving. To be well rounded is to place importance on your spirituality, family, job, fun, vacation—all of the things and people that mean something to your life. You have to find balance so you can be a complete person. If your values lie only in material things, remember that those things will come and go.

I've met many real, caring, and deep people in Hollywood. Often we've met by working together. One of the first people in the industry with whom I truly connected was Taraji P. Henson. We met during the filming of one of my favorite videos from *Be*, this joint called "Testify." In the song, I'm telling a story about a woman who cons a judge and jury into finding her husband guilty of a crime that she actually committed. The song is already so cinematic that I was excited to see it brought to the screen. I wanted either Taraji or Kerry Washington to play the conniving girl in the video. I didn't know Taraji at all, just admired her work. I had my agent get her number, and I called her up to ask her to do the video.

"I'm sitting by my pool," she said.

Damn, she got a pool? "She's doing her thing," I thought. I didn't know much at the time about acting and how much actors got paid.

She said that she was open to doing it but would talk to her manager. For the rest of the conversation, we were just feeling each other out, even flirting a little bit. At the end of the conversation, she said, "I wouldn't date a rapper. I stay away from you rappers."

Eventually we had some cool conversations. And we shot the video. She said that I was looking at her some kind of way during the entire shoot, which I probably was. I was just a man looking at an attractive woman. I invited Taraji to this thing for my Common Ground Foundation in 2005, and from there we started seeing each other.

Taraji was the one I truly, truly loved. I never even told Rashid that until after they were already broken up. I knew from the start that he wouldn't stay with Taraji. Part of it was that their personalities were so different. She's a little more outgoing. Even though Rashid is gregarious and personable, he's really sort of a private person. And you can't be too out there for him. I'm not sure that he ever really, really loved Taraji. At the time, he was looking for love. But he was comparing everyone to Erykah. Taraji was the anti-Erykah in some ways.

On top of all of that, Rashid was in such a delicate place then. He was watching one of his best friends, Jay Dee, die before his eyes. And he was still hurting from his lost relationship with Erykah. He was more running away from something than running to something when it came to Taraji.

I'M NOT SURE OUR RELATIONSHIP ever really had a chance. She met me at one of the most difficult times of my life, as I was watching my close friend Jay Dee pass away. She supported me through it all, and I'll always love her for that.

I had no greater friend at this time than Jay Dee. When I found out that Dilla was sick with a rare blood disorder, I invited him to move in with me in LA. I thought Southern California would be good for his spirits—the sun, the warmth, the beautiful women. Jay Dee would be well, then he would be sick. He was in a wheelchair. It was tough. He would lie on the couch all day sometimes, watching Maury Povich, Springer. It was hard for me to see him sick and lying around, not feeling good and physically deteriorating. Mrs. Yancey, his mom, would be there. To see him rolling through the hall in his wheelchair at a moment of my professional success, it was hard.

Be was a great time in my life as an artist. I felt like I had risen to another level of artistry and fame. People knew me from "The Corner," from "Go!" hearing my records on the radio and the streets. I would go to movie meetings, and some people would be up on it. My songs were getting heard in places that I never would have imagined. Especially coming off *Electric Circus*, which had me wondering, "Will I ever be able to make another album? Is my career over?" When *Be* came out, it was getting glowing reviews, attaining commercial success, and my songs were being used in movies. This is what success is supposed to feel like.

But for all the highs, I was dealing with the lowest of lows. Knowing that Jay Dee would pass, watching him pass before my eyes—it was one of the most difficult things I've ever experienced. Jay Dee died on February 10, 2006. The house became a lonely place, a scary place, a sad place. One day in the months before his death, I came home to find that he had ordered me a TV stand for my room. It was just one of those small gestures, an act of friendship. I moved the stand in there, but after he died, I gave it away because it was too big for the space. As soon as I let it go, I regretted it. That's the sort of thing that you leave in your room no matter what. Dilla bought that. No matter how it looks, it was a gift from someone you love. You leave it in there. It sounds like a silly thing to focus on, but I think about it to this day. I wish I had never given up that thing.

His funeral affected me deeply. It affected all of us: ?uestlove, Q-Tip, Pete Rock. Jay Dee's mother and his four-year-old daughter had been staying with us. Before we headed off to the funeral, we gathered in a circle and clasped hands, ready for prayer. Jay's daughter said she wanted to say the prayer. Her prayer was for everybody. You felt like God was speaking through her. "Bless my daddy's soul. Thank you for my daddy. I know he's with you. May we all be happy in this circle." The power in her voice was for real.

> *Watched gangstas turn God in the midst of war*
> *No matter how much I elevate, I kiss the floor*
> *It was in the wind when she said Dilla was gone*
> *That's when I knew we lived forever through song*
> —"FOREVER BEGINS"

Mrs. Yancey had Jay Dee's MPC there and this hat he used to wear. Black Thought was sitting next to me. I had broken down, and he was comforting me. Then Erykah got Taraji to comfort me. People came to our place after the service. We had food, fish, and stuff. Good food.

Jay Dee's legacy was that he created a sound in music that was so funky, so organic and timeless. His work gives you a feeling of joy, of why we love music. He's the god of producing. Where the god at? He could do so much. He could play instruments by ear. He innovated a sound that had what you'd call a hump to it like nobody else ever did. Every now and then, I hear a beat and think, "It feels like Jay Dee."

Jay Dee commanded respect. I've witnessed Pharrell Williams get down on his knees and bow down to Jay. Kanye came by the house on a Mother's Day when Jay Dee was in here making beats. Jay Dee gave Kanye a 45 with some drum breaks, and Kanye cherished that joint like he'd received a gift from one of the prophets.

I loved him as my brother, a creator. Waking up in the morning and walking past knowing that he was making a beat gave me such joy: "Aphrodisiac," "Thelonious." I was trying to get him on this song called "Funky for You." The label didn't seem too motivated, so Jay Dee dropped me off at the hotel. The next morning, he picked me up and had what became "Thelonious" humping in the truck. He and I went and wrote that joint in his basement. His private legacy? A warm, quiet, and good-hearted friend.

Like Dilla, Kanye is someone I would consider more a brother than a friend. Kanye and I can talk about anything: life and love, whatever's on our minds. Even our mothers became friends. It's hard to make friends—true friends—in the entertainment industry. You want to find someone who's open enough to get to know you in a genuine way. Kanye is that person.

It wasn't always like that, though. I met Kanye back in Chicago through No ID. Kanye was that young dude who used to be in Dion's basement talking about, "My beats is the coldest. Check these out!" We would just laugh at him. Don't get me wrong: his beats were strong even then. But I used to think, "If I got No ID in here doing higher-level beats, why am I gonna mess with you when your beats aren't on that level yet?"

Kanye was cocky as hell, but you had to love him. He could be like a mosquito in your ear, though—straight get on your nerves. My guys used to come with me to the studio, and Kanye would be talking nonstop as usual. "We gonna beat his ass," they'd say. "Nah, cool out," I'd have to tell them. "He's good." Kanye's always had that raw speak-your-mind thing. My boys didn't like that.

I'm not going to sit here and tell you that I knew Kanye would become a superstar. But I knew he was talented. I knew he had a gift for sound. He could rhyme, too. We'd sit around the studio freestyling, and he'd say some clever stuff.

I finally ended up working with Kanye on *Be*. He produced most of the album. Kanye and I would have the best conversations in the studio. I would go digging for records and bring them in, and Ye would listen to them for samples. We cooked hard together. It was an amazing creative process. We became brothers. New York to LA, we were brothers. He was proud to see where he had taken me. And I'll always acknowledge that he played a significant part in elevating my career. Being on his Good Music label was a rebirth for me.

I remember one night I had the rental car from Dave New York, and I was driving to catch Ye at the studio. He was working on a session for someone on Interscope Records—I think it was Eve—and he was working on a beat. I called him, and he said, "Come on through the studio." I got there and walked in, and he was playing this beat that turned out to be "The Food." He played it and then started this little chant. "This yours. Man, you want that?" Once I said I was coming, he just divinely made it for me even though he was in another artist's session. I took that beat, and I was riding out to it. I started getting in on that beat. "Man, I'm coming home on this beat." Life is cycles. *Can I Borrow a Dollar?* was the root. This was the second revolution. I had to go out, come around, and go through the cycle to get back to *Be*. *Be* was the future, but it was back. The future of the retro.

To see how far Kanye has come is amazing and great for the Chi. It's great for all of us. Yes, he's found himself in the middle of controversy—the "George Bush doesn't care about black people" thing, the Taylor Swift jack move—but it's really no different from what he used to do in Dion's basement. It's just that now the spotlights are on. I may not agree with everything he does, but I support him and unconditionally love him. He's a genuine person, a gifted spirit, and a creative force just beginning to find his expression. The last few years have been difficult for him. I can't imagine what it's like to lose your mother. I can't imagine what

I'd do. That tells me Kanye needs his family now more than ever. We're brothers, so that's family.

I met Donda West when we sat on a mother-and-son panel. This was before Kanye had really blown up. I was at Chicago State University, where she was teaching. The three mothers on the panel were Donda, Talib's mom, Brenda Greene, and me. All three of us were English majors, English professors, had our doctorates, and had sons in the industry, rappers who didn't finish school. From that day on, she and I connected. She wanted me to share with her what my experiences had been. I would say, "Girl, they ain't nothing like yours gonna be." Because I hadn't been into the celebrity world. She dove headfirst. Kanye blew up so fast. She would invite me to everything she and Kanye did. That's how we became close. And Rashid and Kanye were close, too, so it became natural.

It was so sad when she passed. We talked a lot before she had the surgery. I did not want her to do it. She didn't need to do it. She was beautiful. She was smart. I told her one time, "Why don't you come back from LA?" I don't think Donda would have been talking about plastic surgery if she hadn't been out there. I can remember when this women's organization honored us, mothers in the industry. We were downtown for the first event that they did, and they sent in a makeup artist. We both said, "We don't really wear makeup. We don't want that." We let them do a little something. She went from that to wanting to get plastic surgery. So I know it was the environment. I know it was the en-

vironment. She wasn't Hollywood. She wasn't anything like that. She was wearing African braids. You can get caught up in that world. I don't know. I just think it made a difference. She would come stay at my house, here in Chicago and down in Florida. We had so much fun. She was smart, spirited, and down to earth. She was my friend.

I try to stay in touch with Kanye too. But he's sort of hard to reach sometimes. He's just hurting. He's a much better person than he's been portrayed to be. You can't even begin to know. That boy's heart is so good. But he's just hurting. He never faced her death. He ran from it. He was in Europe when she died and as soon as the funeral was over, he went back. Kanye has always been the type of person to say what he thinks. I don't judge him. As a matter of fact, I defend him.

I think he's in a much better place now. The past six or seven months, though, he's really been dealing with it. Every now and then I'll text him or email him or talk to him. She was my best friend. Truly. She was his good friend. And she was in the music with him from the day he started—dragging him around, going places. She was all up in it from the very beginning. She knew every word to his songs while I was still trying to remember some of the titles to Rashid's!

And the other thing is that Kanye, in my opinion, is a musical genius. I told Rashid, stay close to him. Help him keep good, regular people around him. People who are willing to tell him wrong from right. I worry about him sometimes. I always love him.

KANYE HAS HELPED ME become bolder as an artist. I see the risks he takes. I see the confidence he has in his own abilities. Being around him, it's hard not to feel the same. The other great influence on my music has been acting. Acting has allowed me to be more open as a human being, to dig into the depths of my own person. It's also allowed me to dig into the psychology of different people, to get into the mentality of others. I think it's made me more open to taking on characters when I rap. I'll tell this story, and I'll put in more of the character's history of why they did what they did. As an actor, you don't judge. So writing from that perspective is a lot of fun. It really allows me to be a screenwriter, actor, director. It allows me to dream and to make that dream come true.

I'm open to trying more things. Once you get into acting, you're not as afraid of embarrassing yourself. You're showing a lot of emotions in character, which helps you show your emotions when you're out of character, too. I always thought of myself as an open rapper, an expressive artist, but I've never been as expressive on the mic as I've been since acting. I'm more in tune with who I am. I'm not afraid. "Man, look, I feel free. Y'all can be restricted if you want. I'm an actor; I can do this." It's really me saying I'm not afraid to try things. Bring on the new.

11 "THE LIGHT"

Dear Omoye:

I love you. I cherish you. I miss you when I'm away. You are such a bright and beautiful young lady. Sometimes I look at you, and I can't believe that I have a daughter as mature, as loving as you. It's still surreal at times that I'm a father, and when you say "Dad," it's like I am Daddy for real. I have a life to help shape, a person to listen to and to give to. I have a responsibility to you, to help you to be the best human being you can be.

I know that I have not always been there. My life keeps me on the road. It seems like there's always a new album or a film. I fight with myself because I know that sometimes I just have to stop and be. Be there for you. Be there with my time and attention. I think one of the hardest things I have experienced is finding a way to balance my dreams with yours. I know I can be selfish because my dreams mean so much to me. I figure that once I attain my goals, I can take care of all my loved ones. But, of course, there's no end, there's no stopping place. That's why I have to find the balance.

I hope you realize that all throughout my journey, you have been in my heart, in my spirit. I feel wonderful when you call me from school on your teacher's assistant break. I think it's so funny that you are a T.A., and our conversations are just free and honest. That's what I want for you, Omoye. I want you to be a free person—free in her thoughts, free in her emotions, free to hear and to love with your whole being. I want you to have the freedom to discover, the freedom to believe, the freedom to fail, and the freedom to keep going in the face of challenge. I want your spirit to stay free always.

Along with that, I pray that you will follow truth. It's an old saying from the Bible, but the truth will set you free. If you follow truth and act in its name, you will be a happier person for it. Truth is what God gave us. Truth is what you feel in your spirit, not what someone tells you or what someone expects you to be. Truth is yours to live.

I know your heart is pure, and I pray that you will be allowed to stay that way. Stay courageous enough to be the person you are. I'm watching you grow. Our conversations are changing. You really do have your own perspective, your own way of thinking. I hope you continue to let that grow. I will give you all the love and guidance and support and prayers and understanding and lessons that I have, and I know you will take that and learn in your life. You will experience peaks and valleys, joys and hurts, but through these experiences, know that God will always be with *you. You are God's child, and with His love, you will always make it through. All is possible.*

And, Omoye, right after God's love is my love. I am there. Your mother is there. Your grandmother and grandfather are there. You are loved. You are loved, and you are cared for as a queen. We all unconditionally love you. Daddy loves you beyond all measure.

Love,

Dad

GAZING AT THE NIGHT SKY HELPS YOU UNDERSTAND WHAT STARS really do—they shine down bright on the world. For a star, the spotlight doesn't have to be on for it to shine. Being a star doesn't necessarily have to do with popularity or exposure. I know some stars whose names aren't known at all except to the people in their immediate circles. Sometimes you'll see a child saying or doing something, and you'll think, "That little person is a star." They just illuminate their own area.

I think Kanye is a self-illuminating star. Even if he had never gotten famous, he'd still be shining his light. I know that I am such a star and always was. I just had to find my light and let it shine. My star and Kanye's star were in entertainment, an area that our society gives extra attention. But there are stars illuminating all sorts of fields, all sorts of galaxies of human experience. They may not be as glorified by society at large as athletes and entertainers, but they shine bright regardless.

There are certain people who are supernovas that just light up the universe. People like Michael Jackson. He influenced so many people with his music. Look at how people were connected to him, were affected by him. It crossed all borders, all barriers of race and language and politics. Even through the controversies, his light continued to shine upon us and bring joy. When he passed away, look at how many people felt connected to him, like we knew him, like he meant something specific to our lives. He shined on us in a way that only God could have created. The same is true for other supernovas. Oprah Winfrey. Harry Belafonte. Muhammad Ali. They shined, they still shine so bright. What all stars have in common, though, no matter how bright they shine, is that inner light. That's God shining through: using stars to bring joy. That's the reason that stars can heal, even.

I once heard a story about a woman diagnosed with terminal cancer. The doctors said she had only months to live. Rather than shrink away in despair—which many would have done, and which would have been her right—she chose to live the end of her life surrounded by love and laughter. She invited friends and family over, and they'd tell stories to one another and watch movies, almost always comedies. She laughed night after night, watching Steve Martin and Eddie Murphy and Whoopi Goldberg on the screen. She laughed so much that she started feeling stronger. She laughed so much that when she went back into the hospital, the doctors said that her cancer was in remission. She laughed her way back to life. Now, no one can say exactly what healed her—perhaps the cancer would have receded on its own—but I can't help believing that the joy she found in loved ones and laughter made the difference.

I remember the moment I first felt like a star. It wasn't when I went on my first tour or made my first music video. It wasn't the first time I saw myself on television or on the cover of a magazine. It was early in the summer of 2000, and "The Light" had just come out. That was a big song for me—not just because it was a hit but also because it was one of my first love songs. I was doing a radio show in Los Angeles for the Beat. When I was rapping, I remember looking out in the crowd and seeing little black girls singing along, singing "The Light." I'd never had that.

After the show ended, a bunch of girls came running after me. What made me feel like a star was that I was rapping about loving a woman and her being the light and how she reflected God's light, and these little black girls were singing my words along with me. That suddenly made my purpose clear. I have a goal that's bigger than myself. That's when I felt that I'd finally begun to fulfill the promise I made to Emmett Till so many years earlier in that tunnel. Do something bigger than myself. That's the definition of a star.

One of the biggest stars I've ever been around is Oprah Winfrey. She's brought so much good to the world, and that makes her great. I've been on *The Oprah Winfrey Show* twice: once when I was supposed to be, for a show she did on hip-hop, and once when I wasn't. Let me tell you about November 29, 2005, the time I wasn't. Earlier that year, I had received a call from Jamie Foxx, who was working on an album, fresh off his Oscar win for portraying Ray Charles, and he wanted to collaborate with me.

"Rash, I got this song, and I think you'd be perfect," he said. "It's about a girl having a baby. Come on and bless it with a verse. We'll record it, and then we'll go perform it on the *Oprah* show."

"Man, you don't even need to say that. If the vibe is right for what I do, I'll do it for you."

Of course, I wanted to go on *The Oprah Winfrey Show*. Who doesn't? Plus, I knew that my mom would be there. It would be in the Chi. It would be a big deal.

Jamie and I went on to record the song, "U Still Got It." The time came for the taping of *Oprah*. I flew to Chicago with a brand-new suit and a fresh haircut. I was clean! I made it to the studio and was taken to a dressing room. Showtime was getting close, and I could hear Jamie and the band rehearsing. I listened, and it sounded like they rehearsed every song of the album except for the one I was on. If that wasn't strange enough, I saw Jamie's manager walk past my door. He turned right around when he noticed me.

"Common? What's going on, man? It's a surprise to see you. What are you doing here?"

What was going on? Had Jamie forgotten? Was this one of his practical jokes? I explained the plan as Jamie had explained it to me.

"Jamie didn't say a word about that to me."

"Let me go talk to him," I said.

"Actually, man, he's about to go on. Oprah just went out on-stage. Let me check."

He came back ten minutes later to say that they might be able to get me on the untelevised after-show. The after-show? I bought a new suit. I got my hair cut. For the *after-show*? Man, this couldn't be happening.

So there I was in the green room, watching the show like I was on my couch back in LA. They were halfway through and in a commercial break when I noticed Jamie lean over and whisper something to Oprah.

"Common's here?" Oprah said. "I love Common. Yes, we have to get him out here!"

In the last segment, they rushed me up to the stage, and we just did the damn thing. No rehearsal at all. We rocked it.

My music has opened up so many opportunities for me to meet new people and travel to new places. I was invited to perform in Cuba for Black August, promoting human rights through music and culture. I was one of the few hip-hop artists invited. In order to perform at the festival, I had to write down my lyrics for the Cuban government to approve them. Despite the challenges, I knew this would be an amazing experience. This means something. I'm representing hip-hop. I'm representing black America. It was a special time.

> I start thinking, how many souls hip-hop has affected
> How many dead folks this art resurrected?
> How many nations this culture connected?
> —"THE 6TH SENSE"

Like most Americans, I associated Cuba with a handful of words. *Castro. Ché. Revolution. Crisis. Embargo.* I left Cuba with other words resonating in my mind. *Love. Rhythm. Kindness. Richness.* I saw some of the richest people there that I've ever seen—rich in spirit, even if they were poor in wealth. Cuba is one of the most beautiful cultures in the world: art, food, and life there are so profound that neither financial circumstances nor their politically complicated relationship with the United States can deprive who they are as a people. They have great pride, but also great generosity. The things they value are family, food, art, culture. They stand for something.

Next to Cuba, one of the most dramatic trips I've taken was to Beijing, China. We were there only for maybe a day and a half. Right outside my window, though, I could see the Great Wall of China. We, the band and me, also had some of the best food I've ever tasted.

I was happy to be in Beijing because its culture is so different from ours. So often when I travel I see so much of how other countries have adopted elements of American culture—and often the worst elements of it, too. That the Chinese didn't really seem to give a damn about American culture was refreshing.

But they were very strict. Just like in Cuba, we had to write down our lyrics for that show. The organizer was telling us we were one of the first hip-hop acts to appear in Beijing and at this festival. And he was telling us how much he had to go through to get us permission to perform. We were supposed to have a forty-five-minute set, but because we couldn't get the sound right—the translation was crazy—we probably got to perform for only ten, fifteen minutes. The way the venue was set up, government officials sat ten feet away from us; the police, twenty feet away; and the audience, thirty or forty feet away. The promoter said he had to ask permission even for the fans to put their hands up and dance. That made me appreciate the freedoms we enjoy in America, freedoms we often take for granted. To have to ask if you can put your hands up at a show? And the way that the police were stiff-arming and elbowing and pushing back fans trying to come up to speak to me—I mean, just to speak to me. It was *women* they were strong-arming. We tried to tell them to cut it out, but that was their way.

What a surreal experience to wake up in the morning and walk along the Great Wall, then get on a plane and arrive in Paris in time to have a late dinner along the Seine River. I took that as a sign of an earthly paradox: just how big the world is and just how small we can make it. I crossed borders and cultures and time zones, I walked along one of the wonders of the world and ended the day in the City of Light, all in less than twenty-four hours. Thinking back on experiences like that makes me understand the value of fame—not for what it is but for the opportunities it brings.

> *Sometimes the most famous feel all alone*
> *So we trip to a place that we call our home*
> *I was known as being spaced and outta my dome*
> *Now I know it's all I've known*
> —"EVERYWHERE"

Over the years, my ideas about fame have changed. As I see it now, it's more a process than an achievement. I've acquired it in increments. First I was known around the neighborhood for playing ball or for running with my crew or for being a ball boy for the Bulls. Where I grew up, just being talented would get you fame. You'd get respect from the gangbangers and the grandmothers. After I started rhyming, I started building a name beyond the neighborhood. Once I signed a record deal and had released a couple albums, people outside of the city started knowing my name. As my airplay increased, and as I started touring around the globe, my fame expanded even more. Now, being in movies, I'm recognized by people who would never have known me from the rap game. Just the other day, I was crossing the street, and I heard an old white couple in their car saying, "That's Common!"

When I was preparing for my role as a professional basketball player in *Just Wright*, I spent a lot of time with Baron Davis, the NBA star. One day after a hard-fought game of one-on-one (I lost, but not by much!), I asked Baron what made him want to be a ballplayer in the first place. "When I was a little kid," he said, "I saw the neighborhood react when the Lakers were winning. This is the 'Showtime' era: Magic, Kareem, Worthy. When they were winning, it brought the whole neighborhood together. I wanted to do that."

I knew exactly what he meant. From the very beginning, I've measured my talents by the reactions of those around me. If I said a rhyme, I'd wait for my friends to say, "That's cold!" That recognition was the best reward. When people come up to me today and say, "You're a dope MC," that's fulfillment. Now when people come up to me and say they loved a film I've been in, that makes me want to keep going. It fuels my passion to create.

Fame is a wonderful thing. I never run from it. Obviously, I love the attention, or I wouldn't have gone from rapping to acting—I would have gone from rapping to carpentry or something. I can get tired of the recognition sometimes. I might be having a nice dinner with my lady, and somebody comes up and asks to take a picture. Or I might be having a bad day, and a parent and a child stop me on the street. I might not want to be Common at all that day, but I'll still show people the love and respect they deserve. I chose this life. When you are putting out music and films, you want to touch the world. Well, there's a chance that when you touch the world, the world is going to want to touch you back. When the world reaches out to me, I embrace it. That is the responsibility of stardom.

Having a little bit of fame is a form of fulfillment for me. Ever since I was young, I knew I wanted to leave a mark on this earth so that the world would know that I was here. I want what I create to survive well past the limits of my own life. Every time I record an album, every time I make a film, I'm striving to create something that people will want to pass on. I know I don't always achieve that, but it's my goal every time. The times I fall short I take as opportunities to learn. But I strive to create timeless art every time. That's what I meant by finding forever. I want my art to be my legacy. I want to walk that forever line.

In my mind, fame has always been directly linked to greatness and greatness to hard work. I've never quite understood the concept of a "reality star"—someone who's famous for getting drunk or losing weight or just living his or her life on the TV screen. For me, fame has always been about talent. Celebrity or notoriety is one thing. But fame and stardom come from the public's recognition of your gift. My goal from the beginning was to take whatever spark of greatness God granted me and bring it to light. Let that greatness be illuminated.

That's why it's always slightly uncomfortable when people give me attention for what I think aren't the best reasons. "Sex symbol." It's an odd phrase. When you see it attached to your name, it's hard to know what to make of it. Be flattered, I guess. It's not like I've run from it. When you're plastered all over billboards and cineplexes flexing your biceps in a basketball jersey, you can't say you aren't aware of the response you'll get.

What do women see in me? I hope they see their idea of a real man, one who is loving, open-hearted, and expressive. At the same time, I hope they see a nigga who's gonna be strong, who's going to be the man of the house. He'll lead when he needs to lead. He's confident in being different, assured of himself in that way. He's confident enough to be vulnerable, too. He'll express his heart. They see a man who's spiritual and street. They know that if we're out in public, he's going to be the protector. He'll work and provide for them, but also pamper and comfort them too.

At one point in the nineties, it was all about the thug. Then women said they wanted some aspects of that, but they also wanted a gentleman, a man who will be loving and will listen, a man who has values. I'm going to open a door. I'm going to walk on the outside when we're on the street. I'm going to listen to what she likes and give her the best of what she likes.

Sincerity has a lot of seduction. I seduce a woman by using our true connection to open her up. I seduce through being me. Being yourself is seductive. I'm a sexual person, so I'm going to be real. You say sweet things, but you say what's on your mind, too. "I want to brush my lips against the back of your neck." Or maybe "I want to fuck the shit out of you." By the way she responds, you know when it's right.

It took me some time to learn all of these things, to figure out how to be a man with a woman. In my adult life, I've only seriously dated four women: Kim, Erykah, Taraji, and finally Serena. I feel like all the relationships before Serena Williams were leading up to this: to loving a woman with all that I've got.

As men we were taught to hold it in
That's why we don't know how 'til we older men
If love is a place I'ma go again
At least now I know to go within
—"LOVE IS . . ."

I met Serena at a party that Will Smith and Jada Pinkett Smith had to welcome David and Victoria Beckham back in July of 2007. Serena was dating some guy at the time. But we exchanged numbers, and then when *Finding Forever* came out later that month, she texted to congratulate me. I knew I liked her the first moment I talked to her. She had started winding down with her guy. About two months later, she called me.

Our first date was special. I brought her to a rehearsal, and it was like giving her a one-man show. Every song, I was just performing for her. Serena was unlike any woman I had ever dated, any woman I have ever known. On the surface, we were so different. Serena was talking to me at first about how she loved *Harry Potter* and Green Day. That might not have been my taste, but your preferences are less important than your values and how you maintain yourself. In that regard, we couldn't be a better match.

It's kinda fresh you listen to more than hip-hop
And I can catch you in the mix from beauty to thrift shop
Plus you shit pop when it's time to, thinkin' you fresh
Suggestin' beats I should rhyme to
—"THE LIGHT"

Love is in the details as much as it is in the dramatic gestures. I show my love for Serena in small ways. She told me she really loved the shoes the girl wore in the video for "I Want You," so I went and got her those. There's a song we used to hear a lot when Serena and I first met, called "Bubbly" by Colbie Caillat. It was her ringtone, too. Well, I was in the studio with Colbie one day and asked her to do an acoustic version and dedicate it to Serena and me. I like sending Serena cherry pies. I buy her flowers for every tennis tournament. I don't want to tell everything. I want to keep some things sacred—not secret, but sacred.

I'm at a point now where I'm really feeling like I want to be married. Some of the intensity and power and spirit I feel with Serena let me know that a lifetime commitment is possible. I'd like to be in a healthy, loving relationship with a woman. I'd like to experience the comforts of a woman. Unfortunately, I sometimes look for motherly things in a woman. You know, nurturing, caretaking. But by the same token, I want strength. That softness and that strength together is what I've found in Serena.

I'm learning things to build my relationship. For instance, Serena is a Jehovah's Witness. Her faith is central to her life. So to connect with her, I have to engage with her faith—not only for the relationship but also so that when I talk to our kids, I'll know what Serena is teaching them. Right now I'm at a place where I'm letting God handle it. I pray and I make sure that I express my love to Serena. Her strength and my strength together, it feels really good.

This is my vision of marriage: it is the love that you share with another that enhances you both. You can become better students of God and children of the Lord; you can become better yous. You will support whatever dreams and visions each of you has for your life, and you can share common dreams for your future together. A spouse is somebody you can have fun with and argue with, someone with whom you can build a family.

With the right person, you can open up and be all that you are, the good and the bad, and that person will still love you. You join together and become one, as the Bible says. Think of yourself as being in a bond that's spiritual, an eternal covenant. To me, marriage is saying that I choose this person for the rest of my life. God has set me on this earth, and there are a lot of people in my life, but I choose to be with you for the rest of my days. You don't choose your child. But you can choose your spouse. This is a person with whom you can share your life. Your life is the most valuable thing you have. I want to experience this gift that God has given me, and I want to experience it with you. Coming home and knowing that you've got that person you love right there. Those warm legs covering your legs. And then sometimes being like, "Come on, baby, can I get some room in the bed? My back!" It's all of that.

My journey in love has led me to this place: of loving with my whole heart, of embracing the opportunity to build a life with someone else. I read somewhere that on average people have about sixty thousand words in their vocabulary, but that on most days we use only a fraction of them. As someone who creates with language, I'm fascinated by the shades of meaning and the range of sounds that different words can create. For all the words I may use in an average day, though, the most important word in my vocabulary is *love*.

I use *love* to describe my relation to God and to family and to friends. I use it in my music. I use it as a verb. I use it as a noun. I even use it as a way to say good-bye. I picked up that last way of using *love* from my guy Dart. I think he started saying it in the 1990s, when it seemed like everyone was saying "peace"—peace this, peace that. Why not say *love* instead? After all, love is the best means to peace. That idea stuck with me.

Now I use *love* almost every time I say good-bye to someone I care about. I end almost every phone conversation with it too. The way I see it, the more we put the word out into the world, the more it will manifest itself in our daily lives. We can never have too much love.

One of my favorite biblical passages deals with love: 1 Corinthians 13.

> Though I speak with the tongues of men and of angels, but have not love, I have become sounding brass or a clanging cymbal. And though I have the gift of prophecy, and understand all mysteries and all knowledge, and though I have all faith, so that I could remove mountains, but have not love, I am nothing. And though I bestow all my goods to feed the poor, and though I give my body to be burned, but have not love, it profits me nothing.
>
> Love suffers long and is kind; love does not envy; love does not parade itself, is not puffed up; does not behave rudely, does not seek its own, is not provoked, thinks no evil; does not rejoice in iniquity, but rejoices in the truth; bears all things, believes all things, hopes all things, endures all things.
>
> Love never fails. But whether there are prophecies, they

will fail; whether there are tongues, they will cease; whether there is knowledge, it will vanish away. For we know in part and we prophesy in part. But when that which is perfect has come, then that which is in part will be done away.

When I was a child, I spoke as a child, I understood as a child, I thought as a child; but when I became a man, I put away childish things. For now we see in a mirror, dimly, but then face to face. Now I know in part, but then I shall know just as I also am known. And now abide faith, hope, love, these three; but the greatest of these is love.

I LOVE THIS CHAPTER because it makes me think about having all of those things: all the faith, all the hope, but with love still being the most important thing. Every time I read the passage, I understand something new within it. Spending time with my daughter, being in a loving relationship, being in nature—all of those things are worthy of love. To love is the highest purpose we can have. When you have love in your heart, you're able to function as the highest you that you can be. At the same time, love is not just about you. When you really love someone, when you love your community, you're doing something for them too.

When I woke up this morning and I read this chapter, a phrase just popped into my head: "the gift of love." That phrase honestly embodies what matters most to me. My mother's greatest gift to me was love. Her gift enables me to walk the world with love. The greatest gift I can give my daughter is that strength to love.

Omoye has made me a better person, even a better man. As I've seen her grow into a young woman—she's a teenager now—I've also seen myself grow as a man. Whatever my mother couldn't teach me, it seems like my daughter has. At the same time, I've worked hard to pass along to her all of my mother's wisdom.

Waiting for the Lord to rise, I look into my daughter's eyes
And realize that I'ma learn through her
The Messiah might even return through her
If I'ma do it, I gotta change the world through her
—"BE"

What has kept me going through all the struggles I've faced in my life? The love of God. The love of family and friends. The love of hip-hop. Love has driven me. I love what I do. I love rapping. I love acting. I love to see that people are moved.

The things I don't love? Not following my heart. When I'm in the midst of people and I'm not being truthful. Or when I'm in situations that don't feel authentic. I'm doing it just because someone thinks it's the right thing to do. I don't love being afraid of things. I don't love not speaking up. I don't love lying. I love honesty and strive for it. I love work.

Perhaps the greatest love of my life is my daughter, Omoye. The love a parent has for a child is beyond measure. As she's grown older, the two of us have forged a bond of friendship to go along with that father-daughter love. We have fun going to the movies or going ice skating with her and her friends. Her friend just beat me in a little basketball video game. Omoye rubbed it in: "She said she would beat you again!" I love her spirit and her playfulness; it brings out the playfulness in me.

> *Talk about it with my youth so she'd understand*
> *What it is to be loved by a man*
> —"LOVE IS . . ."

Ever since she was little, I'd play beats for her and ask her which beats she liked. And then she'd say, "Rap, Daddy! Rap!" I'd start rhyming, and I'd ask, "Did you like that?" Just the other day, she was helping me with a lyric. "Nah, keep saying it the way you did the first time. That one was good."

Recently, I asked Omoye, "What's the one thing that Daddy said, that he taught you, that you remember most?" "To be respect-ful," she said. She used to tell my mother that the reason she gives money to homeless people is that she's seen me do it all the time. I wanted to show her that it's good to give. To be able to give is a beautiful thing. As much as you're helping somebody else, you should find the joy in it too. I want her to know that. Omoye tells me I'm a good daddy. "You treat people nice." More than anything, she's learned from me that treating people with respect is important.

His greatest virtues are his charity, his spirituality, his humility. Those are his greatest. His love of people. He definitely got that through the family. My mother is a giver. I didn't even realize I was a giver or where it came from, because it was always there. My mother was always giving. Until I got grown, I didn't even think about it. Somebody said, "You're a giving person." I didn't even think about it. It was natural. I think it's natural with him, too. Now it's becoming natural with Omoye. That was something that was in our environment. I thought that's just what people do. No, I learned, everybody doesn't do that. It just goes to show how much your parents can influence you.

I FIGHT WITH MYSELF knowing that I haven't always been the dad I wanted to be for her. I haven't fought sometimes to be around her. Sometimes I took the passive route, avoiding conflict with her mother at the expense of seeing my daughter.

"Daddy, I want to come and see you," she'll tell me. That makes me feel good, but it also makes me feel sad because it reminds me that I'm not in her life every day. As her dad, I want her to know that she is loved to the utmost and that she has that love from a man—the first man in her life. Knowing that, she can go into her future relationships and really be able to love in a healthy way. The love that I can give to Omoye and the ideals and values that I can teach her will be her foundation. They'll be qualities that she can use in her relationships. I know this because I've lived these truths myself. I know this because my mother gave this love to me.

12 "THE DREAMER . . . THE BELIEVER"

Big Aj:

Man, it's tough writing you because things are still so raw for me. Your death hit me hard. Not a day goes by that I don't miss seeing your smile or hearing your laugh or giving you that Chicago (Brothers) handshake. You know you were my best friend. I knew I could come to you for anything, talk to you about anything, and if anyone talked shit about me, I knew you wouldn't stand for it. You, Ajile, Big Aj. You were one of the most charming and loveable people I've ever known.

I have to write about you; I've needed to write this for a while now. It feels good to get it out. I dream about you sometimes. In one dream, Mattie was there, and you had on this leather jacket. I was trying to figure out if you were okay, trying to gauge where your spirit was. It seemed like you were trying to be good, but you weren't. It hurt me, and I woke up sad about it.

I want you to know that I'm doing my best, but I miss you. I remember we took this picture at your birthday party, the last birthday you'd ever see. I knew something was special about that picture, but I didn't know it would be the last one we ever took. That day I saw you at the barbershop, and I walked off with Ramos. You were talking to some guy I didn't know, and I wasn't going to interrupt. That would be the last time I saw you. You know I have a hard time saying good-bye, but I know that one day I will see you and meet your spirit once again.

I'm writing, man. You would be super charged about this new album. It's soulful, raw, pure hip-hop. Dion and I hooked back up, and it's one of my best. I'm excited about hip-hop again, like it's my first record.

You've left your mark on me in many ways. I looked at how you used to surf and snowboard and zip-line and all that type of crazy shit, and I realized I have to be adventurous too. I have to enjoy life more, and I am. I'm going for it.

Big Aj, your life was special, and you meant so much to a lot of people. You did a lot of simple things that helped folks. I watched that in you, and I've seen it even more once you made your transition. Man, Aj, it's tough some days. I'm in Brooklyn right now, and I rode past your apartment yesterday. The day before, I found myself on the street where the accident happened, and I just felt my stomach drop when I realized where I was. I'm going to feel the pain, so I just pray and try to write to get myself in a better space.

But you were never much for sadness, so I'll say to you that things are truly going great for me now. Much better than ever before. And I thank God for each moment. I realized that all that I ask for will be given. All that I want I have already because God is a giving and loving God and vast with His gifts.

I am working to be a better leader, a better artist, a better father, a better man. I'm striving for greatness in all that I do. Man, it's sad sometimes to see Mattie, because you and she were connected in the way that only a mother and son can truly be: divinely bound. My soul holds a loving and compassionate place for you, and I pray your soul is at peace. I pray you are in your Maker's arms. I hope to make you proud of what I do while I'm here. See you on the other side. I love you forever.

Love,

Rashid

AJILE WAS MY BEST FRIEND AND BROTHER. HE WAS MY FIRST cousin, but I grew up with him. He was my living guardian angel. No matter who said what about me, he would always be on my side. He'd tell me the truth about myself, but he also had an unconditional love for me. Aj used to play Jimi Hendrix when we were younger. He was just up on things. He used to go snowboarding and surfing. He had a daredevil in him. I remember calling him after I went surfing with Serena. He was happy and proud of me.

He would have been the best man at my wedding. He was somebody I could talk to. I remember listening to Afrika Bambaataa's "Planet Rock" with him. I wrote my first rap with him. He always had my back with my raps. He thought of me as the best. To have a male figure in your life—and I don't even mean a father, but somebody your own age—love you, it means so much. That's my closest male figure in my life. I remember my aunt Mattie used to make us clean up the bathtub all the time. Mattie was stricter on me than my mother in some ways. Mattie made me clean up that tub.

We used to watch *The Warriors* together. *Grease*. We quoted *The Warriors* all the time. "You guys are good. Real good. The best." We collected baseball cards. Had a nice little collection. On New Year's, when he got older, he would come to Chicago. For some reason, we would always get into a fight with some dudes when we went out. "Can we go out one time without fighting?" he'd ask. One time we got on this elevator, and some dude had something slick to say, threw up some pitchforks or something. One of my guys smacked his hand down, and it was on. We're in the elevator straight brawling. Wasn't no running on an elevator. Ajile was the only one who took a real hit; he came home with his tooth chipped. Aj just couldn't dodge the punch quick enough that night.

One of my fondest memories with Ajile is a recent one. He came and trained with me when I was getting ready for *Just Wright*. It felt good to have him there. It felt good to have his support. It also felt good to see just how far we had come, from shooting hoops in Cincy when we were eight or nine years old to today.

I went to Ajile's birthday party on August 17. He died on September 18, the victim of a motorcycle accident. You know that person who unconditionally believes in you, who has your back? That was him. It wasn't any competition between us. He was a good-hearted friend. I found out a lot of the kind things he did for others only after he died. He was such a bright spirit. I'll strive to honor his memory with all that I do.

I guess knowing I'm weak is when I'm really being strong
Somehow through the dusk I could see the dawn
Like the Bishop "Magic" Juan, that's why I write freedom songs
For the real people
—"REAL PEOPLE"

At the end of 2009, around the time of Ajile's death, I feared I was losing my faith. Maybe it was my way of coping with his loss, but I started fixating on fame. You hunger so much for your career and what you want to achieve in life. When's the next audition? When's the next album? You forget that some of the richest moments are moments of discovery about love, who you are, your spirit, helping others. My mind was so focused on jobs that I wouldn't take the time to stop and think, "Man, that money is going to come. I'm serving God first. Creativity next. The money is going to come. God, I know you created me to do some incredible things. Why would You take me to here? Now I've got to go through this struggle."

I think I've felt most distant from God when I was so bent on my own success that I wasn't really putting the Kingdom first, remembering who I am. I was in such heavy pursuit of the success quest without remembering what's most important.

My strongest wish is to maintain my faith. To me, faith begins by knowing that God's way is the best way, the highest way. His is the way that will create the most perfect results for the world and, if you follow it, for your life. The fundamental demand of faith is a belief in the unseen. When Jesus was walking on water, He was walking on faith. So when I'm walking on faith, that's what I say: I'm walking on water right now. As I write these words, I'm walking on water. I'm one with my faith.

Over the course of my career, I've had to exercise a lot of faith. There were times when people would say, "You should be having a lot more record sales than you do. Why are you so underground?" I had to fight against doubt to keep my faith in what I was doing: that my art would come to the light, that it would reach the masses. Faith is easy at the beginning of any endeavor, before challenge sets in. You couldn't tell me that *Can I Borrow a Dollar?* wasn't going platinum. The same for *Resurrection, One Day It'll All Make Sense, Like Water for Chocolate,* and *Electric Circus.* I just believed it. I just had faith. When they didn't go platinum, then doubt crept in. Your faith is tested. In those instances, I could have lost my faith, lost sight of my path.

Instead I chose to embrace my faith all the more. I have faith now that God had the perfect plan in store. If a record didn't go platinum, then that was simply a part of the journey. I needed to arrive where I am and who I am now. And that's when faith is truly exercised. It's easy to have faith when everything is going your way. But the strength of our faith is tested in the face of disappointment, challenge, setback. God will answer. If you ask, God will answer. God will give you the answer you need, though not always the answer you want.

There have been numerous times when I asked for something, and it didn't happen. As a kid, I sometimes felt like God just hadn't heard me. "God, remember when I said I wanted that bike? What happened?" But He has His plan all along. You should pray for the things that you want, but there has to be a sequence to things. An order. Serena said this to me: "Remember to put the Kingdom first."

Several months ago I went to Honduras, and I was by myself, communing with myself. And I remembered how much I enjoyed feeding my spirit. Allowing happiness to be in your life. You have to feel good already knowing it's coming. That is my path. I take the journey, and I walk with faith. Ultimately, it's in His hands. So I'll keep walking on water, living by my faith.

My faith has led me to a life spent in various acts of creation. I'm not driven by fame. Fame is a fortunate accident that's resulted in part, I guess, from my being driven by other things. What drives me most is the act of creating. That means creating art, creating love, creating opportunities for myself and for others.

I was the first rapper to say Barack Obama's name in a song. Tracee Ross, the actress, had called me up one day and said, "You got to hear this speech. I'm playing it for everybody I know." It was Obama's 2004 Democratic National Convention speech, and it floored me. "This is what we need," I thought. "This man is heaven sent." He was offering up a vision for America that not only tolerated someone like me but embraced me. He wasn't choosing up sides like so many others from both parties; he was talking about unity and healing. And then to find out he came of age in Chicago? And that he went to Trinity, my childhood church? And, of course, there was that name. I couldn't wait to use it in a rhyme.

So when Jadakiss got in touch with me later that same year to lay down a verse for his "Why (Remix)," the lines just came to my mind: "Why is Bush acting like he trying to get Osama? / Why don't we impeach him and elect Obama?" (As it turned out, Obama ended up getting elected *and* getting Osama.) It was a political statement of disapproval for the current administration but also an affirmation of something that would become an important word four years later in Obama's presidential campaign: hope. When I came up with that rhyme, I'm not sure if I really thought we could elect a black man as president. It was more aspirational, I guess.

I first met Barack Obama soon after his election to the U.S. Senate. We were both presenters at an event for the National Urban League. Backstage, one of my friends who also knew the senator offered to introduce us. To my great surprise and joy, Senator Obama knew who I was. He even knew my music, though he's admittedly more into soul than hip-hop.

"Brother," he said, "I loved your song 'The Light.' I have to, because I have a house full of women who are Common fans!"

I don't know what I said in response. I probably just smiled and nodded my head or something. Even then, I could tell he was destined for great things. He exuded it from every pore.

The next time I saw him was late in the summer of 2007 at the annual Bud Billiken Parade in Chicago. By now, he was not only a senator but a potential Democratic candidate for president. He came up to me like we were old friends. "Man, I heard the album is coming out," he said. "I'm going to have to scoop it."

Later on that day, I was taking some promotional pictures, and, without me knowing it, Obama just slid in next to me into the frame. It wasn't like he came up and bear-hugged me or something; he just snuck into the shot. I had no idea he had been there until my boy Brian said afterward, "You didn't even acknowledge that Obama was right there." He's got a sense of humor like that. For as serious as he is—as serious as he has to be—he can still act like a grown-up kid sometimes. When the parade ended, my crew and I approached Obama's Secret Service detail and asked if we could fall in behind his motorcade. Dumb question, but we had to ask! Like a lot of people, we just wanted to be in his presence.

When I was younger, I was part of what we called the "Un-American Caravan." That's what UAC stood for. It was the name I gave to my crew. We were a bunch of young black men from Chicago, and we just couldn't see ourselves reflected in the America that was portrayed to us. We didn't consider ourselves a part of this place. "I'm the un-American Idol, tower like Eiffel." I was part of that because I didn't feel like I was a part of this country, that I was accepted or respected. Even though I think this is the greatest country on earth—the greatest country I've experienced, at least— I didn't feel like I belonged. I guess it felt similar to the dynamics of being a slave: you can be in the slave quarters, but you aren't being respected and recognized and considered in the choices being made that are going to affect the country. So when Obama was elected, that was the first time I ever looked at the flag and said, "Damn, I'm a part of this!"

Since his election, it hasn't been easy—for Obama or for the country. But what he is doing as a leader goes beyond politics. His bearing, his very being, brings a oneness to things. When I look at him and listen to him, I feel like I want to do good in the world.

As soon as he got into office, he improved people's morale, not just here but overseas. I used to go to London, Paris, Sweden, and people would assume certain things about me because I was an American. "You're letting this foolishness in Iraq go on for too long," they said in one way or another. "You're not using your power in the world for good." They held me responsible as an American. And I had to accept it, no matter who I had voted for—or even if I hadn't voted at all. Things changed almost overnight once Obama took office. Now that's all people want to talk to me about when I travel overseas. "There's finally hope," they say. "You're headed back in the right direction."

Back home, of course, it's been a different story. The last years haven't been easy. I think people just got so geeked up that there was no way for Obama to live up to their expectations. "He's the second coming," some of my grandmother's friends liked to say. I think they meant to say that he's come to enlighten and to inspire the world. But it was still too much.

The reality of the political system is such that President Obama—any president—just won't be able to make things happen as fast as people want them to happen. There are just too many obstacles, too many people invested in the status quo, for change to happen overnight. Whatever Obama has failed to do to satisfy certain people's political agendas has been far exceeded by what he's achieved on the level of our spirits. If you don't take heed to that, then that's your choice. If you let politics get in the way of who you are and what you can become, then that's to your own detriment.

The only time I've truly been nervous onstage—well, besides the time I played Tiny Tim in fifth grade—was when I spoke at the

Home State Ball for President Obama. My mother has a picture of me onstage, and when I saw it, I could see how scared I was. "Nobody else could," she said, "but I could." It was in my eyes. Maybe *scared* isn't the right word, because it wasn't as if I had something to fear. No, it was simply my sense of the moment. I was overcome with emotion. Here was a black man who had risen to the highest office in the land. Here was a good man.

Here was a man who through his spirit alone could inspire a nation and even part of the world—all before he became president. I felt that my role, as small as it was in the grand scheme of things, was a way of paying tribute to him, not through some form of idol worship but rather by adding my own energies to his. To me, that's what Obama is all about. Yes, he has considerable influence to affect politics and policy, but more than that, he has the gift to inspire us as citizens to act for the betterment of the nation.

The next time I was with the Obamas was at the First Lady's Christmas tree lighting ceremony. When my mother saw that picture she said, "Rashid, you look so calm and so happy!" And I was. That's what it feels like to be around them. That's the type of energy they radiate. Even through his political struggles, Barack Obama keeps a bright energy about him. The way he handles adversity is a good lesson for all of us. He's calm. He's centered. He's controlled, even when he's upset. He's a humble king. I strive for the same in my life.

I NEVER WOULD HAVE THOUGHT that my invitation to the White House would spark controversy, but that's precisely what happened in the middle of May 2011. It began innocently enough: the

First Lady asked me to join her and the president for an evening celebrating young people and poetry. I'd be onstage with some of the nation's greatest poets—people like Rita Dove, Elizabeth Alexander, and Jill Scott—as well as dozens of kids from local DC schools. This is precisely the sort of effort I support, both personally and through my Common Ground Foundation. So of course I accepted the invitation.

A few days before the White House event, I was wrapping an independent film in Baltimore. It had been an exhilarating experience—one of my best as an actor. The cast and crew had come together as a family and as creators. The energy was electric. I was leaving the set when I got a text from my guy Marlon.

"Fuck the media."

That's all it said. My mind started racing to all the wild things they might be talking about. Did some crazy rumor surface about me and Serena? I honestly had no clue. So I sent Marlon a text with a question mark and a couple minutes later, he sent me a longer message: "Man, they're really tripping about you going to the White House. Fox News is calling you a 'vile rapper.'"

That's when all the calls and texts started flooding in. People were sending me encouraging words. "Hang in there." "Don't let them tear you down." But, honestly, I never watched any of the news reports. I don't generally watch Fox News, so why would I watch just because they happened to be talking about me? Besides, I was in such a different place after the film that the drama just didn't reach me.

Looking back, it seems like the "controversy" amounted to this: some political commentators, led by Fox News' Sean

Hannity along with Sarah Palin and Karl Rove, objected to my invitation to the White House due to the content of some of—really one of—my lyrics. They called me an advocate for violence against police and the former president, George W. Bush. They even called me a thug. To prove it, they ignored my eight albums and dozens of songs and found a lyric I performed called "A Letter to the Law" on *Russell Simmons' Def Poetry Jam* back in 2004.

I had to laugh. The lyrics in question weren't condoning violence at all—just the opposite. They were decrying the violence committed by corrupt cops against innocent black citizens in Cincinnati. In the span of a few years, more than a dozen black men had been killed while in the custody of the Cincinnati police department. It was a national scandal. I believed then, as I do now, that the best response to violence is thoughtful, peaceful protest, something I strive to do through my lyrics.

So when I say, "Tell the law my uzi weighs a ton," I'm speaking in metaphor, exercising the power of poetic language to express emotions that can't always be communicated through direct speech. I'm also referring to Public Enemy's 1987 classic "Miuzi Weighs a Ton," where Chuck D uses the uzi as a metaphor for the weapon of the mind. I was mad at the violence committed against these young men, yes. But was I advocating violence against men and women in law enforcement? Hell, no!

As for the lines about Bush, I was saying I'd had enough: enough war, enough people dying, enough lies. In other words, I was saying what more than half the country was saying around that time. Again, I used my poetry to express my frustrations:

Burn a bush, 'cause for peace he no push no button

Killing over oil and grease, no weapons of destruction

How can we follow a leader when this a corrupt one?

Was I advocating the idea of lighting the president on fire? Of course not. It doesn't take a PhD in English to interpret the tone and the connotations of those words. For starters, there's the biblical reference. As for the political message, I was saying that we as a nation need to make a change. Burn all the lies, burn the deceit, burn the propaganda.

When those lyrics didn't achieve the desired outrage, they focused on another one of my songs—"A Song for Assata." They said I was supporting a "cop killer," but anyone with even a passing knowledge of that case knows that her guilt is far from certain. I and many other reasonable people believe that she was wrongly convicted. Before writing the song about her, I traveled to Cuba, where she has been living in political asylum since 1984, and met with her. I heard her story in her own words.

They're getting on me for speaking out against police brutality and Bush's unjust war? They're getting on me for writing a song about a woman I believe was unjustly convicted of a crime? I can live with that. I'm a child of that. I grew up in hip-hop with the rhymes of Chuck D and KRS-One. I grew up in black politics with the words of Martin Luther King, Malcolm X, and Muhammad Ali.

The motivations behind the controversy seemed transparent: it was all part of the continuing effort by certain voices on the political fringe to brand Barack Obama as the "other." They'd been doing it directly by asking him to produce his birth certificate; now they were doing it by association. "He's a Muslim. He's a foreigner. He's a socialist. And he's friends with vile rappers, too!" Where were these critics the two other times I had performed at the White House? Why now?

It seemed all too convenient that this "story" broke the week after President Obama authorized the successful killing of Osama bin Laden. The president's approval ratings were at an all-time high. I guess they thought it was time for another sideshow like the manufactured controversy over his birth certificate. Man, if the biggest thing they could get on the president was that a rapper and actor was reading poetry to children at the White House, then these critics were really starting to get desperate.

People kept asking me if I was mad that I was being unfairly portrayed. Did it hurt me to have my name associated with the very negativity I had spent most of my career in music—and most of my life—striving to fight? Of course, no one ever wants to be misrepresented and slandered. But I saw it more as an opportunity. If I'm ever going to be involved in a controversy, this is how I want it to be! I don't want to be caught up in dumb stuff. I want people to be talking about my art and my beliefs.

It was surreal. My name was suddenly part of world news. One of my friends was watching the White House press briefing and said that the press secretary answered a question about me and the next one was about Syria. Many people were hearing my name for the first time. And if they were curious enough to look into the situation for themselves, they would soon see what I truly represent. This was a chance for my message to reach people who otherwise wouldn't hear it.

As far as the criticisms were concerned, I kept thinking back to one of the passages of scripture my mother would often remind me of in times like these. When you get criticized for something you believe in, it makes that belief all the more valuable. Be glad when they condemn you for doing God's work. That's something for which you can stand. That's one of the deepest-rooted things you can defend. I was talking about social awareness and now it's being brought to the masses. I'm grateful that my name is being spoken in so many places. When you offer yourself to the world and you want to speak up for people through your artistic expression and your activism, you will undoubtedly be attacked. That's how you know your message is being heard.

Politics will be politics, but when Sarah Palin, Sean Hannity—and let's not leave out Bill O'Reilly—started labeling Rashid a gangsta and a "vile rapper," it was even a stretch for them. Since he broke into the music business, I've heard Rashid described many ways, but never once before have I heard those terms attached to him.

What did I feel initially? Part of me had to laugh. It was funny to me because they had gotten him so wrong. Gangsta rapper? That was funny. Like Jon Stewart pointed out on The Daily Show, *my son was on* Sesame Street *with Elmo! But my laughter turned to anger and hurt when I heard them call him vile. None of those feelings lasted long, though, once I remembered what I had always told Rashid: "Before you weigh in on something that people are saying about you, consider the source."*

I first told him that when he was a child and he looked at me kind of puzzled. I explained that if someone is trying to tell you how to play basketball and they've never picked up a ball, you might want to question their knowledge of the game. If someone is telling you how to rap and they've never picked up a microphone, you might want to take what they have to say with a grain of salt.

So I used my own advice. Sarah Palin and Karl Rove don't know Rashid or anything about his work, therefore I could not give weight to what they were saying. I don't know how anyone else could either. I must say I was particularly surprised that Sarah Palin was a part of this, given what the media had put her own family through. Even though I didn't know her, I felt for her as a mother when that was happening. I wonder if she thought about me when she tweeted her opinion about Rashid without even taking the time to find out what he was about? Her comments fueled negative press against my son and put him at the center of a controversy where he didn't belong. I guess politics will be politics.

When I spoke to Rashid, we both laughed about what was going on. I told him that Derek had said afterward, "If they were going to protest anything, they should have protested that hat he was wearing!" I told Rashid that I agreed with Derek and added that I'd protest the entire outfit down to his shoes, for that matter. We both fell out laughing.

We also discussed how he would respond. I reminded him never to let people back you into a corner for defending your beliefs. "If you do that, Rashid, then they have you against the ropes, and you don't ever want to put yourself in that position," I said. "People who know you know what kind of person you are. Those other peo-

ple, the ones making the accusations? They don't want to know you and won't believe what you tell them anyway."

So that's when he sent that twitter or tweet or whatever you call it. I let him know that I thought he had handled the situation well, but that I was not surprised. I expected no less from him. When my friends and colleagues called to express their sympathy and outrage, I told them thanks, but that I was fine and so was Rashid.

PART OF ME has always wished that I could have been alive in the 1960s. I think I have a freedom fighter somewhere deep in my soul. For those of us born after the civil rights movement, the nature of our struggle wasn't nearly as defined. We didn't march. We didn't stage sit-ins. Our demonstrations had to come through our words and our deeds, through the way we raise our children, and the way we defend our ideals. My march comes through the words I speak, both in my rhymes and in my everyday life.

So the morning of the White House event, I set out from Baltimore toward Richmond, Virginia. I had a detour in mind, an important stop to make. I wanted to visit Shirley Plantation in Charles City, Virginia. It started out as work: I was researching my role as the freed slave named Elam in the new AMC series *Hell on Wheels*, a drama about the people behind the construction of the transcontinental railroad.

Hell on Wheels deals with complex emotions: the passion, the vision, but also the greed that went into building one of the great monuments to the American Dream. It took a nation to build it, too—white folks from Ireland and England and Norway; Chinese Americans, and black Americans, too. There were so many people involved. In making this series, we set out to tell the story of how all of these cultures clash, but of how they ultimately come together to achieve something great.

So to understand Elam, I had come here—to a plantation just a couple hours' drive from the nation's capital. Walking along the paths my forefathers walked, I couldn't help but be struck by the astonishing fact that I was beginning the day on this plantation, but I would end it at the White House as a guest of the first black president of the United States of America. It was as if I was living the story of black America, the struggle of four hundred years, in a single day. The realization overwhelmed me; it also put in perspective whatever criticisms I now faced. It was all worth today's journey.

That afternoon, I found myself alone in a room at the White House, hearing the comedian Steve Martin playing the banjo as he and his group did a sound check in preparation for the evening's event. There was so much in my head and my heart.

After all the controversy, all the resistance, here I was at the White House. That's when I picked up a pen and some paper— White House stationery—and began composing new opening lines for the poem I would later recite.

I hadn't written out my lyrics now for close to two decades, but something about the moment, something about the emotions of it, demanded that I set the words down on the page. They began like this:

I woke up with the sunshine

A sunshine I had never seen

There was light at the end of it

Reminded me to forever dream

I was dreaming I walked into the White House

With love on my sleeve

And love for each and every one of you

Reminding you to believe

The words flowed from the pen in a way I've rarely experienced in all my years of writing. I was writing my story, but also the story of us as a people: mothers and sons, the temptations of violence in the face of disappointment, the lure of the hustle, but finally the promise of a new day, a new life. I found myself ending with the promise embodied in the spirit of one man—our president, Barack Obama. My words weren't meant to put him on a pedestal or to deny him his human weakness, but rather to acknowledge the transcendent power that even one person can carry when so many others are helping to bear the weight.

Like a thief in the night, I write for beacons of light

For those of us in dark alleys and parched valleys

Street hits spark rallies of the conscious

Conquerors of a contest that seems beyond us

Even through the unseen I know that God watches

For one King's dream, He was able to Barack us

One King's dream, He was able to Barack us

One King's dream, He was able to Barack us

It was an out-of-body experience being backstage, waiting to go on. My heart was beating out of my chest. I could see that the president and the First Lady were five or six feet from the front of the stage. When I was introduced, the audience applauded so loudly it took me by surprise. They were with me, but also with the president. Even before I started speaking, I kept thinking: "This is a victory." This is a victory because here is a crowd full of people coming together to say: "We are going to support you and the positivity and love that you bring." That let me know there are many people in this world who thrive on positivity instead of negativity, light instead of darkness.

So I sat on my stool, looked at the president and Mrs. Obama, and began my poem—at first reading from that White House stationery, then reciting off the top of my head. On certain lines, I looked the president right in his eyes. He looked back with attention and affirmation.

It was one of the greatest artistic experiences of my life. I felt a rush that I haven't felt onstage in a long, long time. I've performed in front of tens of thousands; I've rocked the mic in front of celebrities and childhood idols like Michael Jordan. But nothing can quite match the rush that accompanies a performance for a purpose that's bigger than the song or the style or the game. In that moment, in that place, I knew I was breaking through walls that people had thrown in front of me. I knew that in a humble way, I was standing up for big things: truth, love, and free expression.

The evening came to a close and the president acknowledged each of the participants. As I left the stage, he stopped and embraced me. It was a small gesture, but a significant one. It told me something about the depth of his integrity and of his appreciation for the efforts of artists of all kinds—even a rapper from the South Side of Chicago.

The controversy, both in its absurdity and also in its unexpected importance, confirmed one thing in my mind: I'll always be a rapper. Yes, I'm an actor, too. I'm sure I'll do many other things as well before my time is up, but as long as I'm blessed with the gift to put rhythms and rhymes together, I'll be an MC.

I left the White House that evening and flew to Calgary to start filming *Hell on Wheels*. I was traveling across borders but also across time. All of a sudden, it's 1865 and I'm a freed slave trying to find my place in a new society. All of a sudden, I'm living in a frontier America driven by selfishness, greed, and personal gain.

The surprising thing about it, though, was that it didn't feel all that different from today. Sure, our country has changed dramatically since the time of Reconstruction. But more surprising are the ways that it has stayed the same. We're still quick to stereotype, particularly across racial lines. What was happening to me was what had happened to so many black people throughout history, only in much harsher terms for them. "He's just a thug. He's a vile human being. He doesn't belong here." They were speaking about me in the twenty-first century, but they could just as easily have been talking about my character, Elam, back in the nineteenth.

That's where we still suffer in this country. Too often we look at a piece of somebody—maybe it's their skin color or their religion or what they do for a living—and we say that's who they are. "I've seen a person like that before. I know what to expect." Mix those assumptions with the power to enforce them upon society and you have prejudice. That same prejudice is alive and well in America today; it just comes out in slicker ways.

That's precisely why we need artists. We need people to imagine other ways of being and other ways of living than what already exists. Writing a poem or a story or a song helps you not only to better understand yourself, but to better understand others too.

The poet, writer, and activist Maya Angelou once expressed the power of creation in more powerful terms than I ever could: "If one is lucky, a solitary fantasy can totally transform one million realities." What a joy—and what a responsibility—it is to live a life dedicated to creating fantasies for others to inhabit, be it in film or in music. That's why on my latest album I've made a conscious effort to write rhymes from the perspective of others. In creating characters, you build a bridge to understanding other people. Maybe through art you can even build a bridge from here to a better future.

I've had the privilege of learning from Dr. Angelou firsthand, even sharing the stage with her. I count her as one of my greatest influences, both as a writer and as a spirit. I met her in late October 2008. I remember that day because it was warm, probably sixty degrees outside. I got my hair cut at Junior's and then I walked across Fulton Avenue and hopped in the truck that took me to Dr. Angelou's house.

Upon arriving I immediately felt a spirit of culture in her home, a history of heart. I sat at the table with her, and I looked around and saw all the pictures, the beautiful pieces of art. She asked me questions, and we were laughing about different things. She talked about the writers she loved. How she got into writing.

She loved the African-American poet Paul Laurence Dunbar. She read me some of his verse. I sat at her table talking about life, and she kindly gave me some books. The next time I went to her house, I took Serena, who looked up to her too.

When I'm around Dr. Angelou I remember who I am. I am a child of God first, a young black man, and if I strive for it, perhaps a beacon of light for others. I had a moment of awareness like this onstage with Dr. Angelou at the National Urban League 100th Anniversary in 2010. She had written a poem for the occasion and she had chosen me to perform it with her. She'd read a stanza or two and then have me offer a freestyle interpretation, a kind of call and response.

Here we were in a black church in Maryland creating art together. Jesse Jackson was there. So were Cornel West and many other familiar faces. It was an honor to perform for them, but more than anything, it was an honor to perform with Dr. Angelou. "They call Common a rapper," she said to the audience, "but I call him a poet." As I learned onstage with her, as I would learn the next year at the White House, being a poet is a powerful thing.

EPILOGUE

Dear Reader:

There's so much in a name. My father gave me his name: Lonnie Lynn. But he and my mother also gave me another—Rashid—the name I go by to my friends and family, and the name I go by with you. (After all, you know just about everything about me now!) Rashid means "guide to the right path" in Arabic. By giving me that name, my parents saw fit to fuse the Muslim with the Christian. That's what I am, a fusion of spirit. I embrace the name in all that it means; I accept it as a birthright. I want to be that guide to the right path. I want to illuminate that path through my victories and my mistakes, my laughter and my cries, my strong days and my fears, my darkness and my light.

Rashid is a name mostly hidden from public view. I rose to fame on another name. Common is a name of my own creation; I brought that particular me into being. There's a power in that. Every superhero has an alter ego, a name he attaches to his powers. Peter Parker is Spider-Man. John Stewart is the Green Lantern. Perhaps there's something to that transformation that brings them power. Common is my vessel; Rashid is my anchor. It connects me to the people who know me and love me the most. It connects me to my soul.

So nowadays they call me Common. They used to call me Common Sense. People close to me have always just called me Rashid. Of course, Common is Rashid—they both are me. And Rashid is often Common these days. I have a tough time not letting Rashid come out through Common. I guess the only difference is that Common allows me to be more boastful, more vocal with my thoughts, and bolder with my actions. Rashid would never say how nice he is, but Common sure would.

People who know me only as Common might find it hard to believe some of the things that made me Rashid. That's partly why I've written this book, so that I can show myself as a man in full. That means telling some tough truths, revealing my faults and vulnerabilities. But it also means showing the true strength of my character.

As Common, I've often been classified as a conscious artist. I take that as a compliment. Conscious means aware. When I think about the conscious artists throughout history, I think of Bob Marley. I think of John Coltrane. I think of KRS-One. These artists are conscious artists because they spoke up when silence would have been the easier route. They were the nerve center of our culture— awake when others were sleepwalking. I'm committed to being that kind of artist, both as a rapper and as an actor. I want to be a voice of awareness pushing us all to stay awake.

The only problem with being labeled a conscious artist is that people assume that's all you are, that you're not also a complex and flawed individual. Just because I might write a song that speaks up for awareness doesn't mean I haven't made mistakes and that I'm not going to continue making more mistakes on my journey through life.

Sometimes Common isn't big enough—isn't broad enough—to fit Rashid. Yes, I'm a conscious artist, but I've also seen some street shit—even done a little bit of it. But what's the purpose of talking about the dirt I did in my rhymes? I didn't grow up with the mind-set that you should take pride in your wrongs, that your dirt should be the subject of public discussion. Just the opposite. In Chicago you kept your dirt underneath your feet. No matter what side of the law you call home, you keep your business on a need-to-know basis. Like my father used to say, the real gangsters are in church with their families on Sunday, not out on the streets talking shit.

I'm not saying I'm any type of gangster, but what I am saying is that I've been witness to life from every angle. I made a conscious decision early in my career to focus on growth and positivity. I wanted to talk about the light at the end of the tunnel, not just the tunnel. If I don't talk about us making it to the light, then some people may never see it. And talking about it reminds me that it's there, too. I choose to make music and films with positive vibrations because that's what I want for my life and the lives of others. In my own life, I still deal with the negativity sometimes, but I don't choose to reflect that in the art I put out into the world. I strive to be a conscious artist because I strive to be a balanced human being on my path toward the light.

What are you here for? Like anybody in the entertainment industry, I want the attention and accolades. I want the awards and the recognition. But I also know that my greater purpose goes beyond all of that. A long time ago I made a conscious decision as an artist and as a human being that I would strive to do things with purpose. From then on, my aim has been to inspire and to raise consciousness.

I knew that I wanted to work for the betterment of others. It started with seeking the betterment of black people because that was my community. You start by doing for your people, for your tribe. That doesn't mean that you have to do so at the expense of others. As I've grown, as I've traveled, as I've broadened my views, I've begun working for the betterment of all people. This is the story I've strived to tell you. This is where Rashid and Common become one.

Love,
Rashid

ACKNOWLEDGMENTS

I thank the Almighty Jehovah God for Your blessings and gifts and for Your everlasting love. I thank You for Jesus Christ, my Lord and Savior.

I thank my loving mother, my father, Omoye, Grandma, Ralph, Derek, Serena, Cristen, Saunte, Rhea, Nicole, Malaika, and the rest of my family, friends, and loved ones who have shown me support and love throughout my life.

Adam, you made this experience a once in a lifetime. I am truly inspired by you, and I know this wouldn't be without you.

Finally, to all my fans and supporters throughout the years—I am grateful. I appreciate you all. May God bless you.